P9-CFV-601

𝔓resented by

the

𝔊overnment of 𝔠anada

———

𝔒ffert

par le

𝔊ouvernement du 𝔠anada

Introduction to New France

MARCEL TRUDEL, D. ès L., F.R.S.C.,
Member of the Académie Canadienne-Française
Professor and Chairman of the Department of History,
University of Ottawa

Holt, Rinehart and Winston of Canada, Limited   Toronto : Montreal

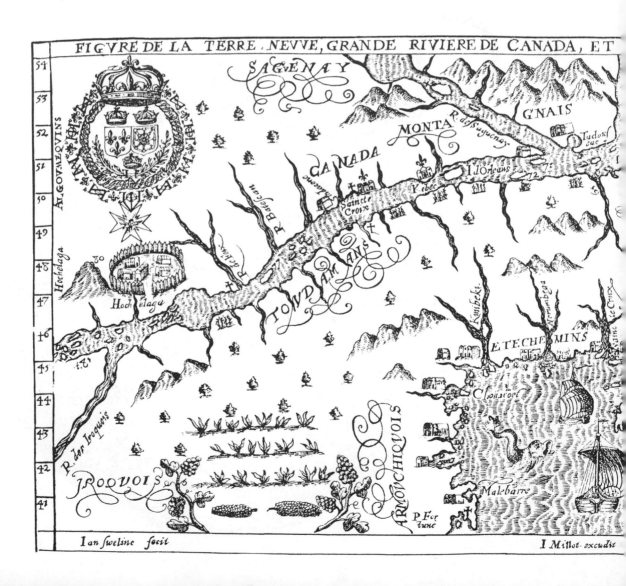

Introduction to New France

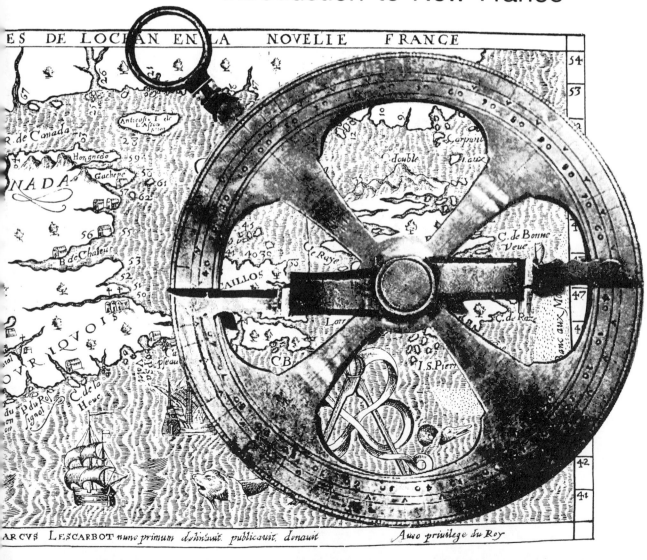

à mon petit-fils

JEAN-PHILIPPE

By the same author

L'Influence de Voltaire au Canada. Montréal, Éditions Fides, 1945. 2 vol. Second prix *David,* 1945.

Vézine. Montréal, Editions Fides, 1946. Reprinted in 1962 in the series "Alouette bleue."

Louis XVI, le Congrés américain et le Canada, 1774-1789. Québec, Éditions du Quartier Latin, 1949. Premier prix *David,* 1951.

Carte seigneuriale de la Nouvelle-France (moins la Côte-Nord), 1950.

Histoire du Canada par les textes. Montréal, Éditions Fides, 1952. In collaboration with Guy Frégault and Michel Brunet. Reprinted in 1962 in two volumes, the first of which was written in collaboration with Guy Frégault.

Le Régime militaire dans le Governement des Trois-Rivières, 1760-1764. Les Trois-Rivières, Éditions du Bien Public, 1952.

L'Affaire Jumonville. Québec, Presses de l'Université Laval. 1953. Published in English in 1954 under the title *The Jumonville Affair.*

Chiniquy. Les Trois-Rivières, Éditions du Bien Public, 1955.

Le Régime seigneurial. Ottawa, Canadian Historical Society, 1956. Published in English in the same year, under the title *The Seigneurial Regime.*

Champlain. Montréal, Éditions Fides, 1956. In the series "Classiques Canadiens."

L'Eglise canadienne sous le régime militaire, 1759-1764.
 Vol. I: *Les problèmes.* Montréal, Les Études de l'Institut d'Histoire de l'Amérique française, 1956.
 Vol. II: *Les institutions.* Québec, Presses de l'Université Laval, 1957.

L'Esclavage au Canada français. Histoire et conditions de l'esclavage. Québec, Presses de l'Université Laval, 1960. Prix *Casgrain,* 1961. Reprinted as extracts, in 1963 by Les Éditions Horizon.

Atlas historique du Canada français. Des débuts à la Confédération. Québec, Presses de l'Université Laval, 1961. Abridged edition in the *Collection de cartes anciennes et modernes,* published in 1948. New edition in 1968 under the title *Atlas de la Nouvelle-France—An Atlas of New France.*

Histoire de la Nouvelle-France.
 Vol. I: *Les vaines tentatives, 1524-1603.* Montréal, Éditions Fides, 1963. Premier prix des *Concours littéraires et scientifiques du Québec,* 1963. Reprinted in 1965.
 Vol. II: *Le comptoir, 1604-1627.* Montréal, Éditions Fides, 1966. Premier prix des *Concours littéraires et scientifiques du Québec,* 1966. Governor-General's Award, 1967.

In Preparation

Histoire de la Nouvelle-France. Vol. III: La seigneuriè des Cent-Associés, 1627-1663.

Cover design: R. Campbell

Copyright © 1968 by

HOLT, RINEHART AND WINSTON OF CANADA, LIMITED

All rights reserved

PRINTED IN CANADA

70   3   2

Foreword

This book contains a summary of what I have taught my history students for more than fifteen years. After a brief review of events, there is a description of the structure of society during the French regime. Although this book has the defects inherent in all works of this kind, I believe, that considering the limited importance history books usually give to institutions, it may be of use to people wishing to have an introduction to a comprehensive study of New France.

Throughout my teaching, I have put students on their guard against the attitude of magister dixit. *In history, the teacher must not impose a single, one-sided interpretation because the purpose of historical studies is too complex for anyone to presume that he can encompass it as simply as that. Therefore, I have been careful to get students to verify my statements for themselves, and to reject the ones they discover to be ill-founded. This book is written in the same spirit.*

In this book, I do not claim to give definite answers to the problems posed by New France, in the area of institutions, in particular, society under the French regime has scarcely been touched upon. Many aspects of society are still unknown because specialized studies are lacking and my explanations in this area are often no more than working hypotheses. For this reason, I have mentioned, in the bibliographical notes appearing at the end of each chapter, studies that not only offer variations of opinion but sometimes even contradict the explanation that I have presented. This book is intended only to stimulate the reader to the further study of New France. I shall be happy if it can give rise to new interpretations or to more detailed reconstructions, even if this results in my own becoming out of date. Such is the progress of history.

Lucerne, May 14, 1966
Marcel Trudel

Contents

List of Maps and Illustrations

Bibliography

Sources

Even though the material presented here places more stress on sources than on their interpretation, this book is not primarily intended to serve research; rather, it is meant to give the reader information on the history and institutions of New France. For this reason, the bibliographical notes following the chapters contain no direct reference to sources. However, in the numerous studies cited here and at the end of each chapter (most of these studies being complemented by a bibliography and references) the reader who is interested in research will be able to locate quickly printed or manuscript sources.

In this field, the *Guide de l'étudiant en histoire du Canada* (see below) gives the essential information. In addition, students of the French regime should have at hand copies of four historical texts:

G. FREGAULT and M. TRUDEL, *Histoire du Canada par les textes*. Montréal, Editions Fides, 1962. This covers the years, 1534-1854.

C. NISH, *The French Regime,* Vol. I in *Canadian Historical Documents Series*. Toronto, Prentice-Hall, 1965. Published in French by the same house in 1966 as *"Le régime français"*.

J. H. S. REID, K. McNAUGHT and H. S. CROWE, *A Source Book on Canadian History*. Toronto, Longmans, 1964.

J. J. TALMAN, *Basic Documents in Canadian History*. Toronto, Van Nostrand, 1959.

Further Reading

In addition to the specialized works mentioned in their appropriate location, the reader will profit from an examination of some general works, which are indispensable for a study of New France.

General Bibliography

J. HAMELIN and A. BEAULIEU, *Guide de l'étudiant en histoire du Canada*. Québec, Presses de l'Université Laval, 1965. This textbook is essential for study and research as it indicates the principal archives, libraries, works of reference, publication of documents, general works and monographs.

General Histories

The following works are mentioned because of the quality and diversity of interpretations they offer:
D. G. CREIGHTON, *Dominion of the North, a History of Canada*. Toronto, MacMillan, Rev. Ed. 1957.
L. GROULX, *Histoire du Canada français depuis la découverte*. 2nd Vols. Montréal, Editions Fides, 1960.
G. LANCTOT, *Histoire du Canada, des origines au traité de Paris*. 3 Vols. Montréal, Beauchemin, 1962-64. Published in English by Clarke, Irwin, 1963-65.
M. M. LONG, *A History of the Canadian People*, Vol. I. Toronto, 1942.
A. R. M. LOWER, *Colony to Nation: A History of Canada*. Toronto, Longmans, 1959.
E. McINNIS, *Canada, A Political and Social History*. Toronto, Holt, Rinehart and Winston, 1959.

Biography

Dictionary of Canadian Biography. Québec, Presses de l'Université Laval; Toronto, University of Toronto Press, 1966. The first volume, the only one that has appeared to date, covers the year, 1000-1700. Each article is followed by a list of sources and studies. This work is under the direction of George W. Brown and Marcel Trudel.

Cartography

MARCEL TRUDEL, *Atlas de la Nouvelle France, An Atlas of New France*. Québec, Presses de l'Université Laval, 1968. This atlas contains general maps of the sixteenth, seventeenth and eighteenth centuries, maps relating to the seigneurial regime and to settlement, as well as town plans relating to the French regime.
D. G. G. KERR, *A Historical Atlas of Canada*. Toronto, Thomas Nelson and Sons, 1961. This is less documentary but more explanatory than the above work. Published in French in 1966 as *Atlas historique du Canada*.

Iconography

C. W. JEFFERYS and T. W. McLEAN, *The Picture Gallery of Canadian History*. Toronto, The Ryerson Press, 1964. The first volume illustrates the period of the French regime. The drawings lack artistic merit, but the description of utensils of the period is very helpful in studying New France.
Le Boréal-Express, published in Trois-Rivières by a group of historians from the Centre des études universitaires, is an imaginary version of a newspaper at different periods in history. It reproduces a host of contemporary illustrations or reconstructions, all carefully chosen. The issues from 1524 to 1760 have been collected in one volume, with an index making for easy reference.

PART ONE

HISTORY
1524-1764

Public Archives of Canada

The fifteenth century view of the world between Europe and Asia
(according to Martin Behaim's Globe made in 1492, before Columbus made his voyage)
Beyond the Canary Islands and the Azores, lie the fabled islands (Antilia, Saint-Brendan, Brasil)
near to Cipango.

CHAPTER I

On the route to Asia: a continent

When Christopher Columbus landed on an island previously unknown to Europe, he thought that he had reached Asia and that he would soon give letters to the Great Khan from the princes of Spain. Columbus believed that he had answered a question that had perplexed mankind for thousands of years: what lay on the other side of the Atlantic?

The Ancient World and the Atlantic

The question of what lay across the Atlantic haunted scholars of the ancient world. Plato had discovered an oral tradition concerning a land from which a great army had supposedly come. Aristotle, Eratosthenes, and Seneca were convinced that the sea separating Europe from Asia was comparatively narrow and could be crossed in a few days. However, the countries of ancient Europe centred on the Mediterranean and were not impelled by any intellectual or economic necessity to solve this question. The science of the day, as propounded by scholars like Strabo, affirmed that an hypothesis was sufficient and saw no advantage in discovering the lands west of the Atlantic.

Furthermore, the nations of antiquity did not have the technical ability to send a fleet across the ocean: ships' rudders were still controlled by the human arm, and there was no precise instrument to aid in steering, nor any reliable method of measuring distances at sea. Certainly there were great navigators in ancient times: the Carthaginian Hanno circumnavigated Africa in the fifth century B.C.; the Greek, Pytheas of Marseilles, reached the Arctic Ocean in 330 B.C. and made reference to a frozen land (Iceland, or perhaps Greenland), which became the ancient Thule. But these explorations amounted to little more than navigating by hugging the coastline from one port to another, or from one island to another, without losing sight of the mainland. Asia was still reached only by the Eastern overland routes. For this reason, when Claudius Ptolemy of Alexandria published the sum total of the geographical knowledge of antiquity (about 150 A.D.), he mentioned that there was only an ocean between Europe and Asia.

Medieval disinterest in the Atlantic

During the Latin Middle Ages nothing was contributed to the solution of the problem of what lay beyond the Atlantic. Cartography at that time was inspired princi-

3

pally by the Church Fathers, the Bible, and the dreams of mystics, and the chief concern of the cosmographers, who placed the centre of the world in Jerusalem, was the location of the Earthly Paradise. (Certain men of the Renaissance, such as Cardinal d'Ailly and Columbus, were also preoccupied with this idea.) They added nothing to the maps of the Atlantic except fabulous islands—the island of Brasil, the island of Antilia, the Seven Cities, Saint Brendan's Island—which proved an attraction until the sixteenth century. Certainly, during these times, Europeans often travelled towards Asia, but they still crossed the continent or skirted its coastline. It was these Europeans, though, who made an important contribution to the techniques of navigation. In the twelfth century, they invented the pivoted rudder and fixed the compass on a needle-point; in the fifteenth century, they invented or perfected the astrolabe; the log was soon to enable navigators to measure distances at sea. The men of Europe were capable of crossing the Atlantic whenever a scientific awakening or economic necessity should urge them to do so. But the great ventures of the Christian Middle Ages were directed exclusively towards the Holy Land.

America and Scandinavia

Although America was unknown to the Latin Middle Ages, the Norsemen of the same period were aware of its existence. In fact, America received immigrants. The Celts were possibly the first wave of that migration. While England, still bearing the marks of Roman occupation, was struggling to find an identity, the Celts of Ireland were extending their control over the lands of the North Atlantic. A century or two before the year 1000, these Celts apparently occupied a land south of Greenland, called Albania or Greater Ireland, which could only have been America. Certain characteristics of Irish civilization appear to be present in the Algonkian civilization; however, these hypotheses are based upon only extremely tenuous or obscure evidence. If there ever were Celts in America, they had disappeared before the Vikings landed.

The Vikings (first called Northmen, later Norsemen) ruled the seas and terrorized Europe. In the ninth century, they occupied Normandy, a region of France, from where, in 1066, they launched the conquest of England. In the North Atlantic, they passed from island to island, occupying Iceland about 874. In 877, Gunnbjörn discovered a land further west—a land rediscovered in 982, by the Norwegian Erik Raude (Eric the Red) and named "Greenland" to make it appear more attractive. Greenland soon attained a population of several thousand, and by 1126, it had a Catholic bishop. The colony maintained direct relations with Norway until 1369. The voyage from Greenland to America was no more difficult than that from Iceland to Greenland. In 986, Bjarni sighted the American coast. Leif, the son of Eric the Red, took advantage of this discovery in 1002, and settled in America with some fellow Norwegians.

The new land was divided into three territories—Helluland, Markland, and Vinland—and there may have been almost continuous settlement until the fourteenth century. Historians are still seeking answers to some of the questions concerning the Viking in America: Who were the Skraelings who fought the immigrants? What journeys did the Vikings make into the interior? Did they, in fact, penetrate as far inland as present-day Minnesota?

The country of Vinland according to a medieval map
A medieval map, dated before 1440, shows an island to the west of Greenland. A Latin legend calls this
island *Vinland* and attributes its discovery to Bjarni and Leif Erickson.

The disappearance of Vinland itself is still clouded by mystery. According to a recent hypothesis, the inhabitants may have been dispersed by the Black Death that was ravaging Europe. The survivors may have mingled with the Huron-Iroquois, who seem to resemble Viking civilization in their political traditions, in their military defence, and in some of the characteristics of their artistic and linguistic life. Nowadays, there is no longer any doubt that the Vikings discovered and settled America. On the island of Newfoundland, archeologists are beginning to confirm the hypotheses of the historian.

This discovery and settlement was practically unknown to the Latin Middle Ages. Adam of Bremen made about the only reference to Vinland in 1075, although a map has just been discovered, dated before 1440, the title of which attests to the discovery of Vinland in the western Atlantic to the south of Greenland, besides proving that a bishop wintered in this new land. Furthermore, the eastern coast of Vinland, as this map shows, seems to correspond to the North American coastline from Hudson Strait to the northern peninsula of Newfoundland. There are many explanations for Europe's ignorance of this Viking settlement in America: the isolation of Norway; the desire of Norway to conceal its maritime activities; and also, perhaps (as cartography leads us to believe), the conviction that Vinland and Greenland were joined in an immense semi-circle in the North Atlantic and formed a single extension of Norway.

The urgent need to discover the world

The fifteenth century marked the eventual rediscovery of antiquity. Through the *Ymago Mundi,* published in 1410 by Cardinal d'Ailly, Christopher Columbus read of Aristotle's belief that a narrow sea separated Europe and Asia. Ptolemaic geography, the most advanced cartography of the time, was enriched by the Arabs and provided one of the sources for the Renaissance. It was to be the sixteenth century that contributed most to man's knowledge of his world.

Scientific curiosity was combined with economic necessity. Asia was pouring luxury products into Europe (spices, silks, precious stones). The middlemen were making a fortune, especially the Venetians who monopolized the transport of Oriental merchandise. Europe depended on the Mediterranean, and even though the fall of Constantinople, in 1453, did not close the route to Asia (since the Middle East still found it profitable to continue this trade), it was becoming necessary to reach the producing countries directly and thus reduce the cost of Asiatic products. Europe was also being depleted of gold in this process, since it lacked goods to barter with and had to pay in gold. But European mines were no longer sufficient to cover the export of precious metal currency to the Orient. Europe had to find new deposits abroad: the Portuguese, for example, were searching in West Africa.

The necessity of meeting these needs was one of the main reasons Europeans undertook lengthy voyages across the Atlantic. They now possessed the necessary techniques: the pivoted rudder, the compass, the astrolabe, the log to measure distances; and although it was not yet known how to calculate longitude at sea, it was possible to determine latitude with great precision. An important school founded at Sagrès in Portugal, by the scholarly Prince Henry (called the Navigator), contributed to the development of nautical knowledge.

Eventually, a new force—that of the great merchants—appeared. Its influence was to transform the economic life of Europe: the German "Függer" are well known, and special mention must be made of the Italian merchants—businessmen with influence throughout Europe and managers of companies in every country. At Lyons, in particular, these men established a crossroads of commercial routes between Germany and the Mediterranean. As bankers and creditors of kings, they were able to support or even initiate trans-oceanic enterprises. Italian became the international language of business. It was the merchants, much more than the princely courts, who spread humanism throughout Europe.

Europe in search of Asia

Not all the European nations were ready for the great world adventure: Norway had become a province of Denmark; Denmark was at war with Sweden for supremacy in the Baltic; the countries of the Holy Roman Empire lacked a unity of interest with respect to the Atlantic; and the little Italian states, of which some were dependent on Spain, remained centred on Mediterranean trade. There remained four Atlantic nations. England, with a population of four million, was becoming unified under the strong rule of King Henry VII. France, since Louis XI, had regained its territorial unity, and with its fifteen million inhabitants and its economic independence, was the foremost power in Europe. Spain had also attained unity, having united its three divided kingdoms. It was difficult to feed the country's seven million people, but Sicily served as a granary. Portugal, a small nation of about one million people, only constituted in 1385, was famous for its nautical knowledge and its bold sailors.

Portugal was the first nation to begin the search for Asia via the Atlantic. Diaz disembarked in the Azores in 1432 and reached Cape Verde in 1446. Then, in 1488, he sailed to the southernmost tip of Africa, rounding the Cape of Good Hope and finally opening the way to the productive areas of Asia. However, from Portugal to South Africa and thence to India is an interminable twelve-thousand-mile voyage through dangerous waters, while the overland route is only half that distance. If Asia were opposite Europe, as had been believed since ancient times, why not go straight across the Atlantic? Martin Behaim calculated the distance to be 126 degrees or approximately nine thousand miles. Columbus maintained that the distance was only 79 degrees, or close to six thousand miles. To offset the advantage that Portugal had gained, Spain undertook, with Columbus, the greatest maritime adventure of modern times.

On October 12, 1492, after a voyage of over five thousand miles, Columbus landed on an island that he believed to be near the continent of Asia. He died in 1506, Viceroy of the Indies, still convinced that he had fulfilled mankind's ancient dream of reaching Asia by crossing the Atlantic.

Portugal and Spain divide the world.

To ensure that only they would profit from their discoveries, the two rival nations appealed to Pope Alexander VI. In 1493, he approved the drawing of a line that cut the world in two from the North Pole to the South Pole, passing one hundred leagues from the Azores and Cape Verde. Everything to the west of this line was to belong to Spain, and everything to the east was given to Portugal. In 1494, Spain and Portugal agreed to shift the line farther west, thus putting Brazil, an area about which nothing was yet really known, into Portuguese territory.

Spain and Portugal now claimed a monopoly of all territory still not under the jurisdiction of Christian princes. With the exception of Europe, the entire world was strictly reserved for two small states with a combined population of scarcely eight million. Whoever did not respect this division as sanctified by the Pope was liable to be excommunicated. Spain and Portugal, who profited most from the affair, were themselves the first to challenge the Pope's power; for in 1494, by common agreement and their own initiative, they decided to alter the line. Other states, namely England and France, were to show the same independence towards the Pope, at the expense of the Portuguese and Spanish claims.

The English claim to have reached "Asia"

Although she was still subject to the religious authority of Rome, England did not recognize the Pope's power to apportion "the riches of this world." In 1497, she attempted in her turn to reach Asia. English seamen had had about thirty years' experience of making long voyages. The Bristol merchants had visited Iceland and Greenland frequently. Then, after being expelled from these rich fishing areas, they had made several attempts to reach the "island of Brasil" mentioned in old legends. The Spanish and Portuguese discoveries appear to be the reason for Henry VII's decision to launch an important expedition. In 1497, he authorized the departure of the Venetian, Giovanni Caboto (better known under the name Cabot). Coming from Spain, this navigator possibly knew a lot about the Atlantic routes.

On board the *Matthew,* Cabot may have reached land after a voyage of seven hundred leagues, and disembarked on June 24 to take possession of the area in the name of England. Afterwards, he may have explored the coastline for a distance of three hundred leagues, returning to England in the month of August. His friends enthusiastically maintained that he had discovered Asia. We have no actual proof, however, that Cabot reached Asia (that is, America) by a western route. Cabot's account of his voyage and the original map he drew no longer exist. There is not even a copy of his map, but only a map by La Cosa drawn from a copy. This map of La Cosa has come down to us in a retouched form, for material discovered twenty-five years after Cabot's voyage has been added. Besides this, the only direct testimony is a letter from the Italian Soncino to the Duke of Milan (Soncino had met Cabot on his return from the voyage), which would lead us to believe rather that Cabot tried to reach Asia by sailing around the north of Europe. Finally, no English place name has survived Cabot's visit; and it was not until the last quarter of the sixteenth century that England based her claims on the work of Cabot. Be that as it may, history has traditionally maintained since the sixteenth century that Cabot landed in North America on June 14, 1497. Historians have suggested Labrador; St. John's, Newfoundland; Cape Breton; and Prince Edward Island as possible sites.

We have no definite information on the second voyage Cabot may have made in 1498 when, it is claimed, he visited the coasts of Greenland, Labrador, and Nova Scotia.

A third exploration is attributed to him, made perhaps in 1500 or 1501, with the Portuguese João Fernandes, who was a *lavrador* ("landowner"). The place name Labrador appears at this time, first to describe Greenland, then the Canadian coast. In any case, while searching for Asia, England had found neither silk nor spices and the merchants of Bristol had to be content with the fisheries of the "new-found land".

Newfoundland remains Portuguese for a long time

During this period Portugal was engaged in establishing trading posts along the route to the Indies (East) around the Cape of Good Hope, but she did not neglect the North Atlantic. The Portuguese, in partnership with the Danes, had already been seen on the routes the Vikings had once followed.

The Portuguese Gaspar Corte-Real, who already had other voyages of exploration to his credit, left the Azores in the spring of 1501 and approached a new land in the Northwest Atlantic. His brother Miguel in his turn undertook another voyage, early in 1502. Only two ships returned to Portugal, the leader of the expedition having disappeared.

The details of their explorations are still unknown, but there is reason to believe that they visited the east coast of North America (Labrador, Newfoundland, and Nova Scotia). Perhaps they even went up the Saint Lawrence and became lost there. The voyages of the Corte-Real brothers, in addition to providing our earliest knowledge about the natives of North America, gave to the new-found land the first place names we can identify: these are Portuguese.

During the same period, cartographers also began to use the name of the Bretons to designate an area that may correspond to Cape Breton: This is almost the time (around 1504) that Bretons are known to have visited the fisheries of Newfoundland. One thing is certain: Thomas Aubert from Dieppe went there in 1508 and was the first Frenchman to return to Europe with some natives. After this, it becomes easy to verify the presence of French fishermen in Newfoundland. Fishermen from England, Spain, and Portugal also came regularly.

However, during the first twenty years of the sixteenth century, the Europeans coming to Newfoundland for the cod fishing made no attempt to explore. About 1520, the Portuguese resumed their efforts and established a colony in North America, an experiment not previously attempted by any European power. João Alvares Fagundes was in charge of this project. During the first six months of 1520, Fagundes explored the coast of Newfoundland, particularly the south. In 1521, he obtained the concession of the area he had visited, and later, he returned there with two ships carrying Portuguese families. But, the colony established, it is believed, at Cape Breton, failed, either because of the climate, or because of wars with the natives.

The work of Fagundes marks an essential step. Before Fagundes, the coasts of Nova Scotia and Newfoundland were almost unknown. After his exploration, maps presented a much more accurate picture of these regions. Moreover, Portuguese cartography of this period increased the knowledge about Nova Scotia and the southern coast of Newfoundland. Numerous place names are Portuguese and many of them have survived down to our time in a French or English form. After Fagundes, to whom we are indebted for this progress, Portuguese fishermen continued to frequent Newfoundland, but Portugal had ended her explorations of North America.

The exploration of North America stops temporarily

In the first quarter of the sixteenth century, Europeans were preoccupied with South America and a wave of explorers, adventurers, and missionaries made for this continent. Of course, they did not find the spices and other products of Asia, but these new lands were overflowing with gold, silver, pearls, rare woods, and dyestuffs. All these resources resulted in Spain's becoming the richest power in Europe.

The crossing of the Isthmus of Panama by Balboa, in 1513, and the discovery of a new ocean meant that these lands undoubtedly formed part of a new continent. To the south of Panama, the eastern coastline was known as far as Rio de la Plata and the western coastline as far as Peru. By 1507, scholars had adopted the habit of referring to this southern area as "America" (now South America). There is some dispute as to whether this name originated with Vespucci, or from the Nicaraguan word *Amerrica*, which apparently means "land rich in gold", and may have been used at first to refer to the *Castilla del Oro*.

Central America was already known. The Spanish had completed the conquest of Mexico by 1521 and established there the vast province of New Spain. The West Indies were being actively exploited. Cuba, Hispaniola (today divided into two parts: Santo Domingo and Haiti), Puerto Rico and Jamaica were together almost sufficient to make the fortune of Spain. The northern coastline of the Gulf of Mexico was visited several times by the Spanish, and Florida was discovered in 1513. It is not known whether there was any connection between Spanish Florida and the "new lands" used as fishing grounds by the Europeans. The cartographers, generally, just placed the ocean between these two regions. Some, such as Cantino, Waldseemüller and Schöner depicted the "new lands" as an island; others, like Ruÿsch in 1508, saw them as simply a cape of Asia.

What exactly is known about the beginnings of North American history, between 1497 and 1521? The historians of the twentieth century have not advanced much farther in this area than their nineteenth-century predecessors. What were the itineraries of John Cabot, the Corte-Real brothers, and Fagundes? Did these explorers go any further inland? Were the Saint Lawrence river and its Gulf already known? A perplexing number of problems still appear insoluble. However, the period of Verrazano begins a chapter of history where the details are much better known. The exploration of North America, which up till 1521 appears to have been undertaken exclusively by Portugal, now enters an important stage. For over half a century, beginning in 1524, this task is assumed by France.

The beginnings of New France

Although the fishermen of Brittany had been coming to the "new lands" since 1504, at least, France could not yet claim any rights to territory in America, for the fishermen did not come here for any scientific or political purpose, and fishing on the Grand Banks added nothing to the knowledge about the New World. France was busy

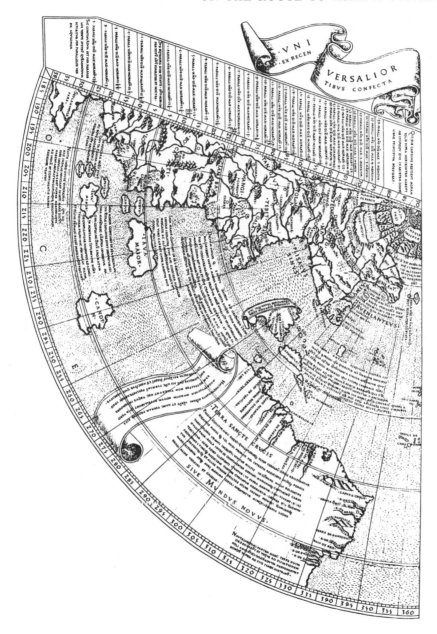

RUYSCH, UNIVERSALIOR COGNITI ORBIS TABULA

Public Archives of Canada

The "New-found land," a cape of Asia
(according to a map by Ruÿsch, in 1508)
Between Newfoundland and Spanish America is a sea extending as far as the
East Indies. This is the route that Verrazano intended to follow.

acquiring territory in Italy, until 1523, when she suddenly became interested in the Atlantic. This was the time when the expedition of Magellan, a Portuguese, had just returned to Spain after circumnavigating the globe. During this voyage, Magellan had discovered to the south of South America a passage leading to Asia. Since Magellan had found a passage to the south of the Spanish colonies, France considered the possibility of another, much shorter passage lying to the north of those same colonies, between Florida and the "new lands."

The discovery of such a passage was the aim of Giovanni da Verrazano, an Italian from Florence, who entered the service of France financed by an Italian syndicate in Lyons. In 1523, he organized the first official French expedition to search for the Atlantic route to Asia. He set out in 1524, after a false start, on board the *Dauphine*. His intention, so he wrote, was to reach Cathay and the eastern extremity of Asia. He took a direct route across the Atlantic (being the first to do so) and reached land on March 25. He states that this place was below 34 degrees latitude and it has been identified as being in the area of Cape Fear, North Carolina. It is there that he saw in the distance, beyond a strip of land, a vast expanse of water, which he took to be the Asian Sea but which was, in fact, only Pamlico Sound. His attempts to cross this narrow obstacle preventing him from reaching the "happy shores of Cathay" were unsuccessful. Maps were eventually published showing an Asian sea in this area touching the Atlantic.

Verrazano continued to sail along a coastline stretching from Florida to the "new lands," which presented an impassable barrier across the route to Asia. To the region of Virginia, he gave the name Arcadia, which was later moved by cartographers farther north and became "Acadia." The *Dauphine* reached the region of New York, which Verrazano called "Angoulême"; and then continued in this way up to the 50th parallel, perhaps to the 54th, without finding a passage across the continent.

Verrazano's voyage represented a great advance over previous explorations, for he had proved that the mainland extended from Florida to Cape Breton. For the first time, the Atlantic coastline was accurately shown on a map, and what is more, Verrazano boldly concluded—in opposition to certain cosmographers of his time—that this land was not attached to Asia but formed a separate continent. The whole of this region, from Florida to Cape Breton, had been discovered by a French expedition; so France acquired a basis for her claims. The name "New France," was given to this area and French place names were scattered along the coastline. The first New France, that of Verrazano in 1524, covered the whole of North America, and it was this interpretation of "New France" that Richelieu would still be claiming in 1627.

Spain, however, maintained that the French had invaded her empire to the west of the line of demarcation. So, in 1524-1525, she sent the Portuguese Esteban Gomez to explore this coastline and look for the passage to Asia at the same time. He sailed along the continent from Newfoundland to Cape Cod. In 1526, the Spaniard Vasquez de Ayllon sailed from Florida up to Chesapeake Bay, where he founded the short-lived colony of *San Miguel* and then died. Henceforth, Spanish maps made no mention of New France but only of a New Spain divided into two parts: the Land of Gomez to the north, and the Land of Ayllon to the south. A long list of Spanish names added during the course of the sixteenth century led to the omission of Verrazano's French place names.

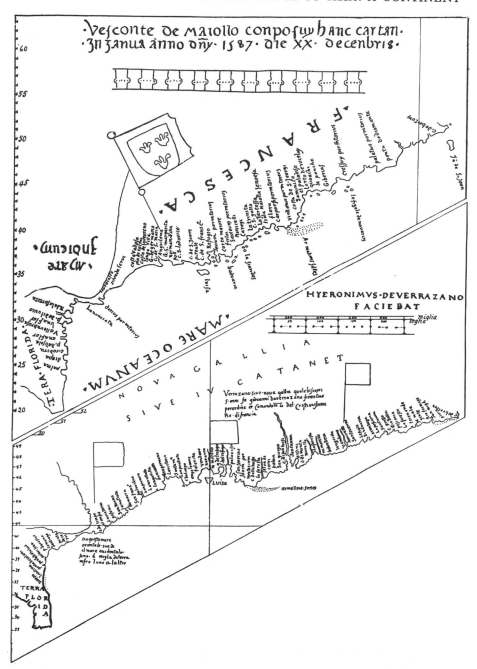

Public Archives of Canada

The New France of Verrazano, in 1524
(according to Maggiolo's map in 1527)
From Newfoundland to Florida lies a continental barrier sometimes called *Nova Gallia*, sometimes *Francesca*. The Asian Sea *Mare Indicum*, which Verrazano believed he had seen, was placed in the present-day region of the Carolinas.

England, in her turn, intervened in 1527, when Henry VIII sent out the *Mary Guilford*, commanded by John Rut, and the *Sampson*. The Englishmen probably entered the Gulf of Saint Lawrence and visited Cape Breton, and then the area which, in the following century, became New England. John Rut retraced Verrazano's voyage from the opposite direction and perhaps went as far as the West Indies. The route to Asia across the continent had not yet been discovered, but by this expedition, England had laid a foundation for her claims to North America.

The discovery of a great waterway to the interior

In spite of an attempt by the shipowner Jean Ango to establish an Asian trade route via South Africa, and in spite of the appeal of the products from Brazil, France did not overlook Verrazano's findings or give up her search for a passage. With the King's financial backing, Cartier set out with two ships on April 20, 1534, heading for the Baie des Châteaux (Strait of Belle Isle), which had been given as his known objective. Newfoundland was reached after twenty days, and on May 27, he entered the Baie des Châteaux, a hundred miles further on, where he still found fishermen.

On June 15, he steered towards the south, beginning his exploration with the gulf behind Newfoundland. The existence of a strait between Newfoundland and Cape Breton remained unrecorded, and he reached the Madeleine archipelago on June 25, believing it to be the beginning of the mainland. Prince Edward Island, where he arrived on the 29th, was thought to be a headland. On July 3, he saw the Bay of Chaleur, which led to the hope of finding a passage. On the 8th, he noticed that this opening narrowed into a bay *dont fusmes dollans* ("which disappointed us").

Proceeding on his way northward, he entered Gaspé Bay, where he stayed from July 16 to 25. There, he set up a cross as a sign that he had taken possession in the name of France. He also established the first European contact with an Amerindian nation, the Iroquois, who were to play a major role in the history of New France until the end of the eighteenth century. Since it was important to have guides who could learn French by spending some time in France, Cartier cunningly captured two sons of Chief Donnacona. The chief was quite willing to let him keep them, on condition that he promised to bring them back.

Cartier continued exploring the Gulf. From Gaspé, he came to a large expanse of land, Anticosti Island, which he took to be a peninsula. Because of a mirage or the fog, he could see only land instead of a river flowing through a strait 40 miles wide. Sailing around Anticosti, he discovered a strait, but he decided to return to France because the winds were unfavourable.

Cartier had not found any gold, metals, spices, or passage to Asia. However, the discovery of an inland sea behind Newfoundland had contributed to the knowledge about North America. Cartier was the first to make a map, but he put only one outlet for this sea: the Strait of Belle Isle, since neither Cabot Strait nor the river had yet been discovered.

In the fall of 1534, the navigator from Saint-Malo was commissioned to set out again on a second voyage of exploration. With three ships, the *Grande Hermine*, the *Petite Hermine*, and the *Émerillon*, taking back the two natives and perhaps two secular

Public Archives of Canada

The oldest picture of the Saint Lawrence
(from the so-called Harley map of the world just after Cartier's discovery, even, perhaps, from 1536)
Throughout the sixteenth century until the time of Champlain the Saint Lawrence (then called *Rivière de Canada*) would be represented in this manner. On the south shore (here the south is placed at the top) the person wearing a cloak is intended to be Jacques Cartier.

priests, he left France on May 16, 1535, and resumed his explorations from where he had left off the previous year. It was at this time that he gave the name of Saint Lawrence to a small bay on the north shore of the Gulf. This name would be extended, in 1569, to the Gulf by the geographer Mercator, and in 1613, to the river flowing into it.

On August 13, Cartier reached a most important stage in his exploration: he sailed beyond Anticosti Island and into a river which was, as he was told, "the way to Canada." On September 7, 1535, he reached the Orléans archipelago, "the beginning of the land and province of Canada." So Cartier discovered on that day, September 7, 1535, the small region of the interior that was then called *Canada* (that is, "town" or "village"). The capital, Stadacona, was situated on the heights of Cap-aux-Diamants.

Cartier still had before him a magnificent opportunity—to pursue his exploration as far as Hochelaga, which his guides had mentioned—but Donnacona tried to turn him against this and keep the advantages of a European connection for Stadacona. In spite of some witchcraft, intended to prevent Cartier from going upstream and from wintering in Canada, the French went up as far as Hochelaga, where they were prevented by rapids from going any farther. Moreover, the absence of interpreters made it impossible to obtain any information.

The Laurentian climate proves to be an ordeal

It was close to Stadacona, on the *Sainte-Croix* River (today the Saint-Charles River) that Europeans spent their first winter in the Saint Lawrence valley. Accustomed to the temperate winters of Brittany, Cartier had not believed the warnings of the natives. Their first experience of a Canadian winter was disastrous, not only because of the extreme cold, but because of scurvy. This sickness, which used to appear on both land and at sea, is caused by a diet deficient in vitamin C, and the Europeans knew of no protection against it. Cartier lost 8 men, and by the middle of February, there were not more than 10 members of the crew of 110 remaining in good health. By the use of cunning, Cartier eventually learned the secret of curing scurvy from the Indians. The remedy was an infusion of the *annedda* (which Jacques Rousseau has identified as the *thuya occidentalis*, or white cedar). This *annedda*, later to be called the "tree of life," restored everyone to good health. However, relations between Cartier and his allies from Stadacona very soon deteriorated because of his visit to Hochelaga and their mutual mistrust. Neither Donnacona nor his sons could be trusted any longer, and Cartier tried to take advantage of a disagreement to remove from Stadacona those who might harm the French alliance. At the celebration in honour of the Holy Cross, he took prisoner Donnacona, his two sons and some other Iroquois. On the homeward journey in 1536, Cartier discovered the strait separating Newfoundland from Cape Breton.

The results of this voyage of 1535-1536 were much more important than those of the previous one. Cartier was the first to use a new passage to the Gulf (by Cabot Strait), proving at the same time that Newfoundland is an island. Above all, he has the honour of discovering the great waterway by which the French would reach the heart of the continent. Going upstream, he discovered the main tributaries that would serve as routes for the building of a French empire: the Saguenay, the Saint-Maurice, the Richelieu and the river coming from the west (the Ottawa), by means of which one could reach a freshwater sea. The farther men penetrated this coastline blocking the route to Asia, the more the land assumed the proportions of a continent.

The first French colony in America

The wars of Francis I delayed this colonial enterprise for some time. Meanwhile Donnacona, now in France, talked of a wonderful land, rich in gold, that he had visited beyond Hochelaga. Finally, in 1540, Francis I put Cartier in charge of a new expedition, but he later changed his mind. He decided on a large-scale attempt at colonization to be directed by a gentleman of the Court, the Protestant La Rocque de Roberval. A lofty official aim was given to this great undertaking by the French King: the propagation of the Christian faith. Since the Pope's division of the new lands between Spain and Portugal in 1493, there remained only one way for France to intervene without offending the Holy See. This was by giving herself a missionary role. That this was only a diplomatic pretext is obvious since the first baptism administered by Frenchmen in New France did not take place until 1610.

Members of the nobility and criminals were recruited, and provisions for two years were bought, together with some cattle. Then the departure date was set for the spring of 1541. Only Cartier was ready by that time so he went ahead, expecting the leader, Roberval, to join him later. On August 23, he reappeared at Stadacona with five ships. No doubt because the fort of Sainte-Croix was too close to Stadacona (where the natives had become hostile), Cartier decided to settle at the mouth of a small river (the Cap Rouge), which flows into the Saint Lawrence on the far western side of Cap-aux-Diamants. This place, he named *Charlesbourg-Royal,* and he established two forts there, one on the

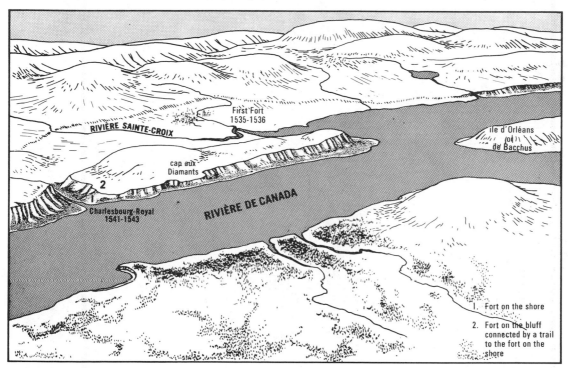

The site of the first French colony in America 1541-1543
An oblique view of the area from Cap Rouge to Île d'Orléans: on the left is Charlesbourg-Royal (today called Cap Rouge); in the centre the site of the "wintering" of 1535-1536.

shore, the other on the headland. When the men began tilling the ground, large quantities of what they believed to be gold and diamonds were discovered. Two ships left for France to announce this excellent news, and Cartier returned to Hochelaga in an attempt to reach the wonderful Saguenay. He was unable to cross the rapids, however, and without interpreters, he learned no more about it than he had in 1535.

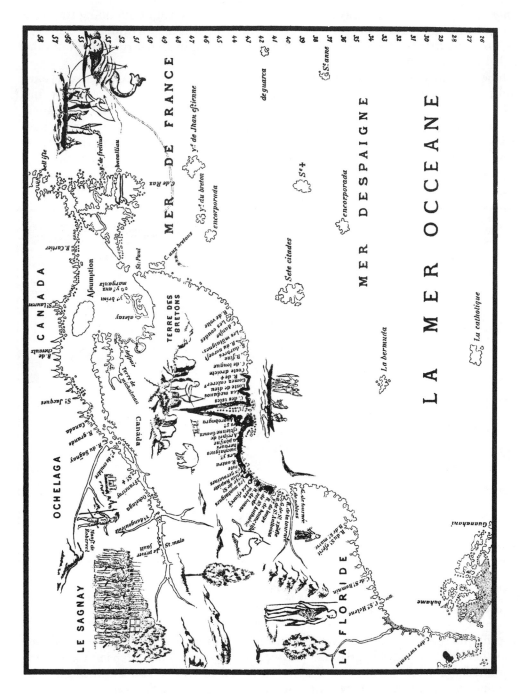

Another drawing of the Saint Lawrence from the sixteenth century
(according to a French map of 1543)
On the north bank the map-maker has tried to show Roberval addressing his troops.

The following spring, Cartier decided to return to France with the entire colony and his treasure, but reaching the Gulf in June, he met his leader Roberval who was arriving at last with the rest of the colony. Cartier was ordered to turn back, but he slipped away during the night and returned to France with his cargo that turned out to be merely quartz and iron pyrites.

Roberval went up the river with his three ships and occupied Cartier's site calling it *France-Roy sur France-Prime*. Sorely tried by scurvy and disappointed with a fruitless exploration of the Saguenay, the colony took advantage of the arrival of a supply fleet, in 1543, to return to France.

The attempt to create a New France in the new northern lands had failed. The French had discovered neither gold nor a route to the Indies, and their relationship with the natives had deteriorated. A good relationship with the natives was essential, however, to the success of any European settlement. This failure discredited American colonization. Cartier's third voyage added nothing to his fame as a navigator. The work of Roberval and his pilot Alfonse produced accurate information on the Gulf and the river, but the great questions that had been asked since the voyage of 1535 still remained unanswered. An aura of mystery came down over the "great river of Canada" and lasted for a good half-century.

The Spaniard Hernando de Soto was, at this time, improving the knowledge of the rest of the continent. Between 1539 and 1542, he explored South Carolina, Georgia, and Alabama. Then, after crossing the Mississippi 450 miles from its mouth, he reached Oklahoma. When compared to this great journey, the voyage up the Saint Lawrence as far as Montreal demanded very little daring from Cartier and Roberval.

The continent of vain endeavours

For the rest of the sixteenth century, America north of Florida remained a continent where Europeans vainly tried to gain a foothold.

After Roberval's failure, France abandoned North America for some time in favour of Brazil, that other Cipango of the sixteenth century. The French were on excellent terms with the Brazilian natives and could engage in barter there even more easily than the Portuguese. The products (such as redwood) taken back to France aroused much enthusiasm. When Coligny wished to establish a place of refuge for his fellow Protestants, he sent Villegaignon to Brazil, in 1555, to settle in Rio de Janeiro Bay. But internal dissension and military intervention by Portugal brought this Protestant New France to an end in 1560.

Two years later, Coligny was still worrying about finding a place of refuge for his people in America. He sent Jean Ribault and Goulaine de Laudonnière to the north of Spanish Florida, the coast where Verrazano had landed in 1524. There, in the Beaufort archipelago between the present-day cities of Charleston and Savannah, the Protestants founded a New France that lasted until 1564. Then, moving farther south and inland from the Saint John's River, they built Fort Caroline. The Spanish, however, who fought Protestantism wherever they found it and who believed their West Indian possessions were threatened, destroyed this New France.

After these systematic attempts at colonization, which had no parallel until the seventeenth century, confusion resulting from the Wars of Religion reigned in France. However, during this politico-religious struggle, the fishermen from Normandy, Brittany, and the Basque country continued their annual expeditions to the Banks of Newfoundland, and traders frequented the Saint Lawrence. Despite her interest in Brazil, France did not lose interest in North America, and from time to time, attempts at colonization were made. The Breton Marquis Mesgouez de La Roche came in 1578. In 1584, Jacques Noël (Cartier's nephew) came. Étienne Chaton de La Jannaye arrived in 1588; Pré-Ravillon, in 1591; and the Marquis de La Roche, again, in 1597. This time, he chose Sable Island, 90 miles east of Nova Scotia. This colony received supplies regularly up to the end of 1601. When it was revisited in 1603, the leaders had been murdered and only eleven colonists remained. During the same period, in 1600, the Protestant Chauvin de Tonnetuit built a habitation at Tadoussac, where the fur routes ended, leaving sixteen men there. This new attempt at wintering turned into a disaster and the settlement was abandoned.

England has no better success

For England, the sixteenth century was also a century of vain endeavours. For the first fifty years, English intervention in America was delayed for various reasons. First, it was necessary to obtain unity in the kingdom. The English did not dare, in the beginning, to invade this continent deliberately, since Spain claimed it all. England's calling was still exclusively European, and her merchants were particularly interested in the Mediterranean trade. It was only during the last quarter of the century that England finally thought of establishing herself in America. She abandoned the Mediterranean trade for the Atlantic trade. Since she was becoming increasingly industrialized, it was necessary to find new outlets for her products. She also needed new sources to supply raw materials. Furthermore, war had now been declared between Spain, the representative of Catholicism, and Protestant England so that Queen Elizabeth no longer needed to respect the claims of her adversary. She wanted to frustrate Spanish aims in America, benefit from her wealth, and perhaps at the same time, discover the western route to Asia.

John Hawkins and Francis Drake were attacking and plundering the Spanish colonies in America while Frobisher was seeking for a northwest passage to Asia. Financed by the Cathay Company, Frobisher reached Baffin Land in 1576, and made a fruitless exploration of the large bay, from then on known as Frobisher Bay. During a second voyage in 1577, he discovered some ore deposits that were considered of sufficient value to warrant a third voyage in 1578. This time, he planned to establish a settlement in Frobisher Bay, but the construction wood that they brought was lost at sea and the proposed winter sojourn was abandoned. In any case, it was soon realized that the ore was worthless and the exploitation of the northwest was neglected for some years. John Davis returned there in 1585, and during the next two years, proceeded beyond the 72nd degree, through the strait now called Davis Strait. Frobisher and Davis had not found the passage to Asia, but in spite of everything, the hope of finding it still remained and considerable progress had been made in mapping the North.

England had bad luck both in her search for a route to Asia and in her attempts to colonize North America. Humphrey Gilbert, who set out in 1583 with five ships, took official possession of Newfoundland and then left to look for Norumbega. Unfortunately his ship sank in a storm. In 1585, Walter Raleigh sent a hundred colonists to settle in Virginia, where he had received a grant of two hundred leagues. The leader of this first group, Richard Grenville, chose Roanoke Island, but all the colonists returned to England in 1586. The same year Grenville, for a second time, brought fifteen people to Virginia, but they were never seen again. In 1587, a new group of 150 colonists settled with John White on Raleigh's land, but when supplies arrived in 1590, there was nobody left. Then events in Europe and the foundation of the East India Company discouraged the colonization of North America for a dozen years.

A new attraction: fur

When the sixteenth century—the great century of exploration and cartography—ended, Europeans had still not succeeded in establishing a permanent settlement north of Florida. In Canada, the known area included only the coastline of Acadia (shown very vaguely), Newfoundland, the Labrador coastline, the opening of Hudson Strait and the southern part of Baffin Land. The only entrance to the interior was the Gulf and the river (still called the "river of Canada"), and even there, progress had been stopped by the rapids upstream from Hochelaga. No exploration had been made of any tributary, not even the Saguenay. Anything else shown on the maps was either pure speculation or an attempt, sometimes a skilful one, to reproduce information obtained from the natives.

At the end of the sixteenth century, no European was living in what is now Canada. However, during the summer, Europeans were present not only on the coastal fishing grounds, but also in the interior of the Saint Lawrence where trade was carried on. A new phenomenon had appeared in the last quarter of the century, which was to direct the destiny of New France for a long time to come.

The beginning of the fur trade constitutes the most important element in the economic history of North America. Since ancient times, Europeans had come every year to catch cod, but they gradually realized that fur, an article for which they were not searching, might bring in an excellent profit. On July 7, 1534, when Cartier made the first barter transaction that we know about, the behaviour of the natives leads us to conclude that trading in furs with Europeans was already a familiar activity.

However, it was some time before this trade was organized. The men involved in "green fishing" (so-called because the only treatment given to the cod was salting) worked at sea, without landing on the coast, and then left for Europe again. It was the fishermen using the dry-curing method who settled on shore for the season. From their bases they went out fishing, then came back and began the long operation of drying, either on the shingle, or more commonly, on scaffolds. These fishermen had to go quite far inland to stock up with wood and game, and as a result, they became familiar with the country.

In addition to the amount of fish they had contracted to take back to Europe, the fishermen who stayed to dry the cod also took back some furs. Then, since furs were plentiful and found a good market, the fishermen brought them back in increasing quantities each year. In France in particular, where merchants wished to be free from the restrictions of a European internal market, fur arrived just at the right moment. It can be said that, after 1580, merchants organized complete trading expeditions up the Saint Lawrence looking for furs. By the end of the century, furs had become the main item of trade and the Saint Lawrence the main trading area.

From now on, colonization was to be dependent on the fur trade. In 1541, colonization was attempted at State expense. However, in the future and for a long time to come, colonization would be financed by private citizens. In order to obtain lasting results from these individuals, exclusive trading rights had to be granted, that is, a monopoly on furs. The first monopoly was granted in January, 1588, to a nephew of Cartier, Jacques Noël, in partnership with La Jannaye. This action was to produce the first conflict between trade and colonization: between the merchants who wanted free trade without any responsibility for colonization, and the colonizers who wished to apply part of the profits from the trade (guaranteed to them alone) to founding a new country. So in 1588, for the first time appeared this dilemma: either everyone should be free to trade, in which case no colonization could be expected, or a monopoly should be granted requiring its holder to undertake the business of settlement. As early as 1588, the decision was made in favour of freedom of trade. Until 1627, the problem for New France would take the following form: sometimes a monopoly would be set up, in the hope that systematic colonization would result; sometimes freedom of trade would gain the upper hand and the country would become no more than a seasonal trading post. One can well understand why New France, dependent on a single export product (fur), took such time and effort to become organized. In any case, the symbol for Canadian history, whether French or English, from now on would be the beaver.

Bibliographical Note

Much more detailed information on this period of discovery will be found in the following general works:

L. GROULX, *La Découverte du Canada*. Montréal, Éditions Fides, 1966.

T. J. OLESON, *Early Voyages and Northern Approaches, 1000-1632*. Toronto, McClelland and Stewart, 1963.

M. TRUDEL, *Histoire de la Nouvelle-France*, Vol. I, *Les vaines tentatives, 1524-1603*. Montréal, Éditions Fides, 1963.

The cartographical studies of W. F. Ganong have been brought together by T. E. Layng into one volume:

W. F. GANONG, *Crucial Maps in the Early Cartography and Place-Nomenclature of the Atlantic Coast of Canada*. Toronto, University of Toronto Press, 1964.

In the *Dictionary of Canadian Biography*, Vol. I, the articles CABOT, CARTIER, CORTE-REAL and VERRAZANO present various points of view on the discoveries.

There is an important thesis by the Jesuit Lucien Campeau on the real destination of Cabot:

L. CAMPEAU, S.J., "Les Cabot et l'Amérique." *Revue d'histoire de l'Amérique française*, XIV, 3 (Dec. 1960), pp. 317-352; "Jean Cabot et la découverte de l'Amérique du Nord." ibid., XIX, 3 (Dec. 1965), pp. 384-413.

Another article, by the same author, discusses the Portuguese discoveries:

L. CAMPEAU, S.J., "Découvertes portugaises en Amérique du Nord." *Revue d'histoire de l'Amérique française*, XX, 2 (Sept. 1966), pp. 171-227.

For the map of Vinland *circa* 1440: see the studies of Thomas E. MARSTON, Farley MOWAT and Melvin H. JACKSON, in *The Cartographer*, III, 1 (June 1966), pp. 1-17.

CHAPTER II

The Amerinds of northeastern North America

The inhabitants of America are called *Amerinds* because the word "native" becomes confusing when Europeans begin to settle permanently in America. This term also avoids using the word "savage," which has disparaging connotations.

These Amerinds are related to the Mongolian race and their skin is a natural yellow or copper colour like that of Asiatics. In a period when Europeans were still living in caves, the Amerinds' ancestors crossed Bering Strait, taking with them only one domestic animal, the dog, and they spread across this continent. In the course of this migration, the Athapaskans and the Eskimos, who have retained their Mongolian features more clearly than the others, were probably the last to arrive; the Algonkians were probably the first. These natives were important because they supplied furs for export to Europe.

The Amerind families of the West

Because these families emigrated so long ago, and because their racial origins can no longer be found in Asia, it has been impossible for us to establish a direct connection between the Amerindian languages and the present-day languages of the Asian continent.

However, the Amerinds of Canada have been divided into eleven linguistic families. Of these eleven families, six lived on the Pacific coast, hardly venturing beyond the Rockies: the Tsimshian, the Wakashan, the Haïda, the Kootenay, the Tlinkit, and the Salish. These six families had, to some extent, a common culture. They all lived in a limited area, and their livelihood depended on the salmon and the cedar. The totem, which reproduces effigies of guardian spirits or family emblems, remains the best-known manifestation of this culture.

In the Rockies, the Mackenzie River valley, and the Hudson Bay area, lived the Athapaskan family who spoke a language that appears to have been similar to Tibeto-Chinese. The Athapaskans were primarily forest dwellers, very much like the Algonkians of Eastern Canada. They hunted the caribou and the beaver and used the bark canoe. Their religion was animistic (they believed that spirits inhabited all things), and their religious organization was as rudimentary as their social organization. Among the Athapaskan tribes, it was the Chippewas who assumed the leading position in the eighteenth century, when they gained the monopoly of English trade on the Churchill River.

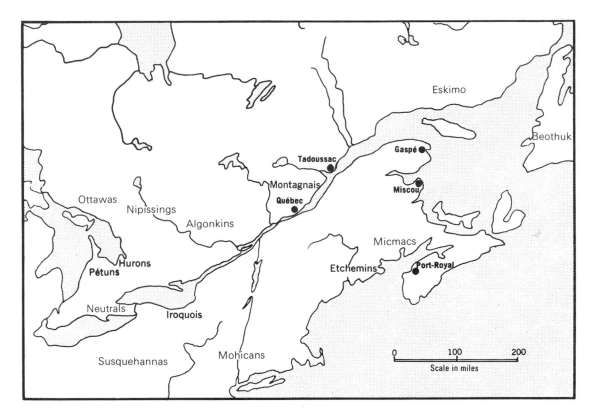

The first native peoples encountered by the French at the beginning of the seventeenth century

The Beothuk and Eskimo

The remaining four linguistic families (the Algonkians, Huron-Iroquois, Eskimo, and Beothuk) lived in the rest of Canada and they occupied eastern Canada during the sixteenth and seventeenth centuries.

The Beothuk, who lived in Newfoundland, were probably the first northern Amerinds to come into contact with Europeans and are responsible for the name "red-skins" because of the colour they used to paint their skin. Unfortunately, the white man did not take the trouble to learn their language, and no missionaries lived among them, with the result that nothing is known of their language or their origin. It is by way of hypothesis that they are considered to form a distinct linguistic family. Driven off and even hunted like animals by the English, they ended by disappearing completely in the nineteenth century. The last one died in 1829.

The Eskimo take their name from a term of contempt applied to them by the Montagnais: *estimeow,* or *aisimeow,* which means "eaters of raw meat." Their own name for themselves was *Inuit,* meaning "Men." They were formerly found, not only in the Arctic regions and on the Labrador coast, but also on the north bank of the Gulf of Saint Lawrence from the Strait of Belle Isle to the Sept-Îles area. Everyone was their enemy: the Montagnais—their neighbours to the west,—the Micmacs who attacked them from Gaspé, and the Europeans with whom they had little contact over a long period of time. It was really only in the second half of the eighteenth century that permanent relations could be established with them. Their religion was animistic. They were small in stature, and nomadic according to the requirements of hunting (caribou, seal and sea lion). They lived in tents (*igloos* during the winter), and for travelling by water, they used the *kayak,* a small boat of sealskin.

Continuous contact with the white man was maintained by the last two families, the Huron-Iroquois and the Algonkians, who were, therefore, more subject to the influence of European culture than the others.

The Algonkian family

The terms *Algonkian* and *Algique,* recently suggested by the ethnologist Jacques Rousseau (to whom we are indebted for the elucidation of many problems) specify a large number of tribes. These tribes, spread out from the Atlantic to the Rockies, constitute a cultural community, and their languages, while individually distinct, have a common origin.

The Algonkian family consists of the following groups, which are here examined in their geographical order from east to west:

1. The Micmacs (Souriquois) lived in the Acadian Peninsula, the eastern part of New Brunswick, and the Gaspé Peninsula. They are sometimes called *Gaspésiens* or *Gaspéïquois.*

2. The Etchemins were also known as Malécites or Penobscots. In the seventeenth century, they lived on the Saint John River, in the western part of New Brunswick, and in Maine. During the first half of the seventeenth century, another nation was encountered. This was the Abenakis who lived on the Kennebec River. This nation, of unknown origin, became the faithful ally of the French against the English. They were found in Maine and New Brunswick and seem, later, to have assimilated the Malécites.

3. The Montagnais-Naskapi group comprises two distinct tribes, the Montagnais and the Naskapi, who nevertheless had a common culture.

Montagnais (from *montagne,* meaning "mountain") is a generic term applied to the natives of the Tadoussac area who wandered as far as Quebec and Cap Rouge. The term is also applied to the various tribes of the same culture who were settled in the area from Tadoussac to Sept-Îles. They called themselves *Ilnout,* meaning "Men." They were primarily hunters of the moose.

The Naskapi—perhaps identical with the Papinachois of the seventeenth century —were moose hunters and lived to the north of the Montagnais in an interior region situated between Lake Saint John and James Bay. The Mistassins are included in this group. Their name, "Naskapi," was a disparaging word originating with the Montagnais.

The Naskapi called themselves *Nenenot,* meaning "True Men."

Also included in the Montagnais-Naskapi group are the Attikamègues who lived upstream from Saint-Maurice. Little is known about them.

4. The Algonkins occupied two points on the Ottawa River (known as the "River of the Algonkins" in the seventeenth century): the present-day region of Montebello, inhabited by the Algonkins of the Petite-Nation, and Allumette Island, a strategic point of the first importance on the fur route, occupied by the tribe called Algonkins of the Island.

5. The Nipissings lived around Lake Nipissing and controlled the passage between the Ottawa River and the Great Lakes. They had acquired such a reputation for magic that they were given the surname of "sorcerers."

6. The Ottawas (Cheveux-relevés or Andatahouats) lived mainly to the north of Lake Huron, but in the time of Champlain, they were also found in large numbers in the southwest of Huronia, on the banks of the Detroit River. After the destruction of Huronia, they dominated the fur trade and thus gave their name to the Ottawa River. These Ottawas were perhaps identical with the Ojibwas.

The Cheveux-relevés or Ottawas

7. The Ojibwas (Chippewas) were a large tribe living around the Great Lakes. Included among them are the Saulteux (so called because they lived near Sault Sainte-Marie) and perhaps the Ottawas. Non-nomadic, and living primarily on what they could gather, they took their distinctive cultural traits from the "wild oat," a type of wild rice, which they consumed in great quantities.

8. The Crees lived in the Lake Superior area.

9. The Blackfeet and the Gros-Ventres lived on the Prairies.

In addition to having the same linguistic origin, these groups of the Algonkian family had common cultural characteristics. Being hunters (except perhaps for the Ojibwas), they lived exclusively on the products of the forest. Their culture was based on the birch, which they used to make canoes, tents, and kitchen utensils (they did not produce pottery for cooking). The band was, in a manner of speaking, their political unit.

The Huron-Iroquois

The picture is completed by an Amerindian family, the Huron-Iroquois, who were completely different from the Algonkians in culture and language.

A village fortified in the Huron-Iroquois manner
Many families shared the longhouses, which were covered with large pieces of birch bark.

The origin of these Huron-Iroquois is unknown. They probably came from the south, for they traditionally cultivated corn, pumpkins, and tobacco. In the time of Cartier, they were found in the Saint Lawrence valley at Hochelaga (Montreal) and Stadacona (Quebec). They also went on fishing expeditions to Gaspé where Cartier met them in 1534. He later found them again at Quebec in 1535. They were subsequently driven out of the Saint Lawrence valley in circumstances that remain mysterious. By the beginning of the seventeenth century, they had joined the remainder of their family on Lake Ontario, where the group was distributed in the following way—north of the lake

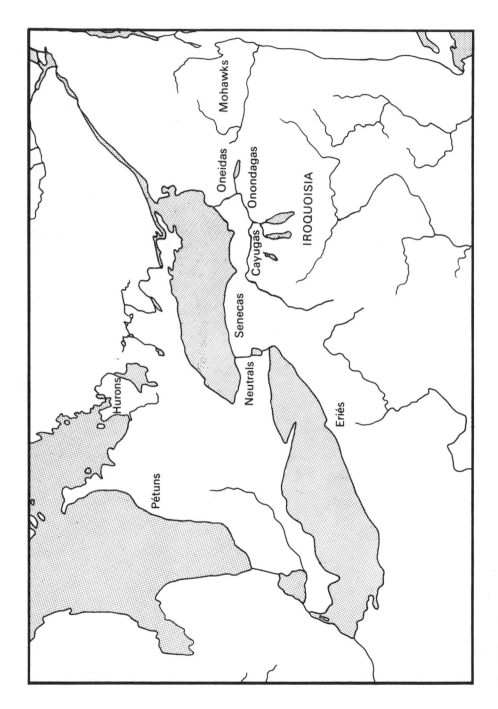

The Huron-Iroquois group
The Hurons, Pétuns, Neutrals, Eries and Iroquois formed a cultural group.

were the Hurons and Petuns; to the west were the Neutrals; to the south were the Iroquois; and to the southwest were the Eries. Most important were the Hurons and the
Iroquois.

The name *Hurons* was given to these people by the French because of their hair-
style, which was bristly (the name derives from the French word *hure*). Their own name
for themselves was *Wendats*. Living on Georgian Bay, cut off from Lake Ontario by a kind
of no man's land, the Hurons occupied a small area about 40 miles by 20 miles in size. In
the first forty-five years of the seventeenth century, however, they were the richest and
most powerful nation on the Great Lakes. The entire trade from the West, at that time,
came into Huronia, and left from there for the Saint Lawrence. Huron became the language of trade and travel.

The Iroquois lived to the south. The word *iroquois,* which is of Algonkian origin,
means "serpents." Their own name for themselves was *Hodinonhsioni,* or "people of the
great lodge." They were divided into five groups that did not form a real confederation
until the eighteenth century. From east to west, these groups were the Mohawks (in
French *Agniers*); the Oneidas (in French *Onneyouts*); the Onondagas (in French *Onon-
tagués*); the Cayugas (in French *Goyogouins*); and the Senecas (in French *Tsonnontouans*).

All these Huron-Iroquois (the Hurons, Petuns, Neutrals, Eries, and Iroquois)
constituted a homogeneous cultural group. They had similar characteristics and spoke
essentially the same language. Their social organization had a rigidity that was completely absent from that of the Algonkians. Normally not nomadic, although they moved
their villages every fifteen or twenty years, they lived in long huts that sheltered several
families. They were great cultivators of maize, tobacco, squash, and beans, and they
introduced the Algonkians to these products.

European influence on Amerindian culture

The Amerinds came under the influence of Europeans in direct proportion to the
amount of contact they had with them. This influence was felt from the sixteenth century
onwards. Some of the tribes that up till then had lived on the coast began to move farther
and farther inland in order to obtain the furs that they exchanged with the white man.
Originally non-nomadic fishermen, they became nomadic hunters, a fact that profoundly
altered their way of life, as well as their traditional culture. From the sixteenth century
onwards, the Amerinds were using tools, weapons, boats and clothes that came from
Europe. This material influence was already penetrating far into the interior of the
continent. Through the Montagnais and the Algonkins, European products travelled as
far as the Great Lakes. This was the beginning of a lengthy transformation that was
accelerated in the following century when the French settled permanently in Acadia and
along the Saint Lawrence.

The European influence also affected the food and drink of the Amerinds. They
very early adopted European beverages, such as wine and brandy, and were soon accustomed to getting drunk. Because of the apparent increase in their strength and the
sudden facility of speech it gave, they saw the new experience as the manifestation of a
divinity.

They also acquired the need for salt, which they had not known before the arrival of Cartier. But, of all the foods to which the French introduced them, it was perhaps bread that they liked best. Once used to bread, they could no longer do without it. On the Saint Lawrence, in 1627, before men were killed for brandy, a Montagnais killed two Frenchmen for bread.

The fashion for imported products

While they were not greatly impressed by the wearing of beards ("hair on the mouth," as they called them), the natives were for the most part dazzled by the French style of dress. They adopted this as soon as possible. From the early years of the seventeenth century, they could be seen wearing hats, hoods, shirts, shoes, and woollen blankets, all of which they acquired by barter. The hat was the most important of these articles, and whoever wore one felt that he had really attained a higher level of civilization. The hat was a necessary accompaniment to the formal bow that the French taught them, and many Amerinds thought that in this way they would realize their dreams of passing for Frenchmen.

Other European products spread rapidly among the Amerinds: seagoing boats (rather heavier than canoes), firearms, swords, iron tips for arrows, pots, kettles, and kitchen utensils. These articles being very much better than the domestically made ones soon replaced them, with unfortunate results for native skill and craftsmanship.

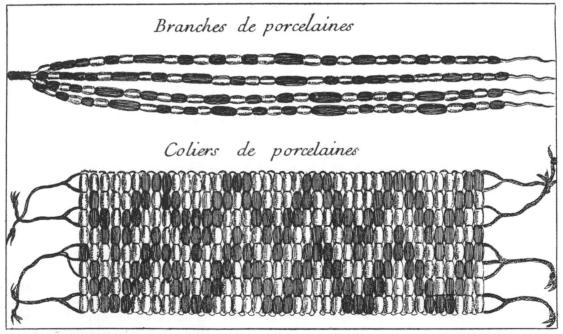

Branches de porcelaines

Coliers de porcelaines

Public Archives of Canada

Shell strands and necklaces
(reproduced from Bacqueville de La Potherie's *Histoire de l'Amérique septentrionale,* 1722 ed.)
Strands and necklaces were used as money, records and jewellery. At first they were made of shell work but later they were replaced by small cylinders made of glass mixed with tin or lead, imported from Europe.

Of all the commonly used articles, the *matachias* best illustrate the way in which foreign products took the place of locally made ones. These *matachias* or shell necklaces (also called in French *grains de rassade*) were made of small, either white, brown, or purple cylinders cut from seashells (the *Venus mercenaria* in particular). The cylinders, the size of chickpeas, were drilled and threaded onto leather thongs, to form shell strands. Several of these strands together formed a "shell necklace" or *wampum*. These strands and necklaces were, therefore, strictly peculiar to the Amerinds and possessed a sacred character, for they were commonly used in treaties. Nevertheless (and this is another surprising example of European influence), the French began to manufacture beads of glass mixed with tin or lead, and this glassware imported from France soon took the place of the original *matachias*.

The struggle between Priest and Shaman

The meeting of cultures also influenced the religious life of the Amerinds. It was often thought, at the beginning of the seventeenth century, that the natives had no religion. The reason was that they did not practise their cult in the European manner, and since certain of their customs were ridiculed, they tried to surround them with an atmosphere of absolute secrecy.

The Amerinds had a religion that corresponded exactly to the society that had produced it. It was animistic in character, and the priest's duty was to invoke spirits. Although they were called *shamans* for the sake of convenience, these priests had various names according to the nations in which they practised their cult: the Micmacs (Souriquois) called them *aoutmoin;* the Montagnais and the Algonkins, *manitou;* the Hurons, *oqui*. The *shamans* had great influence because they were able to make use of natural phenomena. When the missionaries attempted to impose their authority upon the tribes, they had to employ the same procedures. At first, the Amerinds agreed to baptism, which they saw only as a sign of alliance with the French. Subsequently, they came to understand that baptism was much more than this and that the idea was completely different from their religion. At this point, the *shamans,* with the help of their followers, began their long struggle against the missionary, for they realized their whole way of life was at stake.

Christianity triumphed wherever missionaries were able to settle permanently, in spite of the rising death rate which the Amerinds attributed to the practice of baptism. It was not yet known that this death rate was due to European diseases (even to ordinary influenza) against which the natives had no defence. The natives blamed the new religion with its strange rites because, ever since their contact with the French, the death rate had reached alarming proportions.

Christianity caused more of an upheaval in the Amerindian culture than the material goods introduced from Europe. The essential values of Christianity are not in question here, but it should be noted that the defeat of animistic religion by the missionaries meant that Amerindian culture lost its traditional supports. It was unable to integrate the new theology so that it would serve as a supporting and cohesive element as the old one had done.

Amerind influence on the Europeans

Although the Amerind was influenced by the European, we must remember that the European was also subject to the pressures of the American world. The French, for example, were forced to adopt the local methods of transportation. They learned to use the birch-bark canoe on the watercourses of the interior; they wore snowshoes to walk on the snow; and they made use of the toboggan.

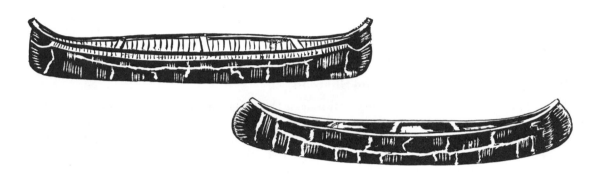

The Algonkian-type canoe made of birch bark

Although in general continuing to eat and drink as they had done in Europe, the French discovered new culinary delights: maize or Indian corn (which the natives ate as *mingan,* crushed and boiled with fish; or as *sagamité,* which is gruel made of maize flour), the meat of the moose, bear, dog, and beaver (beaver tail was a delicacy and both tail and legs were considered as fish and could be eaten on Fridays); feathered game, such as pigeon; Jerusalem artichokes; small wild fruits, such as blueberries; maple syrup; and tobacco, which becomes indispensable to people who adopt the habit.

Besides these foods and techniques, there was a fascination felt by the French that caused the Récollet Sagard to write that the French "become savages after a short time among the savages." The Ursuline Marie de l'Incarnation wrote that it was easier for a Frenchman to become a savage than for a savage to become a Frenchman! Born into a society that constantly imposed all kinds of restraints upon them, the French suddenly found themselves face to face with a civilization where no restraint seemed to exist. Children were raised in complete freedom, and adults were generally free to act and think as they wished. Authority could not be enforced at all. There were no restrictions imposed by the idea of modesty, for the natives went naked in summer, or by the idea of chastity (girls gave themselves to whomever they wanted). As soon as they left immigrant society, the French were overjoyed to escape the traditional norms. For a long time, this new world was to fascinate them, and the Jesuit Charlevoix was justified later in speaking of the special preference that Canadians had for native women.

Language: a check on European influence

The effects of the meeting of cultures, often disastrous for the Amerind, were lessened or at least delayed by the language barrier, an obstacle that took some time to overcome. This problem was far-reaching.

To begin with, the Amerindian languages have absolutely nothing in common with those of Europe. Furthermore, although certain similarities can be found within the Algonkian linguistic family, there were so many different languages that this created small nations. Although the natives of Acadia were less numerous, they had at least three languages. In the peninsula and islands Micmac was spoken; the natives of the Saint John and Penobscot Rivers spoke Malecite; and the Almouchiquois of the Kennebec River spoke Almouchiquois. On the Laurentian fur route, the language barriers increased, making it necessary to employ a greater number of interpreters. There was the language of the Montagnais at Tadoussac and Quebec, the Algonkin language of Petite-Nation and Allumette Island, the Nipissing language (between the Algonkin country and the Great Lakes), and the Huron language which, fortunately, was the key to the whole interior region.

How could one master languages that developed freely and possessed no grammar to check their rapid evolution? How could one translate the abstract vocabulary of logic and theology into languages based on the concrete nature of individual things? These difficulties were, to a great extent, responsible for the length of time it took European civilization to permeate the native culture. What is more, ethnic revolutions sometimes vitiated long effort. In the sixteenth century, the French had acquired some knowledge of Iroquois, but when they returned to the Saint Lawrence, it was necessary to begin all over again, because the Montagnais had taken the place of the Iroquois. Lengthy efforts were made to learn the Huron language, the key to the Great Lakes, but just when it was mastered, Huronia disappeared.

There was a real hope that French would become the means of communication between the Amerinds and the French. In 1667, Colbert deplored the fact that the French were obliged to learn native languages. This was unrealistic, for being independent of the Europeans in the matter of food and free to sell their furs wherever they wanted, the Amerinds never felt any need to learn French. Furthermore, there was no question of forcing them to do so, because it was already hard enough to get them to come to the trading posts of the Saint Lawrence.

In spite of the inconvenience for European civilization and Christianity, it is fortunate that this linguistic barrier existed, for it certainly helped to delay the disappearance of the Amerindian cultures despite the fascinating novelties that Europe provided.

Bibliographical Note

For a general review of the Amerinds of Northeastern North America, see the following three studies:

Jacques ROUSSEAU, "Les Premiers Canadiens." *Cahiers des Dix,* 25 (1960), pp. 9-64.

George W. BROWN, and Jacques ROUSSEAU, "The Indians of Northeastern North America", in the *Dictionary of Canadian Biography,* Vol. I, pp. 5-16. This study contains a glossary of the names of the principal tribes.

Gérard MALCHELOSSE, "Peuples Sauvages de la Nouvelle-France, 1600-1670." *Cahiers des Dix,* 28 (1963), pp. 63-92.

On the life of the Amerinds, the following work is interesting:

R. DOUVILLE and J.-D. CASANOVA, *La Vie quotidienne des Indiens du Canada à l'époque de la colonisation française.* Paris, Hachette, 1967.

Hunt has published an important study of the internal relations of the Amerinds:

George T. HUNT, *The Wars of the Iroquois. A Study in Intertribal Trade Relations.* Madison, The University of Wisconsin Press, 1960.

On the reciprocal influence of European and Amerindian culture at the beginning of the seventeenth century see :

Marcel TRUDEL, "La Rencontre des Cultures." *Histoire de la Nouvelle-France,* Vol. II, *Le Comptoir, 1604-1627,* pp. 373-403.

A. G. BAILEY, *The Conflict of European and Eastern Algonkian Cultures, 1504-1700. A Study in Canadian Civilization.* Sackville, The Tribune Press, 1937.

CHAPTER III

The fur-trading settlement, 1604-1627

In 1604, the French regained a foothold on the North American continent that they had called *New France* since 1524. This time, occupation was to be lasting.

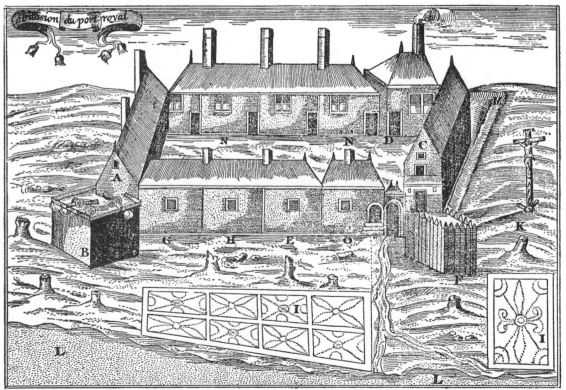

Public Archives of Canada

The Habitation at Port-Royal, 1605-1613
(engraving reproduced in the *Oeuvres* de Champlain, Laverdière ed.)

The search for an ideal location for the colony

At the beginning of the seventeenth century, encouraged by Henry IV, France resumed her efforts in northeastern North America. Admittedly, the unfortunate winter at Tadoussac in 1600-1601, the failure of La Roche to set up a colony on Sable Island (it lasted from 1598 to 1603), and the death of Aymar de Chaste in 1603, shortly after the sending of a new expedition to the Saint Lawrence, seemed as fruitless as the efforts of the sixteenth century. These events were, however, the beginnings of a permanent settlement.

A new leader, the Protestant Pierre du Gua, Sieur de Monts, took over in 1603. He held the title to a monopoly extending from the 46th to the 40th parallels and was backed by a society with ninety thousand *livres* in capital. Reaching Acadia in May, 1604, he stopped on a small island in the Sainte-Croix River (so-called because of its shape) and built a habitation there. Because of a particularly hard winter and the occurrence of scurvy, which caused the death of 35 of the 80 members of his colony, in addition to various other drawbacks, de Monts took his people, in 1605, to Port-Royal, where a four-sided habitation was built.

As the French saw it, however, Sainte-Croix and Port-Royal were only temporary settlements until an ideal site for colonization was found on the Atlantic coast. This site had to combine the best possible advantages: access to the sea, fertile soil, mineral wealth, friendly natives, and a passage to Asia. Twice—in 1605, under the command of Sieur de Monts, and in 1606, under Poutrincourt—expeditions went as far south as Cape Cod in search of this ideal site, but one or another of the required conditions was always lacking. In 1607, when preparations were being made for further exploration in the region of present-day New York, it was learned that the monopoly had been revoked. The entire Port-Royal colony returned to France.

The choice of the Saint Lawrence region

In 1608, de Monts obtained a one-year's extension of his monopoly. But this time he sent Champlain to found a habitation in the interior along the Saint Lawrence, in the region then called *Canada* as opposed to Acadia. He hoped to find there the advantages that had not been found along the Acadian coast and hoped to protect his trade from competition.

After a short battle won by the Basques at Tadoussac (this battle made it obvious that there could be no peaceful occupation of the Saint Lawrence), Champlain, the lieutenant of Sieur de Monts, reached Quebec by river. On July 3, he began to build a habitation. There was no lack of misfortunes. A plot to assassinate Champlain was almost successful. Also, in that first winter, scurvy killed twenty-eight settlers; only eight people survived.

To fulfil former promises, for which he was not responsible, Champlain decided, in 1609, to help his allies of the Saint Lawrence region against their Iroquois enemies. He went up the Richelieu River (then called the "River of the Iroquois" because it led to the area where the Iroquois lived) where he discovered a large lake that he named after himself. Then, in a place near Ticonderoga, he defeated the Indians with ease. This victory was repeated in the following year when he annihilated another group of Iroquois a short distance upriver from the mouth of the Richelieu.

This military co-operation strengthened the alliance between the French and the natives. The alliance he contracted with the Montagnais of the Saint Lawrence and the Algonkins of the Ottawa River was supplemented by one with the Hurons—the nation that controlled trade on the Great Lakes. In order to make his path of retreat more secure, Champlain, in 1611, had the idea of founding another habitation at the foot of the Saint-Louis waterfall, on Montreal Island. He cleared some land, and on a map of 1612, one can see the place name *Montreal* appearing for the first time. However, Champlain's plan would not be carried out for thirty years.

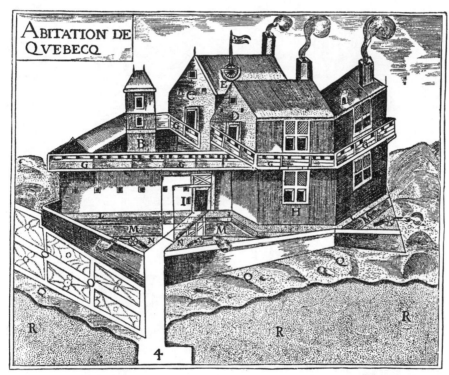

Public Archives of Canada

The Habitation in Quebec, 1608-1624
(engraving reproduced from the *Oeuvres* de Champlain, Laverdière ed.)
The property of Sieur de Monts up to 1612. Reconstructed after 1624.

The reorganization of New France

Except for the establishment of trade, New France was making no progress at all. Because of intense competition, de Monts could maintain only a few men in Quebec, and in 1612, he had to give the settlement over to some merchants from La Rochelle, who used it as a warehouse.

In the fall of 1612, France began the work of reorganization. De Monts gave up his command as lieutenant general, and his settlement and the monopoly went to the Comte

Champlain according to a contemporary engraving
Champlain is the European standing alone facing the Mohawks. This portrait, from an engraving illustrating the battle of 1609 (*Oeuvres* de Champlain, Laverdière ed.) is the only authentic picture of Champlain that has come down to us.

de Soissons. When the count died shortly afterwards, he was replaced by the Prince de Condé who received the title of Viceroy of New France. Champlain now had the protection in high places that he had requested, and he hoped that settlement would begin. However, the year 1613 brought nothing new in this field; it was notable only for a short exploration up the Ottawa River. The purpose of this exploration was to reach the northern sea discovered by Henry Hudson, but it stopped at the barrier posed by the Algonkins. Finally, in 1614, Champlain managed to unite the merchants, who were profiting from Condé's monopoly, by founding the Society of Rouen and Saint-Malo.

In spite of Champlain's hopes, this Society was content with maintaining the settlement at Quebec. The arrival of Récollet missionaries, in 1615, who had transport and maintenance supplied by the merchants, altered the strictly commercial character of the Saint Lawrence. But in spite of Louis Hébert, who arrived in 1617 and tried to live off the land, the colony of the Saint Lawrence was still no more than a fur-trading post.

A single important expansion should be noted. New France was officially extended as far as the Great Lakes. Following Étienne Brûlé, who had gone to Huronia as early as 1610 to learn the native language, Champlain went to Huronia in 1615, in order to help his allies against the Iroquois. After a disastrous expedition, Champlain was obliged to spend the winter with the Hurons. This sojourn enabled him to become more familiar with the natives and with the freshwater sea *(Mer Douce)* he had heard about since 1603. However, he made no use of Huronia as a base for any exploration of the continental interior.

The petition of 1618

The Saint Lawrence colony still numbered only about fifty people, almost all employed in trade. The Acadian colony was now only a small trading area supplying fur to the merchants of La Rochelle. Weakened by the disputes of 1612, Acadia suffered from a division of forces in 1613. Madame de Guercheville ceased to support Poutrincourt and sent La Saussaye to found Saint-Sauveur behind Mount Desert Island in Maine. Then, Virginia, which claimed all the territory up to the 45th parallel, dispatched a warship commanded by Argall. The settlement of Saint-Sauveur was taken by surprise and was razed. Argall also destroyed the settlements at Sainte-Croix and Port-Royal.

The opinion that a definite program of colonization should be undertaken by France was finally heard. In reports submitted to the King in 1618, Champlain attempted, for example, to calculate the income that could be derived from New France if it were exploited in a systematic way. The fisheries, wood and wood-products, mines, furs, farming of various kinds and stockbreeding could bring in 6,500,000 *livres* for New France. In addition, since the Saint Lawrence (as was then believed) could provide a quicker route to Asia than the Strait of Magellan, Quebec could become a customs port through which all the ships of Christendom would pass; and this might become a source of great wealth to France. Champlain, therefore, requested that a colony of three hundred families be established and a town be built in the Saint-Charles valley, established on the principles of "strength, justice, trade and farming." This was the first attempt, later followed by those of the Cent-Associés and Intendant Talon, to transform this fur-trading post into a colony where every resource would be exploited in a rational way.

The Saint Lawrence and the Compagnie de Caën

This petition and other attempts had so few results that Champlain himself was abandoned in 1619 on the Rouen docks by the society that employed him. However, a new Viceroy, Montmorency, tried to co-ordinate the various ventures by granting the monopoly to the Compagnie de Caën in 1620.

This Company was mixed from the point of view of religion. Guillaume de Caën was Protestant, while Ézéchiel and Émery, his associates, were Catholic. The group soon combined with the merchants of Rouen and Saint-Malo, the former holders of the monopoly of the Saint Lawrence trade.

The Compagnie de Caën accomplished more than its predecessors, for the members built a habitation at Miscou and another one thirty miles downstream from Quebec, at Cap Tourmente. This, with Île d'Orleans, was made into a barony for the benefit of Guillaume de Caën. Here, they began stock farming with some fifty animals brought from France by the Company. The Compagnie de Caën replaced the old wooden habitation of 1608 by a new one built of stone. They also helped Hébert and continued to support the Récollets.

A fur-trading colony

When it received its monopoly, the Compagnie de Caën had undertaken to construct five habitations and to install six families in fifteen years. These obligations were gradually fulfilled, but it was evident that, by the year when their monopoly ended (1635), there would still be no colony of settlers. What, then, was the state of New France in 1627, when Richelieu began to take a hand in it?

In Acadia, about fifteen people were living in the habitation at Cape Sable led by Charles de La Tour (the younger), Biencourt's successor. The next settlement was not until Miscou. On the Saint Lawrence, Tadoussac was still only a home port, since ships did not yet sail up to Quebec. The Cap Tourmente settlement, staffed by seven or eight people was a stock farm. Quebec had become the most important centre in New France, but it had only some seventy-two French people. The lower part of this settlement consisted of a habitation, a store, a house serving as a chapel, and some huts. On the heights of Cap-aux-Diamants stood Fort Saint-Louis, which was built of wood and still unfinished, and Louis Hébert's stone house. In the valley, on the banks of the Saint-Charles River, was the monastery of the Jesuits (Notre-Dame-des-Anges), and that of the Récollets (Saint-Charles). Perhaps eighteen or twenty *arpents* had been cleared, but there was still no plough to till the soil.

The total population of New France was about one hundred inhabitants, with almost no European women. In the Saint Lawrence region, there were, in 1627, five women and six girls; in Acadia, not even one. We still know of only two marriages and eight births in New France during this quarter of a century.

What is more, this community was badly organized. Seigneurial arrangements existed (the Cap Tourmente barony, the Jesuit fief and Hébert's fiefs), but these were still vaguely defined. There was no regular parish life and no educational institution, although the Récollets introduced some natives to the French way of life before sending them to be baptized and to study in France. Missionary work had few results. Twelve years of missionary activity along the Saint Lawrence produced only about fifteen native Christians. In Acadia, there had not been a single missionary since 1624.

One success—the network of trade

The network of trade had proved the greatest success to date. In Acadia, the French possessed four trade routes: those of the Saint John, Sainte-Croix, Pentagouët and Kennebec rivers. Although these routes were limited, along the Saint Lawrence the network covered a vast area. Through the Montagnais, furs from the nations of the north reached the Tadoussac trading post. The post at Trois-Rivières, and to an even greater extent, the post at Cap Victoire (near present-day Sorel), was the venue for the annual gathering of the great trading nations: the Montagnais of the Saint Lawrence, the Algonkins of the Ottawa River, the Nipissings and the Hurons. The Hurons, in particular, could be counted upon for an inexhaustible supply of furs, since they lived in the place where the trade routes from the interior reached the Great Lakes.

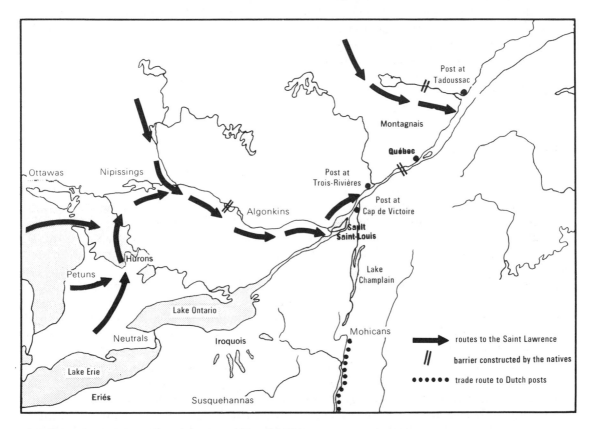

Trading routes and posts in the time of Champlain
The annual fair was usually held on Cap de Victoire (or Cap de Massacre), close to the mouth of the Richelieu River.

It was, of course, not an easy matter to maintain relations with these different nations. The Montagnais could never be trusted, although Champlain succeeded in imposing his authority upon them. He persuaded those who wanted to become chiefs to obtain the approval and support of the French. The other nations were more difficult to control and less receptive to European influence, since they made only brief visits to the Saint Lawrence and lived a long way from Quebec. The normal procedure was to leave interpreters with these natives. These interpreters saw that they came to the trading post each spring and encouraged them to keep the Saint Lawrence as the only outlet for their furs. If necessary, missionaries were sent to exert a stronger influence than the interpreters, while preaching the Gospel. This approach was to be expected in a society where Church and State were closely connected.

The Iroquois, with a confederation not yet as closely united as it would be towards the middle of the century, were still kept outside the great trading network. Commercial rivalry kept them in constant conflict with their sister-nation, the Hurons. Another related nation, the Neutrals, prevented them from moving towards the northwest. The Algonkins cut them off from the Ottawa River while south of Iroquoisia, the Mohicans dominated the Hudson River uplands. For many years, the Iroquois (usually the Mohawks alone) had no alternative but to destroy commerce along the Saint Lawrence. However, the term "Wars of the Iroquois," which was already being applied to these affairs, was scarcely appropriate. The battles of 1609, 1610, and 1615 were in fact no more than skirmishes. Here and there isolated blows were struck, in peacetime as well as in wartime, but the French were not at all inconvenienced.

The need for a new beginning

During this period, other European colonies were being founded on the North American continent. Some of these grew successfully.

Since the foundation of Jamestown in 1607, Virginia was developing rapidly and possessed some two thousand inhabitants. This growth was based on tobacco, which the colony produced at the rate of 500,000 pounds per annum and could sell on a guaranteed market. Virginia was, at this time, the greatest success that any European country had had in North America.

On the Hudson River, there was a population of 200 people, more than half of whom were Walloons. This group was, in fact, the largest French-speaking group in America. Between Rhode Island Bay and Acadia, in an area that the French had in vain scoured for an ideal site for colonization, there were 200 Pilgrims at Plymouth and 110 colonists at Salem. This New England territory was already more populous than New France. Scottish colonists were soon to settle in Acadia which, in theory, belonged to Sir William Alexander and had, since 1621, been called *Nova Scotia* by the English. In Newfoundland, on the Avalon Peninsula, the colony of Ferryland alone was as populous as the whole of New France. It is scarcely necessary to recall that the English had already spent three winters on Hudson Bay, since its discovery in 1610, while the French had not undertaken a single exploration in the north.

New France, with a population of only one hundred and no more than two established families, made a poor showing against the two thousand inhabitants of the other

Armand Jean du Plessis
Cardinal Duc de Richelieu

Fac Lubin sculp.

Public Archives of Canada

Cardinal Richelieu, chief minister of Louis XIII

European colonies. Fortunately, Cardinal Richelieu now assumed the direction of France's only colony. He abolished the office of admiral and took the powers of that office into his own hands, giving himself the title of *grand-maître de la navigation.* He also removed Viceroy Lévy de Vantadour, who had been appointed in 1625, cancelled the monopoly of the Compagnie de Caën, and founded a powerful trading society. The *Compagnie des Cent-Associés* (Company of One Hundred Associates), was granted, as fief and seigneury, the entire North American continent from Florida to the North Pole. It seemed that a better future was, at last, in store for New France.

Bibliographical Note

The period summarized in broad outline here is the subject of the second volume of my *Histoire de la Nouvelle-France: Le comptoir 1604-1627.* This work contains a full bibliography.

CHAPTER IV

The seigneury of the Cent-Associés, 1627-1663

After Richelieu had suppressed the Huguenots, who had become almost a state within a state in France, he began to strengthen French power outside Europe. Following up the reports that Razilly had submitted to him, on the subject of a far-reaching colonial policy for America in particular, Louis XIII's minister took on the task of reorganizing New France.

The Compagnie des Cent-Associés

Instead of small societies founded on the trade of two or three towns, Richelieu decided to form a large-scale company. This new colonial enterprise was to be on a scale unknown up to that time. A society of one hundred members was established, with a total capital of 300,000 *livres* (3000 *livres* was required from each member). To guarantee that the enterprise would last, the profits of the first three years were to be added to the capital; after that, only one third of the profit would be distributed, the other two thirds continuing to sustain the common fund. There was also a new arrangement providing an attractive inducement: any noble or ecclesiastic could join the company without losing the privileges of his status, and since trade could raise one's status to the nobility, it was promised that twelve of the Cent-Associés would be elevated to the nobility. The company was granted the right to fur trading in perpetuity and the monopoly of all trade (except fishing) for fifteen years. It also received, as fief and seigneury, a domain stretching from Florida to the Arctic Circle, and from Newfoundland to the "freshwater sea" (the Great Lakes) and beyond. The claim that all this area could be called New France was based on the discoveries of Verrazano, Cartier, and Champlain.

This immense seigneury was granted with the purpose of settlement. In the next fifteen years, the Associés had to send four thousand people there and support them for the first three years. To encourage the immigration of tradesmen, the rank of master craftsman (with the right to have a shop) was promised to those who practised their craft for six years in the colony and then wished to return to France. Huguenots, were excluded, however, since Richelieu did not wish to see in the colony a repetition of the difficulties that he had found so hard to overcome in France. Finally, in an effort to integrate the native population rapidly, Amerinds who professed the Catholic faith would be recognized as *naturels françois* ("French nationals") without the need for *lettres de déclaration ni de naturalité* ("affidavits or citizenship papers").

Successive setbacks ruin the Company

The greatest possible success was to be expected from such a powerful society of nobles and bourgeois possessing the monopoly of the whole of North America. However, the Compagnie des Cent-Associés soon encountered a number of setbacks that doomed it to failure.

Founded on April 29, 1627, the Company was established at the very moment when a conflict arose between France and England, and at a time when the English were setting up an Anglo-Scottish company that reserved the Saint Lawrence trade for itself. The Associés would have preferred to wait, but Richelieu ordered them to send an expedition in 1628. This fleet of four ships, with four hundred people on board, fell into the hands of Kirke. The following year, Quebec capitulated. The Scots were in control of Port-Royal and Cape Breton, in the area that they had been calling *Nova Scotia* since 1621.

Financial losses to the Associés were thus very heavy. From the beginning, in 1627, the Cent-Associés had been forced to pay 100,000 *livres* to Viceroy Lévy de Vantadour at the time of his resignation. The fleet captured by the English in 1628 had cost 165,000 *livres,* and in 1629, they lost 100,000 *livres* in a second expedition. From 1629 to 1632, the English occupied the seigneury of New France. In 1632, the Company lost its monopoly to the de Caën family and was directed to pay them 40,000 *livres* for ships that it had confiscated from them. In 1635, it had to pay them 80,000 *livres* as compensation for the loss of the monopoly. The Cent-Associés were never able to recover from this succession of setbacks. They lost enthusiasm; members refused, in spite of legal summons, to continue advancing money; and shares began to pass into the hands of indifferent stockholders. When Richelieu, who had a personal stake in the concern, died in 1642, the disorganized company was left without any vitality. Development was left to others, and while it remained the owner of New France, the Company ceded the trade of Canada to the Communauté des Habitants in 1645. In 1647, it also ceded the trade of Acadia to Menou d'Aulnay.

The influence of Razilly

At the time when the Compagnie des Cent-Associés was just being formed, a period of vigorous growth in Acadia was initiated by Commander Isaac de Razilly. He had the ear of Richelieu, whom he had advised on the foreign and colonial policy of France. Razilly, a Commander of the Order of Malta, chose to make Acadia, rather than the Saint Lawrence, the defensive bulwark of New France. As in the time of Poutrincourt and Madame de Guercheville, the Acadian peninsula and the mainland depended on two leaders, Razilly and Saint-Étienne de La Tour (called La Tour the Younger), who shared equally the monopoly of trade. Razilly was joined by his brother Launay-Razilly, his cousin Menou d'Aulnay, and Nicolas Denys. On July 23, 1632, Razilly led three hundred men (accompanied by some Capuchins) to La Hève to build a habitation. From this new capital, he took steps to drive out the Scots from Port-Royal, and he began the construction of a new habitation at Canso. In 1635, he drove the English from their post on the

Signatures to the capitulation treaty of 1629

Penobscot River. In Razilly's opinion, Pemaquid, at the mouth of the Kennebec River, was the place that should mark the extreme limit of New England. He died, however, in November 1635, just when he was giving the Acadian colony a strength that it had never known and a vitality much greater than that of the colony of the Saint Lawrence.

The loss of Acadia

An unhappy fate always overtook the work of the French in Acadia. Just when de Monts was getting his colony on its feet, the revocation of the monopoly, in 1607, put an

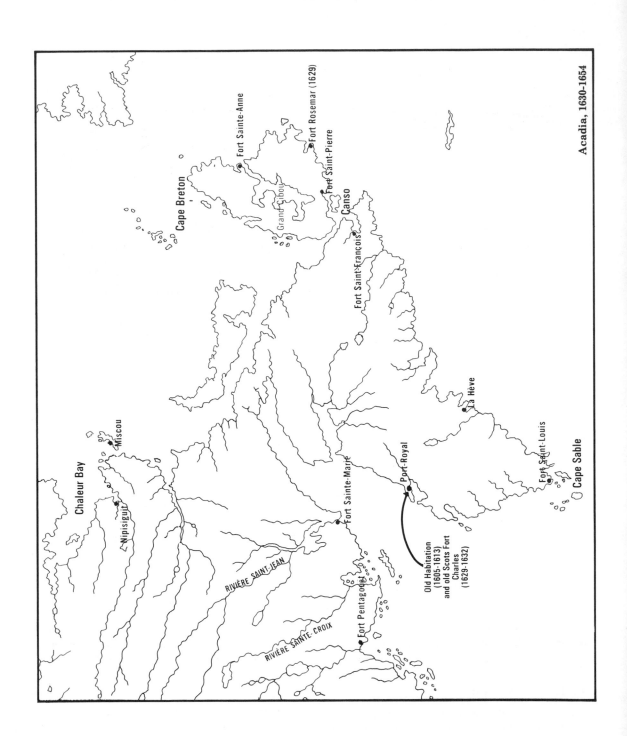

Fort Sainte-Anne

Fort Rosemar (1629)

Fort Saint-Pierre

Cape Breton

Grand Cibou

Canso

Fort Saint-François

La Hève

Fort Saint-Louis

Cape Sable

Port-Royal

Old Habitation
(1605-1613)
and old Scots Fort
Charles
(1629-1632)

Fort Sainte-Marie

Chaleur Bay

Miscou

Nipisiguit

RIVIÈRE SAINT-JEAN

Fort Pentagouet

RIVIÈRE SAINTE-CROIX

Acadia, 1630-1654

end to the enterprise. In 1613, Argall destroyed Saint-Sauveur and Port-Royal, and in 1629, Acadia became English. The colony was, however, reoccupied and had every promise of a fine future, but it lost its dynamic leader in 1635 (he died prematurely). It was to be a place of internal quarrels for a long time to come.

After the death of Isaac de Razilly, Acadia was under a dual authority: Claude Launay-Razilly (Razilly's brother and heir), who possessed the seigneuries of La Hève, Port-Royal and Sainte-Croix; and Charles de Saint-Étienne de La Tour, the owner of Cape Sable, the Saint John River, and the Penobscot River. Both men continued to share the monopoly of Acadian trade. However, because he was detained in France, Launay-Razilly delegated his authority to his cousin Charles Menou d'Aulnay, who, by sale or concession, rapidly acquired the Razilly brothers' share.

Disagreements between Menou d'Aulnay and La Tour soon arose, originating in various ways. There were jurisdictional disputes between the Compagnie des Cent-Associés, which supported La Tour, and the mother country, which favoured Menou d'Aulnay. In addition to the commercial rivalry involved in the exploitation of a vast monopoly, the division of the land had been made against the dictates of common sense. Ignorance of Acadian geography caused land belonging to La Tour to be allotted to Menou d'Aulnay and land belonging to Menou d'Aulnay to be given to La Tour. These conflicts led to a long civil war. La Tour was condemned at Court, as a result of the influence the Capuchins had secured for Menou d'Aulnay, and was soon besieged in his fort on the Saint John River. He obtained the help of the English in Boston and unsuccessfully tried to take Port-Royal in 1643. Menou d'Aulnay, who had greater resources than his rival, captured La Tour's last remaining fort in 1645, and La Tour, still recognized by the Cent-Associés, sought refuge in Quebec. In 1647, Menou d'Aulnay obtained exclusive possession of the whole of Acadia, from the Gaspé to New England, with the powers of a viceroy.

Acadia had recovered its unity for a brief period, but on the death of Menou d'Aulnay in 1650, complete confusion returned. Several people, at the same time, tried to obtain their rights with the support of decrees from the Conseil du Roi. These included the Cent-Associés, the widow of Menou d'Aulnay, his creditor Emmanuel Le Borgne, La Tour who had returned to favour with the King, the Duke of Vendôme (uncle of the King, who entered into partnership with the widow of Menou d'Aulnay), and Nicolas Denys. Denys held the title to the land from Canso to Gaspé and maintained posts in Cape Breton as well as at Miscou and Nipisiguit. The situation was further complicated by a surprise marriage, in 1653, between La Tour and the widow of Menou d'Aulnay. An English expedition from Boston, in 1654, put an end to the jurisdictional quarrel for some time. Robert Sedgwick, who wanted to base the economy of New England on the fishing industry, seized the forts of Penobscot, Saint John, and Port-Royal. While Cape Breton, Île Saint-Jean (today Prince Edward Island), the Bay of Chaleur and the Gaspé remained French possessions under the authority of Nicolas Denys, the rest of Acadia from Canso to the Penobscot was occupied by the English.

Throughout this constant drama, the Acadian population remained small in spite of some well-intentioned undertakings. Razilly hardly had time to settle many colonists, and although the leaders who succeeded him continued to recruit covenanted immigrants, a great number of these recruits returned to France. The Acadian population has been calculated at 120 for 1641, and at the time of the conquest in 1654, it did not amount to more than 300 people settled mainly in the valley of Port-Royal. Although the Cent-Associés had granted several fiefs from the Bay of Chaleur to the Penobscot, seigneurial life did not yet appear really organized. These fiefs served primarily for fishing and the fur trade.

Religious life was strictly on a missionary basis. The Récollets arrived in 1630, and worked in La Tour's domains until 1645. The Jesuits had missions in Cape Breton and on the Bay of Chaleur. The fate of the Capuchins depended directly on the disputes that arose after 1635. Menou d'Aulnay became the administrator of the considerable sum that Richelieu, as a member of the Acadian Company, had left the Capuchins for their work. As a result, they constantly took the part of Menou d'Aulnay and supported him on numerous occasions. When d'Aulnay died, the Capuchins remained faithful to the party of his widow, an action that brought upon them the persecutions of Le Borgne. In 1652, following the English conquest, the last remaining Capuchins in the area were expelled. The seminary they had established at Port-Royal disappeared. This institution, founded around 1644 for the instruction of young natives, had had about a dozen pupils under the direction of Mme de Brice.

In short, the colonization of Acadia had not been achieved. Continual disorder and quarrels paralyzed all progress and caused Acadia to fall back into the same unhappy state as before 1627. Because of the successive failures of the colonizers, Nicolas Denys, in 1644, believed that only the king could succeed in Acadia. This area was given back to France by the Treaty of Breda in 1667, but three more years passed before French occupation became effective.

Canada at a standstill

At the time when Razilly was proceeding with his organization and settlement of Acadia, Canada was hardly expanding at all. When Champlain finally reappeared at Quebec in 1633, in command of three ships, he was leading the first fleet to bring immigrants to Canada since the creation of the Compagnie des Cent-Associés, but even at this time, only two hundred people disembarked, mainly soldiers. Furthermore, because the company had been ruined by its first setbacks, settlement became increasingly the task of private entrepreneurs who received seigneuries on condition that they introduce immigrants. In the beginning, some of these seigneurs played a most important role. Robert Giffard and the Juchereau brothers began systematic immigration, and it was through them that the seigneurial regime, which was still vague before 1629, took on a clearer outline and established its own traditions.

Although one would have expected a considerable expansion (since the country was known as far as Lake Superior), only two unimportant expeditions into the interior are recorded. In 1634, Champlain built a small fort on an island (named Richelieu) lying opposite Deschambault and forty miles upstream from Quebec, in order to control navigation on the river. Then he sent his officer Laviolette (about whom nothing is known either before or after this mission), to construct a settlement at Trois-Rivières, a traditional trading place. For eight years, this was to be the colony's most advanced post upstream.

During the early years of the seigneury of the Cent-Associés, trading policy remained the principal preoccupation of the authorities of New France. This policy made possible the longest voyage of exploration during the first half of the seventeenth century. With the purpose of putting an end to a quarrel between the Hurons, the merchants of the Great Lakes and the Nipissings, the interpreter Jean Nicollet between July, 1634, and August, 1635, went to the west coast of Lake Michigan. He, like so many others, hoped to reach Asia, and he carried in his baggage a large silk robe such as the Mandarins wore. He went perhaps as far as the Wisconsin River, without finding China, but he established peace and became the first European to start from the Saint Lawrence and penetrate that far into the continent.

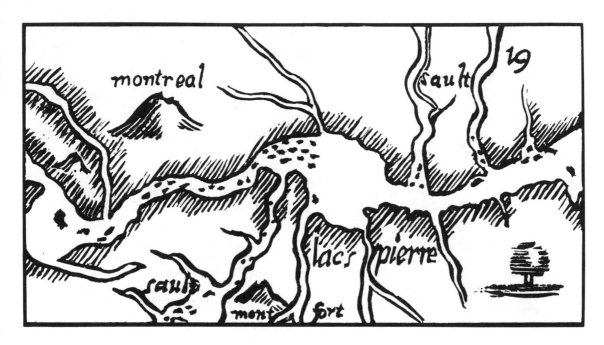

The first appearance of the place name Montréal
(part of a map drawn in 1612 by Champlain, published in the *Oeuvres* de Champlain, Laverdière ed.)

The folle aventure of Ville-Marie

One must wait until 1642 before recording an important step in the occupation of the country, for that was the year when Ville-Marie was founded on Montreal Island. As early as 1611, Champlain had hoped to found a settlement there, and in this he was encouraged by the Algonkins, who stood to gain if the fur route was made safer. However, resources were lacking for this enterprise.

In 1639, as part of the vast religious movement called the French Counter-Reformation, a layman and tax collector Jérôme Le Royer de la Dauversière, along with the barons of Fancamp and Renty and the abbé Jean-Jacques Olier, founded the *Société de Notre-Dame de Montréal pour la conversion des sauvages* (Society of Our Lady of Montreal for the conversion of the savages). With the help of the Jesuits, they hoped to convert the natives and bring them together on Montreal Island. The difficulties were cleared up one after the other in a surprising way, for the Cent-Associés granted them Montreal Island in 1640. The *Société de Notre-Dame* entrusted the leadership to a pious layman Paul Chomedey de Maisonneuve. He counted among his first recruits a young laywoman, Jeanne Mance, who came to found a hospital.

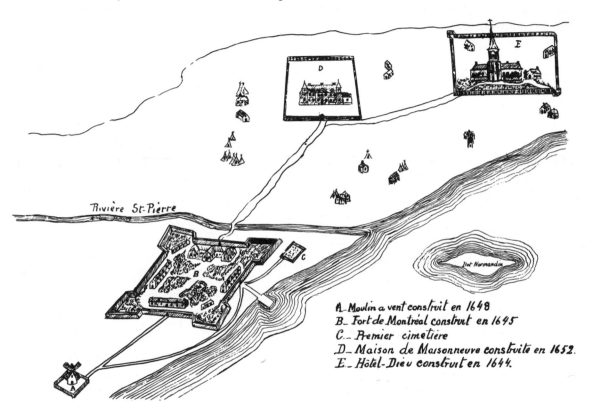

A_ Moulin a vent construit en 1648
B_ Fort de Montréal construit en 1645
C_ Premier cimetière
D_ Maison de Maisonneuve construite en 1652.
E_ Hôtel-Dieu construit en 1644.

Bibliothèque municipale de Montréal

Ville-Marie in 1652
(drawn by Léo Leymarie after an old map)

After a winter spént in Quebec (where the inhabitants were far from enthusiastic about the plan for a new settlement), the *Montréalistes* landed on the island in the month of May, 1642, and installed themselves in a small fort on the very spot where, in 1611, Champlain had cleared the ground for Place Royale. Three months later, Governor Montmagny built a fort at the mouth of the Richelieu River. The purpose of this short-lived fort was to safeguard communications between Trois-Rivières and Ville-Marie (which was, for a long time, the most dangerous outpost of New France) by closing the route to the Iroquois.

The Iroquois were not the only threat to the work of the Société de Notre-Dame. As the first obstruction in the passage upstream and the last stop downstream from the fur country, Ville-Marie was destined to become the most important trading post in New

France; several times the Société de Notre-Dame was reproached with having settled on the island for commercial purposes. Ville-Marie occupied an ideal site for trading with the interior of the continent, but the first generation of *Montréalistes* was actuated by entirely spiritual ends. In the whole history of New France, it is the only colonial foundation with an essentially apostolic character.

The religious motive was, at the same time, a threat to the Society for it wished to remain independent of the State and the other foundations already established; it wished to exist only through the benevolent help of benefactors. However, some of these people had promised help beyond their means, without seriously considering the realities of the situation, while others were very soon discouraged by the slowness of results. The general enthusiasm of the beginning declined rapidly. In 1651, the work was close to being abandoned, and although revived in 1653, it declined again. When the Société de Notre-Dame was dissolved in 1663, it had settled only about fifty families and cleared only two hundred *arpents* of land.

The Communauté des Habitants

The Cent-Associés, after their setbacks, found it convenient to entrust their responsibility to subordinate groups. Now they acted in a manner which was equivalent to a withdrawal. In 1645, they re-granted the monopoly of the Saint Lawrence trade to the *Communauté des Habitants de la Nouvelle-France*. In return, the Company contracted to pay each year, as seigneurial rent, one thousand pounds ($\frac{1}{2}$ ton) of beaver pelts; the Company also agreed to defray the administrative expenses of the country and to establish twenty settlers in Canada each year.

For the first time in the history of New France, the great fur trade would be carried on under the direction of merchants established in the colony, for their direct profit. Certainly, trade still depended on the European market, and the transportation of furs did not yet involve the creation of any industry, but the "Canadians" (as they could already be called) felt less dependent on the mother country. It is this sentiment, perhaps, that explains the overtures the Saint Lawrence colony made shortly afterwards to New England, with a view to concluding a treaty of trade and alliance.

The first years were prosperous for the new Company, as a result of the Iroquois peace in 1645, and because furs had accumulated upcountry. Afterwards, the hostility of the Mohawks made trade more difficult. Civil war in France cut off some of the outlets, and internal difficulties undermined the Company. As Jean Hamelin wrote: "It is unfortunate that unlucky events and rivalry between merchants should have ruined the Communauté des Habitants. Only a system of this kind could ensure the development of a middle class capable of assuming the economic and social role which had devolved upon it." Nevertheless, the shareholders of this Company of 1645, were the forerunners of the great merchant families of the French regime.

Iroquois aggression

The Iroquois peace of 1645 was of short duration. The destruction of Huronia was to upset completely the precious trading network that had been built up on the Great Lakes.

The Huron Indians held the monopoly of trade on the Great Lakes. From Huronia, the furs came by the northwestern river (then called the Algonkin and today the Ottawa) to the trading posts of the Saint Lawrence. The Iroquois, although of the same origin and culture as the Hurons, had always been kept apart from this commercial traffic. The Mohawks, however, about 1626, had set up a commercial route to the Hudson River, in spite of the Mohicans. To the detriment of their fellow Iroquois (the Oneidas, Onondagas, Cayugas, and Senecas), they reserved for themselves the trading post of New Netherland, their closest neighbours. But what now happened was that about 1640 the fur reserves of Iroquoisia became exhausted. The Iroquois wished to seize the trade from the Hurons and decided to force them (the Hurons) to assimilate or be eliminated, if they refused.

Fort Sainte-Marie, missionary centre for the Great Lakes, 1639-1649

As in 1642 and 1643, the Iroquois began by cutting the trade route between the Saint Lawrence and the Great Lakes. For a certain time, this reduced the Laurentian trade to the posts of Saint-Maurice and Saguenay. The peace of 1645, concluded only with the Mohawks, was no more than a short respite. In 1647, the Ottawa fur route was blocked again. Finally, between 1648 and 1650, some two thousand Hurons joined the Iroquois whether they really wanted to or not; the others, who refused annexation, were massacred. About four hundred sought refuge on Île d'Orléans, led by their Jesuit missionaries; a good number of these survivors were also, willingly or by force, soon to take the road to Iroquoisia. Huronia had disappeared from the map.

For a certain time, it was hoped that the commercial rivalries dividing the Iroquois would turn to the advantage of the French. While the Mohawks profited from the Dutch trade, the other Iroquois would have liked to use the Lake Ontario-Saint Lawrence route to trade with the French. From 1656 to 1658, the French even maintained a settlement among the Onondagas, but the Mohawks managed to shatter this new alliance. Total war between the Iroquois and the French again immobilized the Saint Lawrence fur traffic.

The entire trading network of the Great Lakes was destroyed. The Iroquois dispersed the former allies of Huronia: the Neutrals, Petuns, Eries, Nipissings, and Algonkins. Not content with this tribal upset, which perhaps has no equal in Amerindian history, they spread terror among the Attikamègues of the upper Saint-Maurice and even as far as the Mistassins to the north of Lake Saint John. From time to time, the Iroquois sent peace missions to Quebec to try to recover important prisoners. When the Iroquois were at war with the Susquehannas (traditional allies of the Hurons), they even asked for French military aid. The Iroquois victory meant there was no further question of a general peace.

But a new nation, the Ottawas (*Cheveux-relevés*), which had long been an ally of the French, was attempting to take over the role of the Hurons on the Great Lakes. Living mainly to the north of Lake Huron, the Ottawas had connections with the Amerinds of the interior (the Assiniboines and Cree), enabling them to control an international trade supplied by nations living in the area of the "Western Sea." The Ottawas soon took up this position, reserving the trade on the river that now bears their name, exclusively for themselves. Once more, the French found themselves faced with two suppliers, the Ottawas and the Iroquois, each as demanding as the other. In choosing the Ottawas, as formerly by choosing the Hurons, the French opted for war.

Achievements of the Church

Apart from the settlement of Trois-Rivières in 1634, and the formation of the Communauté des Habitants in 1645, the religious foundations were the only important accomplishments. This period is one that has been called an *épopée mystique* ("mystical epic"), which lasted with a certain intensity for about twenty years. It would only manifest itself again through certain rare individuals, such as Marguerite Bourgeoys and François de Laval.

Since 1632, the Jesuits had undertaken the education of the natives in their monastery of Notre-Dame-des-Anges (as the Récollets had done). They also founded in Quebec, in 1635, a regular college that was the first in North America. In 1637, they established the reservation of Sillery, to train the natives to live after the French fashion (this again was a first in North America). Also in this period, the Jesuits began the habit of publishing their *Relations* which, for the years 1632-1673, forms a collection of forty-one small volumes. These are an extremely useful source for our knowledge of the seventeenth century in Canada. In 1639, the Ursulines founded a *séminaire de filles* (girls' school) in

Archives de la province de Québec

Mother Marie de l'Incarnation, superior of the Ursuline convent in Quebec
(post-mortem portrait)

Quebec where, while ensuring the education of young French girls, they attempted to instill French culture into the young *sauvagesses* (one of whom was later to become the first wife of Pierre Boucher). With the Ursulines in the same year, the Hospitalières of Dieppe arrived and opened an Hôtel-Dieu (hospital).

The Ville-Marie foundation of 1642 was an accomplishment of the Church, or more exactly, of a pious society, and religious institutions soon appeared there. In 1644, Jeanne Mance superintended the foundation of an Hôtel-Dieu, and in 1657, the Sulpicians arrived to ensure spiritual ministration. The following year, Marguerite Bourgeoys, who had come from Champagne in 1653, began her first school, and in 1659, the Hospitalières of La Flèche in Anjou came to take charge of the Hôtel-Dieu. While the boldness of these enterprises is to be admired, it must be emphasized that, in a land still poorly organized, they were premature. They were, above all, the work of an unstable ruling class (the case of Madame de La Peltrie is typical), which explains to a great extent the dramatic way in which the enterprises were set up. In any case, the Church rapidly established its spiritual and social services, but it is regrettable that in settling the people and in economic life the same vitality was not shown and the same resources were not available.

Missionary work attained a magnitude that has not yet been surpassed, and this was even more important than the other achievements of the Church. Without underrating the work of the Capuchins in Acadia from 1632 to 1654 (although this was primarily parochial service), it must be remembered that the achievements of the Jesuits (the only missionaries in Canada up to 1657) in trying to convert Huronia was remarkable. From their headquarters of Sainte-Marie (at Midland, Ontario), they spread across the Great Lakes. This missionary effort was accompanied by an excellent mystic element, proving the vitality of this young Canadian Church. All this work in Huronia, however, was to be reduced to nothing by the killing of great missionaries (such as Fathers Brébeuf and Lalemant) and by the dispersal of the Hurons. In 1649, the mission of Sainte-Marie was moved to an island on Georgian Bay (today called Christian Island), and in June, 1650, the Huron Christians moved to Île d'Orléans in the Saint Lawrence region. The Jesuits of the first half of the seventeenth century have written the finest pages in the history of the Catholic Church in North America; to find an achievement even approaching theirs, one must wait until the missionary work of the second half of the nineteenth century.

How far had the settling of New France progressed?

In 1627, New France possessed only about one hundred inhabitants, one group at Quebec and at Cap de Tourmente, and the other at Port-Royal, in Acadia. What stage had French settlement reached by 1663?

There were now settlements on the south coast of Newfoundland. In 1662, Thalour du Perron landed eighty colonists in Placentia Bay. In fact, the French claim dates from 1658, when Gayot obtained a grant there, but the Cent-Associés, calling themselves the owners of Newfoundland, had at first opposed the idea of a colony. In spite of a mutiny, the settlement at Placentia, specializing in fishing, was maintained. New France also had a population of about 400 or 500 settlers in Acadia, but after 1654, only Cape Breton and the settlements at Miscou and Nipisiguit remained under French control.

The most important part of New France was the Saint Lawrence colony of Canada. In 1663, its population numbered some 2,500 inhabitants; whereas, according to the initial plan, there should have been 4,000 by 1642. This population of 1663 was not the direct achievement of the Cent-Associés, but rather the work of individuals interested in clearing their land and of religious societies. Since 1647, shipowners had been expected to transport one immigrant per ton of freight. These colonists came mainly from the Perche area (which provided about one hundred families in the first half of the century), Normandy, Brittany, Anjou, and the areas of La Rochelle and Île-de-France. Only on rare occasions did the arriving group (like that of the colonists of 1653) amount to one hundred people, and since it has been calculated that about 1,300 immigrants came before 1660, the annual average was scarcely above fifty. These immigrants were, for the most part, tradesmen and apprentices who contracted for three years (the origin of their name of *trente-six mois*) before becoming established. Up until about 1656, merchants and private citizens recruited only colonists with some skills; afterwards, the merchants brought mostly unskilled immigrants who had no trade to declare. Among the immigrants coming before 1663, were 220 *filles à marier* (marriageable girls) brought to New France by the female founders.

This population of 2,500 was already widely scattered. In the territory stretching from Île d'Orléans to Montreal, the settlers were grouped in three areas. The first and largest included Quebec and the surrounding countryside (the shores of Beaupré were the most evenly settled); the second corresponded to the immediate vicinity of the fort of Trois-Rivières; the last centred around the fort of Ville-Marie. Seigneuries (forty-five in all) had been granted on the two banks of the river, but the granting of a seigneury did not necessarily mean the settling of colonists; in fact, on the north bank, the land between the three towns was still unoccupied by Europeans. The same condition was to be found from one end of the south bank to the other, because of a shortage of men and through fear of the Iroquois.

New France in need of reorganization

Nothing was less like the New France that had been planned in 1627 than the New France of 1663. Attempts to bring in a large number of settlers had failed; almost the entire population of Acadia lived under English rule; and in Canada, over a thirty-five year period, the number of inhabitants had risen from 100 to only 2,500. Such an increase could certainly be impressive if this were a small country, but the whole of the North American continent was claimed for New France. On this continent, meanwhile, other European colonies were making rapid progress: New Netherland, although it had similar economic conditions, already possessed 10,000 inhabitants; Virginia alone had 30,000. So what could be the importance of New France with 2,500 inhabitants when contrasted with the Atlantic colonies with their total of 80,000 inhabitants?

This small French population suffered military and economic insecurity. Although it was still strong in the time of Champlain, its position became deplorable after the sudden increase in the power of the Iroquois. The announcement of an Iroquois invasion was enough to make all the people barricade themselves in their homes. The years 1660 and 1661, in particular, were years of panic. Furthermore, the fur routes were regularly blocked.

When Radisson came down from the Great Lakes in 1660, along a route that had been opened for a certain time by the Battle of the Long Sault, no furs had been received from upcountry for two years. What then were the resources of New France in 1663? She still did not have to her credit any large fishery or any kind of industry, and the export of very small quantities of plank wood had only just begun. The economy was still based on a single article—fur. Just as before 1627, everything depended on the trading post, and when there were no furs, everything else was lacking. In 1660, there was still talk of abandoning the Saint Lawrence.

Some institutions had been set up, but the civil ones worked badly. A scattered population weakened the country, as did the division of Canada into small parts (the posts of Trois-Rivières and Montreal) desiring to be independent of Quebec. A cabal chose the governor, and the governor's council, although twice reorganized, did not satisfy either the Communauté des Habitants, which assumed the costs of administration and wanted to impose its own laws, or the settlers, who complained that trade had been taken over by a few individuals. The land itself had fallen into the hands of a few powerful families, (Lauson, Legardeur, Leneuf). They had been granted immense seigneuries but did not bother to develop them. Many of the religious institutions (because they depended on the zeal of unstable individuals) had a very uncertain future. Conflicts broke out between the Governor and Mgr de Laval on the subject of the brandy trade with the natives, and jurisdictional quarrels arose between the religious authorities of Quebec and Montreal. The religious administration itself was a missionary one. From 1632 to 1658, it was controlled by the Superior of the Jesuits, and even after the first arrival of the Apostolic Vicar Laval, no parish was formally set up.

Although it was still the owner of New France, the Compagnie des Cent-Associés was now only concerned with collecting its rents. In 1645, it gave Canada over to the Communauté des Habitants, and in 1647, Acadia became the domain of d'Aulnay. The Company itself fell apart. By 1633, it had scarcely forty-five members.

In 1627, a new beginning in New France had been necessary; in 1663 there was a pressing need for a further reorganization.

Bibliographical Note

For this important period of the *Cent-Associés*, 1627-1663, see the summary made by Gustave Lanctôt, in *Histoire du Canada*, Vol. I, *Des origines au régime royal*. Montréal, Beauchemin, 1962, pp. 173-417. I am preparing an extended study of this period, *La Seigneurie des Cent-Associés*, to be published as Volume III of the series "Histoire de la Nouvelle-France."

Special studies are few. Nothing of importance has yet been written on the *Cent-Associés* nor on the *Communauté des Habitants*. In addition to the articles published in the *Dictionary of Canadian Biography*, some very useful works should be mentioned:

On the Iroquois Wars

G. T. Hunt, *The Wars of the Iroquois: A Study in Intertribal Trade Relations*. Madison, University of Wisconsin Press, 1960.

On the Jesuits

C. DE ROCHEMONTEIX, S.J., *Les Jésuites et la Nouvelle-France au XVIIe siècle*. Paris, Letouzey et Ané, 1895-1896.

On Acadia

Rameau DE SAINT-PÈRE, *Une colonie féodale en Amérique*, Vol. I. Paris and Montréal, Plon and Granger, 1889.

A. COUILLARD-DESPRÉS, *Charles de Saint-Étienne de la Tour et son temps*. Arthabaska, 1930.

On the beginning of Trois-Rivières

A. TESSIER, *Trois-Rivières*. Trois-Rivières, Le Nouvelliste, 1935.

On the founding of Montreal

M. C. DAVELUY, *La Société de Notre-Dame de Montréal*. Montréal, Fides, 1965: history and life bibliographies of the members of this Society.

Gustave LANCTÔT, *Montréal sous Maisonneuve, 1642-1665*. Montréal, Beauchemin, 1966.

Ville-Marie, "Poème de la Nouvelle-France." *Cahiers de l'Académie canadienne-française*, no. 8 (Montréal, 1964).

Finally, the long study of the Dollard incident by André VACHON is interesting, see *Dictionary of Canadian Biography*, Vol. I.

CHAPTER V

Continental Expansion, 1663-1713

After Governor Davaugour, Mgr de Laval the Apostolic Vicar, and Pierre Boucher the Governor of Trois-Rivières had all contributed their suggestions, Louis XIV intervened in the seigneury of the Cent-Associés. He introduced a series of measures after 1663, which were tantamount to a new founding of the French colony.

The reorganization of New France

a) *An alteration in the seigneury*

Louis XIV first required the Compagnie des Cent-Associés to give up its seigneury in America in 1663. This brought about the disappearance, in the following year, of the Communauté des Habitants. In 1664, the King granted the fief and seigneury of New France to the *Compagnie des Indes Occidentales* (West Indian Company). This Company was a large association that received the monopoly of navigation and trade, not only in North America, but also in a large area of South America and on the west coast of Africa. The new Company, however, unlike its predecessor, had no part in the administration, which depended on the king through the intermediary of his ministers. Moreover, after 1674, New France ceased to be the seigneurial domain of a trading company.

The mother country even intervened in the operation of the seigneurial regime. Landowners who had acquired large domains without attempting to develop them lost their holdings to more enterprising seigneurs. Montreal Island, which belonged to a group that had completely deteriorated (the Société de Notre-Dame) became an independent fief in the interior. In 1663, it passed into the hands of the Saint-Sulpice Seminary, and this island was at last placed under the same control as the other seigneuries. This action led to the departure of Chomedey de Maisonneuve. The court of justice established in 1651 was replaced by a court of royal jurisdiction. Finally, the methodical examination of the seigneurial system would very soon produce regulations establishing the form of this regime for two centuries to come.

b) *Duality of government*

Upon the seigneurial structure, which was now uniform again, the King imposed a new form of administration that was to last until 1760.

As in the French provinces where, since the time of Mazarin, an intendant had control over "justice, *police*, and finances," while a governor retained military power, New France received, in 1663, a government with two heads. The governor was placed in charge of military activity and external affairs (including Indian affairs), and the intendant supervised the three departments of the interior, justice, *police* (that is, civil administration) and finance.

There was no longer a single, powerful governor, as there had been before; jurisdiction from now on was shared. Before the spheres of influence of each were clearly defined, there would be violent disputes, but in any case, the system had been given its initial impetus.

c) *The Conseil Souverain*

While entrusting the control of the colony to two officials, the King introduced another new organization: the *Conseil Souverain* (Sovereign Council). When it was founded, the intendant had not yet assumed power, so that this Council was under the authority of two heads: the governor and the bishop. Together, they had to choose the other five councillors, but soon this choice depended directly on the king. The Council was a court of justice acting as the court of appeal for local cases (which of course did not exclude an appeal to the king). At first, it took the place of an executive and legislative council, but in the following century, it was finally limited, under the name of *Conseil Supérieur* (Superior Council), to the functions of a court of justice for the whole of New France.

The establishment of this Conseil Souverain brought about, in 1664, the adoption of the customary law of Paris, to the exclusion of all other provincial law systems. This meant that, in principle, New France from then on recognized only a single body of civil and criminal law, and a single system of weights and measures.

d) *The defence of the country*

Up to that time, it had been necessary to rely for the defence of the country on a small troop of soldiers maintained by the Cent-Associés. This system had made impossible any campaign against the Iroquois, and the inhabitants defended themselves, or relied on movable troops that went to the aid of areas under attack. In 1663, a militia system was organized in Montreal, which was to be extended six years later throughout the colony. Furthermore, the King decided to send a whole regiment, the *Carignan-Salières*, a force of about 1,200 men, to try to quell the Iroquois.

Arriving in 1665, the troops built three forts on the Richelieu (the traditional route of the Mohawks): one at the mouth of the river, the site of the old Fort Richelieu; the second, called *Saint-Louis*, in present-day Chambly, at the foot of the rapids; the third, *Sainte-Thérèse*, three leagues higher upstream from the same rapids. The invasion route was thus completely protected. In January 1666, the troops marched against the Iroquois. Unused to winter campaigning in North America, they reached the Mohawk country only after untold hardships. They found only old people and children there, and it was not thought worthwhile to continue the expedition any further. But in the course of the summer, Fort Sainte-Anne was built on an island in Lake Champlain. This fort marks the

Public Archives of Canada

Fort Richelieu and the surrounding area in 1666
(from a reproduction in Sulte's *Histoire des Canadiens français*)
In 1665-1666, the Carignan-Salières regiment secured the Mohawk's traditional
route with four forts—Richelieu, Saint-Louis, Sainte-Thérèse and Sainte-Anne.

point of furthest penetration towards the Mohawk country. During a new campaign in the autumn, the troops had to be content with ravaging a countryside almost empty of its inhabitants, but it at least had the merit of demonstrating the military strength of the French colony. The Iroquois understood that from now on they would be dealing with a well-organized defence; thus, the colony would be able to develop in greater safety.

When the Carignan-Salières regiment re-embarked for France, in 1668, it left behind about four hundred of its members (soldiers and officers), who settled on the land or took up trades. A large number of them would become the nucleus of those families of soldiers, who provided the defence of the country, in the regular corps of the *Troupes de la Colonie*, or in the militia.

e) *The Church*

The Canadian Church also took part in this reorganization. It was already well established, but in this general reorganization, it would reach the peak of its political power. The Apostolic Vicar, Mgr de Laval, succeeded in getting Governor Davaugour recalled, following their quarrel over the use of *eau de vie* (spirits) in trading with the "savages." He chose Mézy, a convert from the Ermitage de Caën, as his successor. The Apostolic Vicar shared equally with the governor the task of choosing the other members of the Conseil Souverain. His position on this council had all the authority appropriate to the ecclesiastical rank he held.

But the Church still lacked an organizational framework. Until 1659, it had remained a missionary church under the authority of the Superior of the Jesuits. Mgr de Laval aimed to provide cadres. It was planned, for example, to transform the office of apostolic vicar into a bishopric, but this project was not carried out until 1674. To bring his clergy together and to provide for their support, Mgr de Laval founded the *Séminaire de Québec* (Quebec Seminary), a community of priests who were to serve the country without being attached to benefices. To support this foundation, he introduced the system of tithes, and later (among other revenues), endowed it with two large seigneuries: the Côte de Beaupré and Ile Jésus. In 1668, Mgr de Laval founded the Petit Séminaire, an establishment that trained candidates for the priesthood.

In 1664, with Notre-Dame-de-Québec, he officially introduced the parochial system, and for the spiritual training of the faithful, he established the Confrérie de la Sainte-Famille.

Finally, during this period, ecclesiastical personnel were rearranged. In Montreal, in 1657, the Jesuits gave up the ministry to the Sulpicians; then, in 1664, they gave Quebec to the secular clergy; and before long, in 1670, they ceded Trois-Rivières to the Récollets.

Systematic settlement

This reorganization was the starting point for important economic development in the area and for vast territorial expansion. This twofold progress was due to the influence of the minister Colbert and the very able intendant Talon. Talon's program can be reduced to the following two points: obtaining the highest possible return from the colony, and extending its frontiers to the limits of North America.

Archives de la province de Québec

Mgr de Laval, as seen by the Récollet painter Frère Luc (Claude François)
This portrait, preserved in the Quebec Seminary was completed during the winter of 1671-1672.

Archives de la province de Québec

Jean Talon, as seen by the Récollet painter, Frère Luc (Claude François)
This portrait, preserved in the Hôtel-Dieu in Quebec, was completed in the winter of 1671-1672.

This program could only succeed if the population increased rapidly. To speed up immigration, the State forced the captains of merchant ships to transport colonists eighteen to forty years of age; but above all, it counted on the seigneurs. These men, who became real entrepreneurs in the matter of settlement, received fiefs on the one essential condition that they settle colonists on them. The number of seigneuries was expanded to produce a corresponding increase in the number of people responsible for settlement and to strengthen the country. For example, the Richelieu route was occupied by settling former officers of the Carignan-Salières regiment there. In a single year, 1672, the authorities granted forty-six seigneuries, the highest total in one year up to that time.

This policy of increasing the population could not succeed unless supported by a policy of increasing the marriage rate. Continuing the work already begun by some founders, the State sent some *filles de roi* ("King's daughters"), orphans raised at the king's expense, and obliged bachelors to choose wives from among them. It has been estimated that, from 1665 to 1673, some nine hundred *filles de roi* came in this way, most of them "perfect young ladies," who found husbands as soon as they arrived. Furthermore, dowries were granted to poor girls, presents were given to those who married very young, and gratuities were distributed to large families. Because Colbert was convinced that French culture would inevitably triumph over native culture, marriages were even encouraged between the French and the Amerinds. His policy was that French and Amerinds should be of one blood and should become one people.

The progress of this settlement was closely followed by means of the annual census of names. That of 1666 is the first of its kind in the history of Canada. The King's Minister studied each census and showed pleasure or disappointment, according to whether the figures revealed progress or stagnation.

A plan to exploit New France completely

Intendant Talon wanted, as had Champlain, total development of the country. Talon accelerated agricultural production, so that the colony could feed itself. In order to help the immigrants to settle on the land, he brought pedigreed animals (cows, horses, sheep) from France, which the colonists tried to acclimatize. He tested seed grain, looking for the kind that would be best suited to the conditions of the Saint Lawrence region.

Working under the orders of a *ministre à manufactures* and encouraged by the influx of tradesmen, Talon saw that circumstances were favourable for the development of industry. He ordered research to be done on every kind of resource. A survey of oak trees was made with regard to starting a shipping industry, and men were sent to look for iron, coal, and copper. He put into operation a tarworks, a tannery, and a brewery. He tried to organize "fixed" fisheries and to interest the population in developing local crafts.

Since a country cannot prosper without trade, Talon endeavoured to establish regular exchanges between Canada and the nearest French colony, Acadia. He even wanted regular trade between Canada and the very distant West Indies.

Talon's dream is unfulfilled

Talon wished New France to be not only self-sufficient, but to provide an abundant supply of raw and manufactured materials for the mother country and the other colonies.

CHARLEBOURG

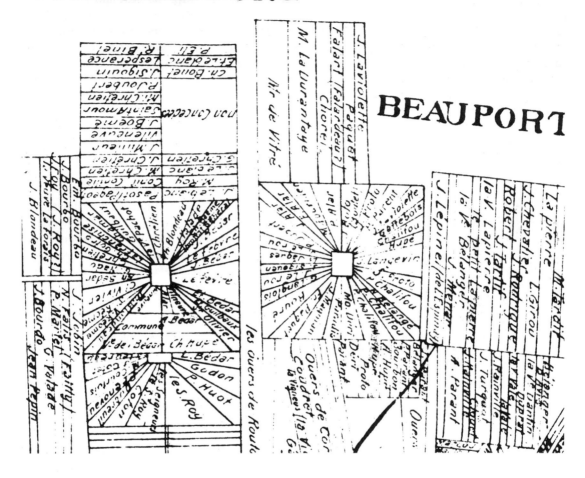

Talon's Villages
(part of a map by Gédéon de Catalogne, 1709)
Instead of using the rows adopted by the seigneurial system, Talon tried to formulate a plan, based on the Charlesbourg experiment, which would improve the grouping of the settlers; this experiment did not gain acceptance at all.

If this policy of total production had been achieved, New France would perhaps have reached the same economic level as the productive colonies, such as New England and Virginia.

But Talon's policy was never more than a beautiful dream in the history of a fur-producing colony. Although Talon was the most forceful of the country's intendants, his stay was too short (five years on two tours of duty) to transform New France into an industrial colony. Also, the lack of specialized workmen ruined the best-prepared projects, and the fur-trading economy still exerted too strong a pressure. Most important of all, the mother country adopted a still more rigorous mercantilist policy. When there was an attempt made at the beginning of the eighteenth century to reintroduce Talon's program, manufacturing (especially the production of beaver hats) was forbidden on the ground that it provided dangerous competition for French manufacturers. In 1704, the King's Minister would recall this fact, that a colony exists only in order to provide raw materials for the mother country that has established it. New France was, therefore, to remain a fur colony.

A New France: as large as the continent

Intendant Talon was to be more fortunate in the second part of his program: that of extending New France to the frontiers of America. Of course, when this policy of expansion involved colonies already organized by the English or the Dutch, Talon's intentions met with less success. There was New Netherland (New York), irrigated by a great river and enjoying the convenience of an ocean port open the year round, whereas Canada was cut off from Europe for six to eight months of the year. Many times, the French policy of expansion included the acquisition of New York, either by purchase or by conquest. In 1689, for example, Louis XIV instructed Frontenac to seize this colony and to deport its population "together or separately" to make room for a French colony. The arrangements for this plan of conquest and deportation, however, failed from the very beginning.

It was easier to expand into regions still unoccupied by Europeans. Here, results were surprising, for in only twenty-five years, New France had expanded as far north as Hudson Bay, west beyond the Great Lakes, and south to the Gulf of Mexico. This was the most spectacular French achievement during the seventeenth century.

It should be observed, first, that this movement towards exploration was not limited to the period when Talon was intendant but had begun before it. In 1647, the Jesuit De Quen finally discovered Lake Saint John; between 1658 and 1662, Radisson discovered the Upper Mississippi, explored Lake Superior, and reached Hudson Bay along the Albany River. But in Radisson's case, these were individual adventures involving no official taking of possession nor any geographical survey.

Talon began to have expeditions organized by the Government and to supervise the others closely. It was no longer sufficient to pass through an area; it had to be formally claimed for France and the natives persuaded to act in accordance with French interests. In addition, each explorer had to return with a detailed report of his trip.

a) *Towards the empire of Hudson Bay*

The English had been the only Europeans during the first half of the seventeenth century to frequent Hudson Bay (discovered in 1610). In 1670, they established their Hudson's Bay Company with the assistance of Radisson. The great waterways (the Nelson, Severn, Albany, and Rupert rivers) flowed northward into the Bay and threatened to divert the furs of the rich areas nearby from the trading posts of the Saint Lawrence to the English trading posts. To ward off this economic disaster, it was necessary to win over the natives of these areas so that they would continue to trade with the French in spite of the more difficult journey to the French posts.

In 1671, Saint-Lusson travelled to Lake Superior. There, he established friendly relations with natives who had travelled great distances. He took possession, in the name

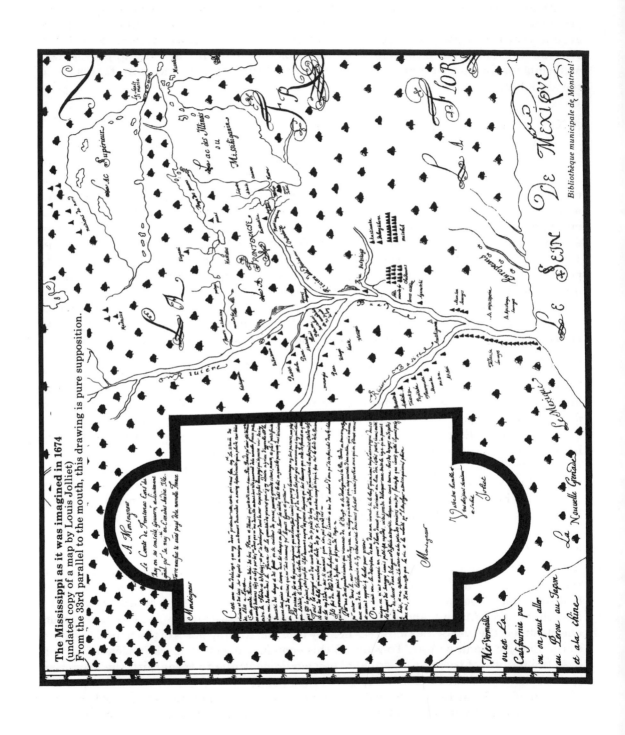

The Mississippi as it was imagined in 1674
(undated copy of a map by Louis Jolliet)
From the 33rd parallel to the mouth, this drawing is pure supposition.

Bibliothèque municipale de Montréal.

of France, of the whole interior of the continent as far as the Pacific Ocean. In the same year, Denys de Saint-Simon and the Jesuit Albanel led an expedition that reached the lake of the Mistassins in 1672. From there, they went down the Rupert River as far as Hudson Bay, taking possession of the lands they crossed and trying to attach the Indians to French policy.

Because of these voyages by Saint-Simon and Saint-Lusson, the boundaries of New France were, in theory, extended as far as the limits of the continent. It was hoped that through a system of alliances, the Saint Lawrence valley, rather than the Hudson basin, would remain the principal outlet for American furs.

b) *The French discovery of the Mississippi*

Although the voyage of exploration by Louis Jolliet and the Jesuit Marquette was ordered by Talon with the purpose of finding the route to Asia, it was only begun after the Intendant's departure. By June 1673, Jolliet and Marquette reached the Upper Mississippi, which Radisson had already visited. Then they went down the river as far as the 33rd parallel (the border between Arkansas and Louisiana), reaching there in mid-July. (This was approximately the point at which the Spaniard de Soto had ended his journey when he went up the same river in 1541-1542.) The French explorers were well aware that this river could only flow into the Gulf of Mexico.

In 1682, it fell to Cavelier de La Salle to reach the mouth of the Mississippi and to take possession in the name of France of this immense river basin still separated from the English colonies by the Alleghenies. However, La Salle committed an error in calculation, which proved detrimental to his undertaking. Determined to discredit the work of Jolliet, and convinced that the Mississippi which he had come down was not the *Rio del Spiritu Santo* that the Spanish had known since at least 1519, La Salle wanted to locate the mouth of "his" Mississippi in the northwest corner of the Gulf of Mexico. When he came back by sea, in 1684, it was, therefore, in this northwest corner (on Matagorda Bay) that he established his colony. He soon realized, however, that the river where he had stopped was not the Mississippi. Unfortunately, he was murdered while attempting to find it again overland.

A renewal of French life in Acadia

During this period of expansion, the French regime returned to Acadia, because the Treaty of Breda, in 1667, gave back to New France its "window on the Atlantic." However, France's oldest American colony, which had just lived for fifteen years under English rule, was to continue the long drama that marks its history, passing at short intervals from one Crown to the other. Restored to France in 1670, the Acadian peninsula was reconquered by the English in 1690. They held it until 1697. The French took it again, only to lose it finally in 1710, so that over a period of sixty years (from 1654 to 1713) Acadia was to experience only thirty-four years of French rule.

The Acadian peninsula was continually neglected by France, for when she was occupying it, she did not bother to send any colonists, but when she lost it, she gave vent to the bitterest protests. During the last quarter of the seventeenth century, Acadia had no more dynamic leaders. However (and this was to the advantage of the colony), the French king set up a strong administration, which put an end to dissension. The intendants of New France, such as Talon and Demeulle, closely supervised the development of the Acadian population.

This was a great period of agricultural development in the peninsula. Its most fertile region (situated on the Bay of Fundy) was cultivated, and by 1707, Port-Royal had become a prosperous centre with six hundred inhabitants who owned three thousand head of livestock. Other centres developed at Minas and Beaubassin. Colonists also settled along the Saint John River and on the other side of the Bay of Fundy. At the same time, the Denys family made progress on the Miramichi, at the mouth of the Nipisiguit (today called Bathurst Bay), and at Restigouche. Faced with an aggressive New England, Acadia found colourful characters to defend it: men like the Basque Baron Saint-Castin who, with his Abenakis, for a long time halted the English advance up from the Penobscot.

In 1707, three years before the final conquest of Port-Royal, Acadia had some two thousand inhabitants who farmed with about eight thousand head of stock. This was the finest period of French rule in Acadia, but this prosperity arrived just when France was forced to retreat from the area.

The conflict of two empires

In Europe, a long political and religious crisis developed into a general war after the League of Augsburg was formed in 1686. This action hurled a coalition of Protestant nations against the Catholic nations. In America, the English and the French spheres would also come to a test of strength.

a) *A small fur-trading colony's need for living space*

When the conflict broke out in America, there was an alarming disproportion of strength. On the English side, there was a population of some 250,000 inhabitants, an empire rich in a variety of products, thanks to the variation in its climate, and colonies drawing strength from a foreign trade favoured by the year-round accessibility of their ports. On the French side, there was a colony of unlimited size, protected by natural defences and possessing only 12,000 inhabitants (scarcely the population of little Rhode Island at that time). It was a colony isolated from the rest of the world for six months of the year, without industries or a fleet, and with an economy still based on beaver fur.

It was precisely because of the beaver that this small French colony, with its 12,000 inhabitants, was continually forced to expand. It had to prevent the merchants of the Atlantic coast from obtaining access to the Great Lakes, particularly the merchants of New York. The colony took part in a commercial struggle, which would not end until 1783, between the trading posts of the Saint Lawrence and those of New York. This small colony also had to stop furs from being directed towards Hudson Bay. If this were not done, the alternative would be to occupy the trading posts in that area. The latter solution was chosen, and the *Compagnie française de la Baie-d'Hudson*, also called the *Compagnie du Nord*, founded at Quebec in 1682, set up a post at the mouth of the Nelson River. However, the defection of Radisson, in 1684, caused this post to fall into English hands.

b) *The first victorious battle*

Thus, even before the mother countries were at war, the colony of the Saint Lawrence, which had sunk a considerable amount of money into the Compagnie du Nord, began the first military offensive in the region of Hudson Bay. In 1686, backed by the merchant Aubert de La Chesnaye, the Chevalier de Troyes went up the Ottawa River with about one hundred men and seized the English forts Monsoni, Rupert and Albany. Helping him were the Le Moyne brothers, one of whom was Iberville. In the course of the next few years, Iberville and his brothers occupied all the English trading posts.

General war began in August 1689, with an Iroquois raid on Lachine, a loading port for the interior. When Frontenac returned from France with orders to invade New York, the only way in which he could protect the weak colony was to send out war parties to spread terror. The English colonies replied with crushing force, sending an army of two thousand men commanded by Winthrop against New France as a first offensive. This army was to invade the Saint Lawrence from Lake Champlain, while a fleet under Phips, with thirty-four ships and two thousand men, was to attempt to take Quebec. Winthrop's army, however, weakened by dissensions and smallpox, had to disband before the campaign began. Phips, after winning Port-Royal in May, met with complete failure at Quebec in October.

The siege of Quebec in 1690
(drawn by an eye witness, La Hontan—engraving reproduced from *Voyages* by La Hontan)

Public Archives of Canada

The treaty of Ryswick, in 1697, recognized French power in America. Although Newfoundland, which Iberville had won in 1696 and 1697, again became an English possession, the treaty gave back to New France a liberated Acadia and the whole of Hudson Bay.

Another major event now strengthened the French positions. The Iroquois prepared for lasting peace with the French and their allies. This decision resulted from commercial rivalries among the natives, and to a lesser degree, from the work of Frontenac. Since the destruction of Huronia, the Iroquois had tried unsuccessfully to keep the Great Lakes trade for themselves. They had braved a powerful league of the Ottawas, the Miamis, and the Illinois, who had French support. In addition, the Iroquois urgently required an escape from the pressures of the only ally whom they could trust at

Quebec in 1700
(extract from La Potherie's *Histoire de l'Amérique septentrionale*)

Public Archives of Canada

that time: New York. Several peace feelers were unsuccessful because there was opposition from the Ottawas, and because governors La Barre and Frontenac sometimes behaved strangely. A set of circumstances in the case of Denonville led to the erroneous conclusion that the Governor had been guilty of "perfidy." Be that as it may, a general peace was signed at Montreal, in 1701, among the Amerinds of the Great Lakes.

c) *A second series of triumphs*

The victory of New France in America could only be a brief respite in the total war between the two commercial empires. A new European conflict, in which the thrones of Spain and England were opposed, provided an opportunity for the English to reassert their rights to the fur-producing area of Hudson Bay, which was the source of their economic strength. The conflict also allowed the English to retake Acadia—which they had called "Nova Scotia" since 1621—and allowed them to make a final effort to eliminate New France on the Saint Lawrence.

Thus, in 1702, war began again on all fronts, but New France, although numerically weaker, won a surprising series of victories once more. New England failed three times in Acadia, and she was not to win it until 1710. From their base at Placentia, the Canadians again conquered Newfoundland, razing Saint John's in 1709, and still kept their positions on Hudson Bay. Then, in 1711, England resumed its plan for a double invasion of New France.

Nicholson was to invade the colony from Lake Champlain with an army of two thousand men, while Walker sailed up the Saint Lawrence River with a fleet of ninety-eight ships, carrying twelve thousand men. However, part of this fleet was lost on the reefs at Sept-Iles and Walker decided to retreat. At the news of this failure, Nicholson did the same.

The colossus with feet of clay

By 1712, New France had reached the highest point in her territorial expansion. She was firmly established in Hudson Bay, and she still occupied Newfoundland. Although she had lost the Acadian peninsula, she maintained settlements in Cape Breton, on the Saint John River, and up to the Bay of Chaleur. She dominated the Iroquois, who had made peace, and by establishing the strategic post of Detroit in 1701, she confirmed her hold on the Great Lakes. She retained absolute control of the Mississippi valley, and Iberville had built forts on Biloxi Bay and Mobile Bay in the Gulf of Mexico, in order to restrain the Spanish who were asserting their claims based on discoveries of the sixteenth century. The dreams of Champlain and Talon had come true.

However, this empire was fragile. Not only did its economic structure remain unstable (one has only to remember the failure of the *Compagnie du Canada*, in a period of full military strength), but its fate depended entirely on the fortunes of the mother country. The disastrous treaty France signed at Utrecht in 1713 sacrificed America. She gave Hudson Bay with all the rivers flowing into it back to England; she gave up all claims to peninsular Acadia; and finally, she recognized the English control of the Iroquois country.

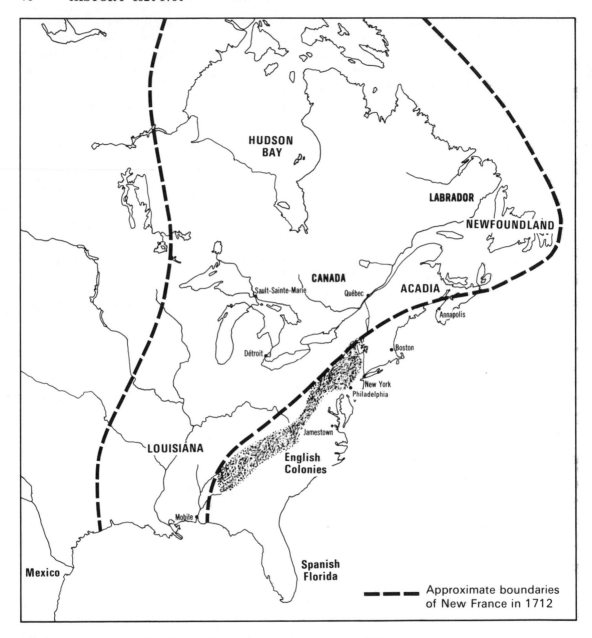

The French Empire in North America at its greatest extent, in 1712

Thus, New France, whose economy was based exclusively on the beaver, lost access to the immense fur-producing area of Hudson Bay. By losing Newfoundland, along with her colony of Placentia, she lost all hope of controlling the Gulf from that side. By abandoning Acadia, with a population of two thousand French colonists, she was eliminated from the Atlantic coast. Also, the fact that Iroquoisia had, in theory, become an English possession meant there was an open breach in the French empire of the Great Lakes, a gap by which it was possible to cut the route going from the Saint Lawrence to Louisiana. Finally, the French defeat in Europe brought an immediate economic disaster, for the mother country would now honour only one quarter of the paper money circulating in New France.

New France was reduced to a long corridor. Her northern approaches along the Gulf of Saint Lawrence were vulnerable to English attack. Her right flank was threatened by the breach in the Iroquois country and by the English thrust across the Alleghenies, a barrier formerly impassable. For half a century, the strength of New France would be dedicated to survival. She fortified the vulnerable length of her frontiers and tried, with a superhuman effort, to prevent economic suffocation by directing furs from far-off Saskatchewan to Montreal. To the 20,000 people of New France, the threat of conquest seemed very near as they faced the 350,000 people living in English colonies from Newfoundland to South Carolina.

Bibliographical Note

On this period, the following general works may be consulted:

G. LANCTÔT, *Histoire du Canada. Du régime royal au traité d'Utrecht, 1663-1713*. Montréal, Beauchemin, 1963.

W. J. ECCLES, *Canada Under Louis XIV, 1663-1701*. Toronto, McClelland and Stewart, 1964.

C. W. COLE, *French Mercantilism, 1683-1700*. New York, 1943.

The most important specialized studies are biographies:

Talon

T. CHAPAIS, *Jean Talon, intendant de la Nouvelle-France, (1665-1672)*. Québec, Demers, 1904.

R. LAMONTAGNE, *Succès d'intendance de Talon*. Montréal, Leméac, 1964.

Frontenac

W. J. ECCLES, *Frontenac, the Courtier Governor*. Toronto, McClelland and Stewart, 1959.

Denonville

T. PRINCE-FALMAGNE, *Un marquis du grand siècle, Denonville*. Montréal, Leméac, 1965.

Jolliet

J. DELANGLEZ, *Life and Voyages of Louis Jolliet, 1645-1700*. Chicago, Institute of Jesuit History, 1948.

Iberville

G. FRÉGAULT, *Pierre Le Moyne d'Iberville*. Montréal, Fides, 1968.

On Cavelier de La Salle, see the study by Celine DUPRÉ, in the *Dictionary of Canadian Biography*, vol. I, which summarizes what is known today about La Salle and is accompanied by a full bibliography.

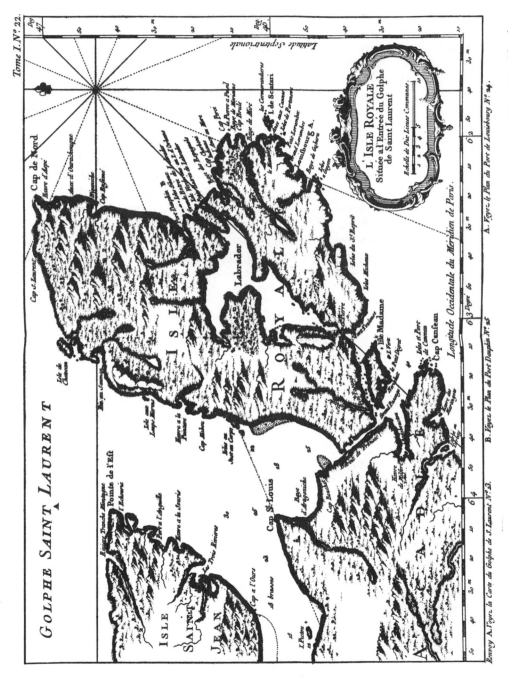

GOLPHE SAINT LAURENT

ISLE SAINT JEAN

Cap de Nord

Cap S. Laurent

Isle de Chicanou

ISLE

ROYALE

Labrador

Ile Madame

Cap Canseau

Pointe de l'Est

Cap St-Louis

A. C. A. D. I. A.

Latitude Septentrionale

L'ISLE ROYALE
Située a l'Entrée du Golphe
de Saint Laurent

Echelle de Dix Lieües Communes

Longitude Occidentale du Méridien de Paris.

Public Archives of Canada

The new French Acadia: Île Royale or Cape Breton Island
(Bellin's *Atlas*)

CHAPTER VI

Resistance, 1713-1754

By the Treaty of Utrecht, New France lost Hudson Bay, Newfoundland, and the Acadian peninsula. Furthermore, the English from now on had access to Lake Ontario because their control of the Iroquois country was recognized in the treaty. Since New France had been deprived of the richest source of furs in America and was threatened in her positions on the Gulf of Saint Lawrence, she now consisted of little more than two long corridors. These corridors, the valleys of the Saint Lawrence and the Mississippi, both pivoted on the Great Lakes, an area that was now within reach of the English. The position of New France was, therefore, that one part, Acadia, had been eliminated and that the other two, Canada and Lousiana, could be isolated at any moment.

The improvement in the situation of 1713

The period from 1713 to 1754 was one of resistance rather than durable achievement. Confronted by an increasingly powerful English empire, New France directed her efforts towards repairing the damage of 1713 and trying to prevent the strangulation of New France.

a) *Reconstruction of French Acadia*

Because New France wanted to restrict Nova Scotia to the peninsula and to maintain her own positions on the Atlantic and in the Gulf, she tried to rebuild French Acadia in a different place.

In 1714, Cape Breton Island was chosen. On the east coast, the Government selected a bay suitable for the establishment of a military port (in spite of the fact that this area was very often covered by fog). The construction of a fortified town, Louisbourg, was begun there. The first inhabitants were people who had been evacuated from their homes in Placentia, Newfoundland.

Cape Breton (soon to be called Île Royale) possessed very little cultivable soil, so that if the Acadians from the peninsula were to be persuaded to regroup elsewhere, fertile land would have to be obtained for them. This land was found on *Ile Saint-Jean* (today, Prince Edward Island) where no Europeans had yet settled. A group of colonists arrived there in 1720, in charge of the Comte de Saint-Pierre. By the end of 1721, about one hundred settlers were living there. The population increased as people came from peninsular Acadia and France. The port of Saint-Pierre, on the north coast, and the port of Lajoie, on the south coast (now *Charlottetown Bay*), became the important centres of this new Acadia. The first missionary, the Sulpician de Breslay, gave the area to the Récollets, who were for a long time the only priests in the new colony.

b) *Fortification of the Saint Lawrence*

The mother country fortified the Saint Lawrence in order to strengthen the defences of New France. During the previous war, an English fleet had besieged Quebec in 1690 and another, that of Walker, had attempted the same operation in 1711. The ramparts of Quebec and Montreal were built after the Treaty of Utrecht.

In Quebec, the work of fortification had been undertaken, at the beginning of the century, according to the plans of Levasseur de Néré and later those of Beaucours. This work had been suspended for a short while but was resumed in 1716. By 1720, Quebec had become a fortress. An added advantage was the elevated position that it occupied on Cap-aux-Diamants. The town of Montreal, up to this time, had been surrounded only by a stockade, which proved difficult to replace when necessary. Montreal was as vulnerable as a completely unfortified city. In 1716, the Conseil de Marine decided to surround the town with a stone wall, flanked by bastions. A battery installed on a small hill did duty as a citadel. Montreal now had the appearance of a fortress.

A traditional invasion route (that of the Richelieu) could easily bring the English into the heart of Canada and allow them to cut communications between Quebec and Montreal. Since the fort of Chambly, strengthened in 1711, was too far from the frontiers that were being claimed, an advance was made much farther south, towards the Hudson River. The construction of a fortress, Saint-Frédéric (later, Crown Point) was begun in 1731, south of Lake Champlain. Thus, by blocking the expansion to the north, the French hoped to safeguard a region that was essential to their protection. In 1733, the authorities began to distribute seigneuries there, in the hope that people would settle.

c) *Guarding the Great Lakes*

By recognizing English control of the Iroquois territory, France had given her enemy access to Lake Ontario. Any English installation on the south shore of this lake threatened the route along the upper Saint Lawrence. On this side also, measures were taken in order to prolong the life of New France.

A small post had, for a long time, guarded the Niagara portage between lakes Ontario and Erie. This corresponded to Fort Frontenac, which controlled the mouth of Lake Ontario. Joncaire—an adopted son of the Senecas (Iroquois who lived in the neighbourhood of this post)—in 1720 received orders to improve the condition of this post. In 1725, in spite of English protests, France built a stone fortress on the right bank of the Niagara (therefore in Iroquois territory), to guard the route to the West. This fortress could also act as a rallying point for the Iroquois, should pressure from England increase. In answer to this French threat, in 1727 the English constructed a fort at the mouth of the Oswego River, in the country of the Onondagas. Lake Ontario had become the stake in an international game; but until war came, the French positions were safe.

d) *The rise of Louisiana*

Louisiana had been explored as far as the 33rd parallel by Louis Jolliet, and to the mouth of the Mississippi by Cavelier de La Salle. However, up until 1685, it had only the small fort of Saint-Louis, in the far west of the Gulf, in Matagorda Bay. This fort disappeared after the death of La Salle. Iberville re-established the French claim in 1699, by building Fort Maurepas on Biloxi Bay, while his brother Bienville constructed another fort, in 1702, on Mobile Bay. However, Louisiana was still not a colony, and both the English from the Carolinas and the Spanish tried to ally themselves with the natives in the Mississippi area, at the expense of the French.

It was not until 1712 that France made a serious attempt to establish a well-organized colony in Louisiana. The financier Crozat received the monopoly of trade for fifteen years. Dauphine Island (at the entrance to Mobile Bay) was at that time the centre of activity. The country was provided with these institutions: a Government, a Superior Council, and the customary law of Paris. When Crozat failed, in 1717, the whole of Louisiana, including the country of the Illinois, became the exclusive territory of the Compagnie des Indes Occidentales, which began a policy of settlement. On its behalf, in 1718, Bienville founded the town of New Orleans, on the left bank of the Mississippi, one hundred miles from the sea. In 1722, this town became the capital of Louisiana. Admittedly, the speculations of Law in 1720 put an end to important preparations for settlement, but the colony had sufficient manpower to overcome the Chicachas and the Natchez and to become an important part of New France, along with the country of the Illinois, to which Canadians were coming. The immense Mississippi valley seemed secure for France for a long time, because the Appalachian barrier cut it off almost completely from the English on the Atlantic.

In spite of the disastrous Treaty of Utrecht, New France had completed its empire in America. It now possessed an enormous crescent-shaped area stretching from the Gulf of Saint Lawrence to the Gulf of Mexico.

In search of a new fur empire

The failure of the Compagnie du Canada during the last war added to the loss of the fur supplies of Hudson Bay and left the economy of New France in a dangerous position. An attempt was now made, in spite of the strength of English competition, to bring prosperity back to the fur trade.

a) *Renewal of trade*

Since the end of the previous century, and even when New France had enjoyed the profitable trade of Hudson Bay, trading (which was forbidden to the settlers) had been carried on only by small or unstable companies. In 1717, when trade became free in the interior of the colony, there was an increase in the amount of fur trading. In the same year, a large company, the Compagnie d'Occident, took over the export of beaver fur. This company was replaced in 1718, by a sounder enterprise, the Compagnie des Indes Occidentales.

The only important trade routes that France still possessed were those of the Great Lakes, where obstacles were endangering the whole fur trade. The Fox nation, who lived on the west coast of Lake Michigan, had almost been defeated in 1712. They were, however, continuing their war against the allies of the French. It was becoming evident that, through the Iroquois, the Foxes and their allies (the Mascoutens and Kickapoos) were attempting to divert the furs from the Great Lakes to the English trading posts at Albany. If this attempt were to succeed, the last great source of furs would be lost to New France. An expedition under Louvigny, in 1716, checked the Foxes a second time, and regular trade was re-established. Then the Foxes created new trouble. After six years, 1728-1734, the French managed to destroy and disperse them for good. Trade returned to normal.

b) *The channelling of furs from the West towards Montreal*

The most spectacular effort to save the economy of New France was that made by La Vérendrye who attempted to bring furs from the West to Montreal.

Since the Treaty of Utrecht, the fur-producing areas of New France had been reduced to the Saint Lawrence valley and the Great Lakes. The Saint Lawrence area was almost depleted, and the great trade routes leading to Hudson Bay were all, theoretically, part of the English empire—Lake Mistassini (to the north of Lake Saint John) and the Rupert River; Lake Abitibi, with the Abitibi and Harricana Rivers; and the Albany, Severn, and Nelson Rivers. These routes drew all the fur, even from the northern coasts of lakes Huron and Superior, to the English posts.

Although trade from the far west would normally flow to Hudson Bay by means of Lake Winnipeg and the Nelson River, the French attempted to compete with the English there and divert the furs to Montreal. This, together with the foolish hope of finally reaching the Asian Sea, was the concern of La Vérendrye.

Backed by a company of Montreal merchants, La Vérendrye began the exploration of the western country in 1731 from his base of Kaministigoya (on the far western side of Lake Superior). As he advanced, he set up posts that served as stages for the new distribution of furs: in 1731, Fort Saint-Pierre, on Rainy Lake; in 1732, Fort Saint-Charles, on Lake of the Woods; in 1734, Fort Maurepas, on the Red River; in 1738, Fort La Reine, on the Assiniboine; in 1741, Fort Dauphin, near Lake Winnipegosis, and Fort Bourbon, to the northwest of Lake Winnipeg; and in 1743, Fort Paskoya, on the Saskatchewan. A long march towards the southwest, from the Assiniboine River as far as South Dakota, led the sons of La Vérendrye to a new barrier: the Rockies. This western trade (in furs, and also in slaves) proved to be irregular for several reasons. These included rivalry among the natives, the difficulty of supplying food and goods for barter to these distant posts, and most important of all, the normal flow of trade towards Hudson Bay. For this last reason, the effects of strong English competition—from north of the Great Lakes and from Albany in the south—were increasingly felt by New France.

The return to Talon's program

The intendants concentrated their efforts on strengthening the colony, which was being threatened on all sides by the English empire. Among these were Bégon (1712-1726),

Essai d'une Carte que M.ᵣ Guillaume Delisle P.ᵉʳ Geographe du Roy
et de l'Academie des Sciences avoit joint à son Memoire presenté à la Cour en 1717. Sur la
Mer de l'Ouest.

La gravure de l'Original n'est
que d'un simple trait, et la Mer
est lavée en couleur d'eau.

Baie d'Hudson

Affinipoils

Canada

Sioux   Lac   Superieur
Pointe du St.
Esprit   Nipiffiriniens

Mer de l'Ouest   Outaouacs

Aouia   Hurons
le Miffouri   Neu
                                          tres
C. Blanc
C. Mendocin   Quivira
                     Riv.ʳᵉ de l'Ouest   Panis

                                          Ilinois

Californie   Cibola
                    Nouveau
                                                    Virginie
            Mexique   Choumans
Mer   L o u i s i a n e
du   Caroline
Mer Vermeille

Sud   Floride
                              Embouchure
                              du Miffiffipi
            Mexique   Golfe du Mexique

Archives du Séminaire de Québec

The location of the "Western Sea," as imagined in 1752
This supposition put forward by the geographer Delisle in 1717 is found again in 1752 in a report by Buache
to the Académie des Sciences in Paris.

Hocquart (1729-1748), and Bigot. Although they indulged in speculation, these top-ranking officials recall in some ways the administration of Talon. They repeatedly tried to obtain a diversified economy for New France and to increase immigration. In addition, a greater stability in institutions made their administrations generally easier for them.

a) *An attempt to reorganize finances*

The period 1713-1754 opened with an attempt to improve finances. At the end of the war, an enormous amount of card money (some two million *livres*) was circulating in the colony. This money was used at its nominal, not its real value; so New France, in addition to agricultural crises, suffered a crisis of inflation. The mother country put an end to the crisis by redeeming this paper money, but only at a quarter of its value. In 1719, she abolished this monetary system. However, the dearth of coins, as in the period before 1685, paralyzed internal trade and all industry. In 1729, paper money was reintroduced. This time the monetary system was helped by a long period of peace, along with stricter regulations. It answered the needs of the economy in a satisfactory way until 1745. Then the War of the Austrian Succession and the Seven Years' War finally led to the decline of the system.

b) *Towards a diversified economy*

It is Hocquart, of all the intendants of this period, who most resembles Talon in his desire to utilize all the resources of the country. He also accomplished the most. Moreover, he was in office for nineteen years, which is the longest term of office in the history of the intendants.

During his ministry, the road network was greatly expanded. Among others, he opened the important Quebec-Montreal highway, which was to increase trade between the far-flung regions of Canada.

Agriculture was developing. In 1721, there had been only 62,000 seeded *arpents* in Canada, but in 1739, there were 188,000 *arpents*. New crops, such as tobacco, appeared; others, like hemp and flax, gained a new popularity. Wheat, the only staple cereal, was more strictly controlled to assure a more reliable food supply and to try to organize an export trade. More was produced. The yield increased from 283,000 bushels in 1721, to 635,000 in 1739.

The intendants were interested in the development and maintenance of small industries (sawmills, cloth mills, tarworks). These small industries were short-lived and provided little profit since they lacked capital, specialist workers, and outlets (because the trade with the West Indies never amounted to very much). There was, of course, the hat factory in Montreal, which could have expanded because of the good supply of furs. It had to be closed, however, in 1736 on orders from the mother country, since colonies at that time existed only to provide Europe with raw materials.

In Quebec, Hocquart established naval shipyards, which were very active from 1739 to 1750 because of royal subsidies. From 1733 onwards, Poulin de Francheville operated the Saint-Maurice ironworks. After the failure of 1741, they became active again under Government direction. Through the influence of Hocquart, "fixed" fisheries multiplied along the Saint Lawrence as far as the Labrador coast, but the Canadians were unable to profit from the great fishing resources of the Gulf.

c) *A great period of settlement*

The most important progress was made in settlement. Because of an extraordinary birthrate and the largest immigration in its history, New France experienced an increase in its population. In Canada alone, the 20,000 inhabitants of 1713 had increased to 55,000 by 1755.

Although it lacked the vigour of Colbert's policies, the State always played a part in directing emigration towards New France. Ships' captains were obliged to transport those who had contracted to settle. From 1720 to 1750, some 1,000 people were sent: young men who were being exiled, a large number of salt smugglers, poachers, and even a certain number of criminals. Soldiers were allowed to settle permanently in the colony. The Government closed its eyes to the arrival of Huguenots. Fugitives from the English colonies were easily naturalized, and even the slave trade made a contribution to settlement, for many slaves left children when they died.

The towns seemed to profit most from immigration, while the seigneurial domains made limited progress. Admittedly, in the single year of 1736, five seigneuries were granted in order to open up Nouvelle-Beauce, but between 1714 and 1732, only five had been granted. After 1733, twelve seigneuries were distributed in the area of Lake Champlain, where it was hoped to speed up the occupation of the land, but no settlement took place. After 1740, in addition to eight new seigneuries on Lake Champlain, sixteen were granted in the area of the Saint Lawrence, but this grant did not lead to immediate colonization. Much more immigration would have been necessary to populate these areas.

New France in 1754

The English colonies in North America had a total population of one million in addition to about 300,000 slaves, who constituted the supply of workers. This population was not spread out, since geographical conditions still limited the colonists to the Atlantic coastline.

Compared to these English colonies, New France was still small, with a scanty population of about seventy thousand inhabitants. This population was split into three groups that remained unattached to each other because of the great distances separating them. In French Acadia, where perhaps some ten thousand people lived, only Île Saint-Jean and Louisbourg possessed organized societies; but since the War of the Austrian Succession, the development of French Acadia had been considerably retarded. In 1745, the English had seized Louisbourg and Île Saint-Jean, which they occupied until 1748. Although the majority of the inhabitants were forced to evacuate, they returned gradually to resettle in the same area. Canada, with its population of 55,000 and its two large fortified towns (Quebec and Montreal), constituted the most compact and the most soundly organized group in New France. Finally, distant Louisiana was divided into two isolated areas of settlement (the country of the Illinois and New Orleans) and possessed about four thousand inhabitants.

Considered by itself, New France seemed to have made remarkable progress from 1713 to 1754. French Acadia had been rebuilt; Nouvelle-Beauce had been opened up; Lake Champlain had been fortified and seigneuries granted there; the West had been explored as far as the Rockies; and Louisiana had been founded and maintained. All this growth

NEW FRANCE

64,500 settlers

ENGLISH COLONIES

1,000,000 settlers

New France, compared to the English colonies in North America, in 1754

confirms the fact that the same amazing vigour that had vitalized New France during the previous century still existed. In spite of an economy threatened with strangulation by the Hudson Bay trading posts to the north and the competition of New York, Pennsylvania, and Virginia to the south, New France offered resistance to the English empire. The success of this resistance, however, seemed progressively less assured from one year to the next.

Bibliographical Note

The history of events in the period 1713-1754 has been little studied. The period has almost always been approached from the perspective of problems or institutions, and the same method is used in the second part of this book. Two works of a general nature should be cited:

G. FRÉGAULT, *La Civilisation de la Nouvelle-France*. Montréal, Pascal, 1944.

G. LANCTÔT, *Histoire du Canada. Du traité d'Utrecht au traité de Paris, 1713-1763*. Montréal, Beauchemin, 1964: pp. 15-199.

N. W. CALDWELL, *The French in the Mississippi Valley, 1740-1750*. Urbana, University of Illinois Press, 1941.

C. E. O'NEILL, *Church and State in French Colonial Louisiana, Policy and Politics to 1732*. New Haven and London, Yale University Press, 1966.

Certain biographical studies also provide a general background to this period:

M. N. CROUSE, *La Vérendrye, Fur Trader and Explorer*. Toronto, Ryerson, 1956.

G. N. FRÉGAULT, *Le Grand Marquis. Pierre de Rigaud de Vaudreuil et la Louisiane*. Montréal, Fides, 1952.

N. McL. ROGERS, "The Abbé Le Loutre." *Canadian Historical Review*, XI, 2 (June 1930), pp. 105-128.

CHAPTER VII

Conquest, 1754-1760

A military clash between the two North American empires became inevitable as time passed. The French exploitation of the Saint Lawrence and the Great Lakes was in opposition to the English hold on the fur-producing areas in the north and along the whole of the Atlantic coastline. The French barred the way to the interior of the continent, and as the English colonies developed, they found it necessary to expand towards the Ohio and the Mississippi. The merchants of England were well aware of the lucrative profit that would ensue from the acquisition of the valley of the Saint Lawrence.

The resulting conflict was, however, not only between two commercial empires but also between two types of society. The two civilizations seemed to be struggling to ensure the victory of their respective institutions. At some points, it appeared to be a direct conflict between Protestantism and Catholicism in North America.

The military position of New France

Although New France could offer only a meagre population of 85,000 inhabitants scattered in small groups from the Saint Lawrence to the Gulf of Mexico, in opposition to the more than one million inhabitants in the English colonies, when war broke out, the French positions were still secure.

From the islands of Acadia, the French still dominated the entrance to the Saint Lawrence. The fortress of Louisbourg, which had been taken in 1745 and had been given back in 1748 without the French having won a single battle in America, held a very strong position in North America. On the edge of the Acadian peninsula, two forts (Beauséjour and Gaspareau) had restricted the English since 1750 to the isthmus of Chignecto and served as links between French Acadia and the Acadians of Nova Scotia.

On the Saint Lawrence, at the two extremities of Canada, the two towns (Quebec and Montreal) had been fortified with stone walls. They resembled fortresses, and the town of Quebec, lying on a cliff-top, seemed to have been impregnable. In addition, the French maintained the forts of Chambly and Saint-Jean on the Richelieu River to guard another invasion route. They had even pushed forward to the south of Lake Champlain, where since 1731, they had been entrenched in Fort Saint-Frédéric.

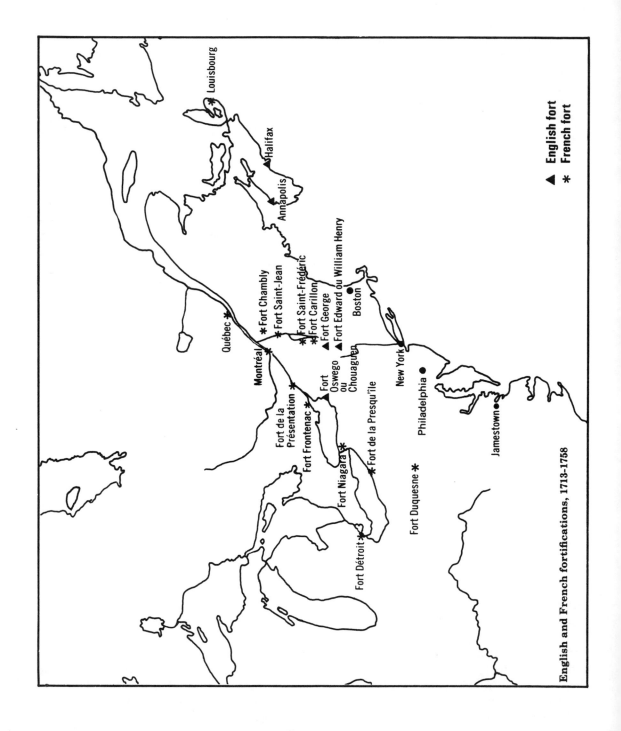

Louisbourg

Halifax

Annapolis

Fort Chambly
Fort Saint-Jean
Fort Saint-Frédéric
Fort Carillon
Fort George
Fort Edward ou William Henry
Boston

Québec

Montréal

Fort de la Présentation

Fort
Oswego
ou
Chouaguen

Fort Frontenac

New York

Fort de la Presqu'île

Philadelphia

Fort Niagara

Jamestown

Fort Détroit

Fort Duquesne

▲ English fort
* French fort

English and French fortifications, 1713-1758

The Great Lakes country was equally well defended. On the route of the upper Saint Lawrence, there was Fort La Présentation, built in 1749; then old Fort Frontenac, at the outlet of Lake Ontario; and Fort Niagara, which guarded the passage between lakes Ontario and Erie and held the Iroquois within reach for rapid intervention. On the south shore of Lake Erie, Fort Presqu'Île had become a port of entry to the Ohio and led to the founding of two military stations in 1753: the fort on Rivière-aux-Boeufs and Fort Machault. Finally, Detroit, with its fort, guarded the essential link between lakes Erie and Huron.

These man-made fortifications were reinforced by natural defences. From the Bay of Chaleur to south of Lake Champlain, mountains and marshes prevented the New England forces from attempting an overland invasion; from New York to the Carolinas, the Appalachian chain still hemmed in the English colonies on the Atlantic coast. All this, with the memory of the English failures in 1690 and 1711, showed that New France—even if she were showing signs of exhaustion—would not be easy to conquer.

The war of conquest on the Ohio

It was on a secondary waterway of New France that the decisive conflict of the two empires was to break out. Flowing southwards into the Mississippi, the Ohio (or Belle-Rivière) served primarily as a connecting link between the Great Lakes and Louisiana. Because the Monongahela, which flowed into it, was the only possible way of getting through the Appalachians for the traders of Pennsylvania and Virginia, the Ohio valley suddenly, towards the middle of the century, became a stake of great importance in the international game. Up to that time, New France really had had to face only New England and New York, but from now on, the powerful English colonies in the south had a direct interest in the conquest of the French empire.

a) *Both the English and the French claim the Ohio valley*

Basing her demand on the fact that La Salle may have discovered and taken possession of the Ohio in 1670 (although this had never been verified), France claimed the entire Ohio valley and maintained that the Appalachians were the eastern limit of her empire. The Treaty of Utrecht, 1713, had not decided the fate of this region, which in any case had not posed an international problem up to this time. The French had been able to set up, without trouble, the post of Vincennes, in 1732, at the junction of the Wabash and the Ohio.

However, after the discovery of a gap in the mountain chain (the Kanawha River flowing into the Monongahela), the English built the post of Pickawillany in 1743, well to the west of the Ohio. In 1744, by the Treaty of Lancaster, they received from the natives half a million acres to the west of the Appalachians and immediately founded the Ohio Company of Virginia. As a result, English tradesmen and surveyors invaded the valley.

Aware of this new prize, England and France, in 1748, agreed to name commissioners to study the American frontier disputes, but neither France nor England waited for their conclusions. In 1749, Governor La Galissonière sent Céloron de Blainville to bury plaques in different parts of the Ohio valley in order to "renew" the claim of 1670. But, as was admitted by the Jesuit de Bonnecamps (a member of that expedition), the valley was "little known" by the French and "unfortunately too well known to the English." Governor Duquesne dismissed the English claims as fantasies, and writing about the Ohio River, he clearly stated French policy: "The King desires it, and that is sufficient reason to advance." In the spring of 1754, he sent Contrecoeur with an army of one thousand men to build a fort at the junction of the Ohio and the Monongahela.

b) *The Jumonville affair*

A small group of Englishmen were already there, constructing a fort, but Contrecoeur forced them to leave the area. However, the English continued to visit the mountains frequently and to pass the frontier line that had been vaguely indicated by the French. Contrecoeur sent Jumonville to demand that they withdraw from the land of the French King. The emissary left on May 23, provided with orders that made him both a soldier and the bearer of a truce-flag. If the English appeared to be stronger than his forces, he was to read the demand; otherwise, he was to expel them.

Washington, who at the age of twenty-two, was already a lieutenant-colonel of militia and a member of the Virginian Assembly, set out to look for this group of Frenchmen when he heard of their arrival from the "savages." After a long search, he found them, on the morning of May 28, in a wooded hollow where they had been hiding for a day. Washington had been informed of the military purpose of the French expedition, and wishing to avoid being surprised himself, he ordered an attack. Jumonville was killed before he had time to begin reading his summons.

Coulon de Villiers, Jumonville's brother, avenged this defeat, by surprising Washington, on July 3, at Fort Necessity, sixty-five miles from Fort Duquesne. Washington agreed to capitulate because he was cut off from all assistance and was threatened with a massacre by the natives accompanying Villiers. Washington, relying on a Dutch interpreter who was in a hurry to finish the business (it was night and pouring rain), signed a treaty in which the death of Jumonville was twice referred to as a murder. Villiers, for his part, also made a mistake: he prohibited the English from entering Ohio for only one year, which was as good as recognizing their rights. This proved most embarrassing to the French authorities, and when they published the treaty among a collection of documents designed to discredit England, it was in a duly abbreviated version.

The English had thus been expelled by an army from the junction of the Ohio and the Monongahela; the French had begun construction of a fort in a disputed area; Jumonville's detachment had been eliminated by force of arms; and Washington had been forced to capitulate. Officially, this was a period of complete peace; but in fact, the Seven Years' War had begun in America two years before its outbreak in Europe.

War on three fronts: 1755

The English colonies viewed as aggression the French advance into country that they had considered as theirs since the treaty they had signed with the natives. Although France and England were still officially at peace, the two North American empires came into open conflict. In 1755, campaigns took place on three fronts: the Ohio, Lake Champlain, and Acadia.

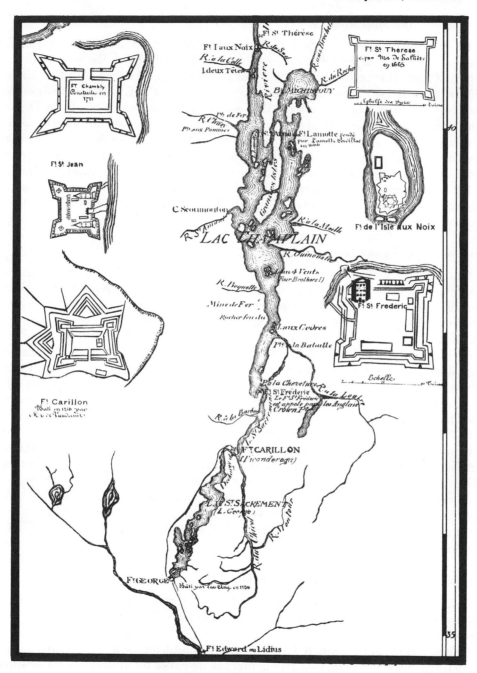

Archives du Séminaire de Québec

Lake Champlain at the time of the Conquest
A sketch map drawn about 1758 based on a drawing by Franquet in 1752.

a) *The battle of the Monongahela*

In September 1754, the English entrusted General Braddock with the task of driving the French from the Ohio and establishing himself there. He led fifteen hundred men against Fort Duquesne on July 9, 1755. To meet him, Contrecoeur sent Liénard de Beaujeu with only two hundred soldiers and six hundred natives, well trained in open fighting. Beaujeu was killed during the first engagement and was replaced by Dumas who stationed his men on either side of a path on which Braddock's men became trapped. From the advantage of the forest, bullets rained down on the English who were forced to flee, unable to protect themselves. Braddock was mortally wounded, and along with his artillery, he lost some papers giving valuable information about the English plans. While the French had only twenty-three dead and sixteen wounded, the English lost almost a thousand men, killed or disabled. The corridor to the Ohio remained closed to the English colonies.

b) *The conflict on Lake Champlain*

The French had less success on Lake Champlain. Goaded by the defeat on the Monongahela, James De Lancey, the Lieutenant Governor of New York, proposed a general plan for the invasion of New France. The first stage of his plan was to destroy Fort Saint-Frédéric south of Lake Champlain, which served the French as a base for attack. In the course of the summer of 1755, Governor Vaudreuil learned that William Johnson had completed Fort Edward (or Lydius), between the Hudson River and Lake George, and was about to march on Fort Saint-Frédéric with three thousand men. The Governor, therefore, sent Baron Dieskau with fifteen hundred men to halt his advance.

On August 8, near Fort Edward, the first encounter routed a force of English troops, but they later entrenched themselves so strongly that they could not be dislodged by the French. The French killed more men than they lost themselves, but their leader had been wounded and taken prisoner, and they had failed to capture Fort Edward. What is more, the English immediately began a new advance northward, indicated by the erection of Fort George, or William Henry, on the south shore of Lake George. The French, on the other hand, protected their positions on Lake Champlain by building Fort Carillon, between Lake George and Fort Saint-Frédéric, in the same summer of 1755.

The English and French fronts thus faced each other, and were separated by only forty miles.

c) *The English colony in Acadia is threatened*

While the French were strengthening their position in Ohio and restraining the English in the area of Lake Champlain, a sizeable French population was disappearing from peninsular Acadia.

During the Anglo-French conflict, this population, which had been ceded to England by the treaty of 1713, was giving increasing cause for concern to its new masters. Long after its cession, Nova Scotia still retained the appearance of a French colony. Annapolis (the former Port-Royal) was, in fact, the only really English part. All the rest remained French: in particular the Bay of Sainte-Marie, the Canso area, and especially the Minas Basin, where the Acadian population was concentrated.

Therefore, in 1749, England decided to bring in a large group of non-French colonists. On Chibouctou Bay, Cornwallis founded Halifax where, in 1754, an assembly was instituted. However, this new colony of some three thousand people developed only on the Atlantic coast, completely isolated from the French population.

This English colony was the object of incessant attacks. In 1749, in an attempt to dislodge it, the Micmacs declared war. Their raids against the English continued for a long time. It is probable that missionaries such as Le Loutre and Maillard played a decisive role in this war. In any case, they wrote in justification of it, and were able to keep the Micmacs in a state of religious fanaticism, which served apostolic purposes and French policy at the same time. They used the same tactics to incite the Abenakis. For the missionaries, the interests of religion were inseparable from the interests of the State, in accordance with the instructions they received from their ecclesiastical as well as their political superiors.

During this period, by means of the Isthmus of Chignecto, the Acadians remained in constant contact with New France. Encouraged by the proximity of Louisbourg and Île Saint-Jean, they refused to take an oath of loyalty that would morally bind them to England. Here again, uniting a spiritual cause (the religion of the Acadians) with the temporal aim of loyalty to France, the missionaries showed themselves more concerned with executing orders from Versailles than with working for the real well-being of the Acadians. (In particular, Le Loutre was to some extent responsible for the drama of 1775.) They encouraged the Acadians to resist and tried to make them emigrate to the mainland. Court orders were often accompanied by threats that the Acadians would lose their priests if they refused to rejoin New France. Eventually, a large number of Acadians joined the French, the Micmacs, and the Abenakis, to take part in raids against the English settlements.

d) *The removal of the Acadians*

Under these conditions, the existence of Nova Scotia was in serious danger, as (it was believed) was that of New England. Since the Acadians refused to become English subjects and were a danger to English settlement, there remained only one solution: to transport them elsewhere and replace them by colonists loyal to Britain.

This solution was not new to America. In 1689, Louis XIV had instructed Frontenac to conquer New York and to scatter its inhabitants "together or separately" in different places throughout the English colonies, but it had not been possible to put that plan of conquest into execution. The English were to be the first in America to deport a population of European origin.

The man who initiated this policy in Nova Scotia was the Lieutenant Governor, Charles Lawrence. With the aid of New England, he seized forts Beauséjour and Gaspareau in June, 1755. Now, at last, the Acadians of the peninsula were deprived of their link with the French. Then, with the approval of Judge Belcher, Lawrence decided to deport the Acadians to the English colonies. Judge Belcher's opinion was that the Acadians had acted simply as rebels. Lawrence was later rewarded for his actions.

The operation began at the end of the summer of 1755 and continued throughout the autumn. Some two thousand Acadians may have escaped and got back to New France, but it is probable that six or seven thousand of them were deported in the first year.

This operation did not, however, remain an accident of English policy. In the following years, as England advanced her conquests, she continued the process of elimination by deportation. In 1758, she eliminated the Acadian populations of Cape Breton and Île Saint-Jean. This program was continued until 1762. The Acadians who had not fled to Canada or to the West Indies were sent to France, where the French Government could do little to improve their position. They numbered some two to three thousand people. In this way, the English were able to settle in Nova Scotia quite peacefully, in the area that had been emptied of its French colonists.

New France still victorious, 1756-1758

Since the Acadians of the peninsula could no longer be counted as an essential element in the French empire after 1713, the massive deportation of 1755 did not impair the strength of resistance of New France. With her positions on the Ohio and on Lake Champlain intact New France would, for two and a half years, hold in check the opposing forces and perform some unexpected feats of arms.

a) *On Lake Ontario*

The English fortification of Oswego (or Chouaguen), which was composed of three forts, still threatened to interrupt navigation on Lake Ontario. The English were planning to use this fort as a powerful base from which they could eliminate forts Frontenac and Niagara, and thus cut off the Ohio and Louisiana from all military communication with the Saint Lawrence.

Faced with this threat, the French took the offensive. During the fall of 1755 and the ensuing winter, Governor Vaudreuil made his plans. In March of 1756, he began with a raid that disabled Fort Bull; but it was not until the following August that Montcalm came to besiege it with a force of three thousand men. On August 14, its eighteen hundred defenders capitulated, surrendering to the French a large amount of artillery, ammunition, and provisions. The military route of Lake Ontario remained secure for New France.

b) *On Lake Champlain*

The French positions were reinforced on the Lake Champlain front. The fortress of Carillon, which faced Fort George, seemed to render impossible any English plan of expansion towards the north. Here again, and even more important, the French were to take the offensive.

After a week-long foray in March, 1757, which destroyed a great amount of war materiel, the French later seized Fort George on the following August 9. Between Carillon and the Hudson River, the only English fort remaining was Fort Edward. Not only did the English lose their most advanced fort, but their sick and wounded were massacred by the natives whom the French had been unable to control.

New York expected a victorious French invasion daily. The murderous raids which the Canadians continued to carry out into the English colonies increased the enemy's fears. However, urged on by Pitt, England, together with the English colonies, decided to strike a decisive blow in 1758. Some fifty thousand men were to be poured into America to

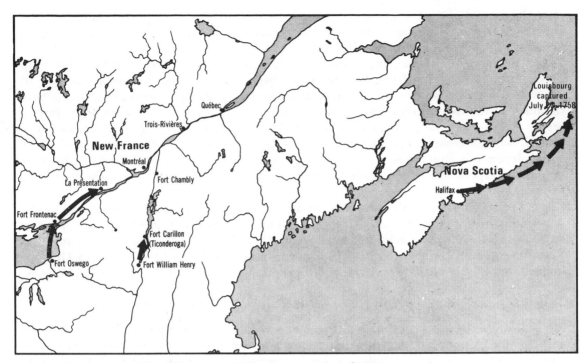

General movement of English troops during the campaign of 1758

attack on three fronts: Louisbourg, from where they would try to take Quebec; Lake Champlain, which would open the way to Montreal; and Fort Duquesne, at the entrance to the Ohio.

The first of these three projected attacks was made on Lake Champlain. In the summer of 1758, Abercromby with an army of seven thousand men moved against Carillon, which was defended by half that number, under the command of Montcalm. Believing that his adversary was about to receive a large reinforcement of troops, Abercromby hastened to make a frontal attack on July 8. The French made a stout resistance, forcing the English to retreat with a loss of almost two thousand men, wounded or dead, while Montcalm's losses amounted to less than four hundred men.

The defence crumbles, 1758-1760

The brilliant French victory at Carillon could check the enemy only temporarily. When the English forces, much superior in numbers and resources, began their extensive campaign on all fronts, New France would be crushed in a very short time.

a) *Economic confusion*

New France, at least until 1748, had lived through a period of prosperity, for her money (even her paper money) remained sound and her economic activity seemed promising; but after that, New France was rapidly on her way towards bankruptcy. For ten or fifteen years, the country's economy was a war economy. Admittedly, consumption rose after the arrival of the troops, but in order to assure both the transportation of military forces and the provisioning of distant posts, it became necessary to conscript the *habitants*, which caused a corresponding drop in production.

As the years passed, the colony produced less and less and was forced to rely increasingly on supplies from Europe, which became costly and unreliable because of the war at sea. The war economy, which was supposed to be only temporary, finally took the place of the regular economy. Other causes accelerated the breakdown. Canada was hit by a severe famine during the winter of 1757-1758. The following summer, food was scarce, because communications with France had been broken. The Grande Société, of which Intendant Bigot was a member, practised fraud on a large scale. Fur, the only important export, could no longer be sent abroad. The result was an alarming rise in prices.

From 1756 to 1759, the price of a hundredweight of flour rose from 12 to 60 *livres*. A pound of beef increased from 3 to 40 sols; a pound of bacon, from 6 to 70 sols; a dozen eggs, from 3 to 70 sols; a pound of sugar, from 12 to 180 sols; a cask of wine, from 70 to 1,200 *livres*. Meanwhile, the daily wage of a workman rose from 2 to only 6 *livres*. Only an immediate peace could save the country from collapse, but in 1758, no peace was in sight.

b) *The isolation of the Saint Lawrence by the end of the summer of 1758*

Despite the battle of Carillon, the immense English campaign was to succeed. On July 8, 1758, Montcalm held up Abercromby's advance; but, on the 26th of the same month, Louisbourg had to capitulate for the second time, before a force of 28,000 men. From Louisbourg, the invader blocked the river and ravaged the French fisheries, while waiting for the attack on Quebec.

During this time, on the Lake Ontario front, the English were carrying out a victorious advance. On August 26, to the great surprise of the French, Bradstreet appeared with three thousand men before Fort Frontenac, which capitulated the next day. The English collected an immense amount of booty. The small fort of La Présentation, which guarded the rapids downstream, fell soon afterwards. Finally, on November 24, Forbes entered Fort Duquesne which, until that time, had blocked the entrance to the Ohio. The French commander had just withdrawn after blowing it up.

c) *The futile resistance of 1759*

The essential posts on the Great Lakes had thus surrendered, and only Fort Niagara remained. The gateway to the Saint Lawrence was in English hands. Although the French were still solidly entrenched on Lake Champlain at the end of 1758, it was believed that the conquest would soon be complete. Yet this would take a long time to accomplish.

While Wolfe, with 39,000 men on board his ships, including 9,000 soldiers, began the siege of Quebec in June, 1759, Johnson seized Fort Niagara, and Amherst proceeded towards the French positions on Lake Champlain. Bourlamaque, who wished to save his small army in order to protect Montreal, evacuated forts Carillon and Saint-Frédéric at the end of July and retreated to the fort of Ile-aux-Noix. He built this fortification up as quickly as possible. On the upper Saint Lawrence, Lévis also erected a small fort on

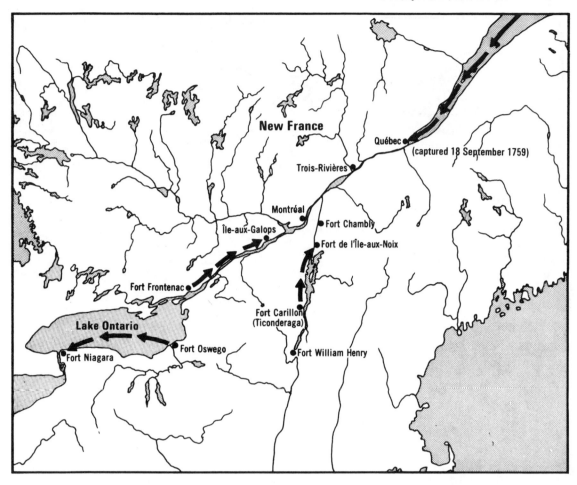

General movement of English troops during the campaign of 1759

Île-aux-Galops below La Présentation, in a supreme effort to block the enemy's path. However, the crushing blow occurred on September 18, when a series of errors by the French led to their defeat on the Plains of Abraham and made a quick capitulation the best course. Quebec surrendered to the English.

d) *The triple invasion of 1760*

What remained of the French army was withdrawn to the Jacques-Cartier River, where it tried to close the route upriver, and to the Richelieu, above Montreal. The French still hoped that a French fleet would bring decisive assistance. For this reason, Lévis went downriver from Montreal to Quebec in an attempt to retake the capital with seven thousand men, in the spring of 1760. On April 28, Governor Murray came out of the town with four thousand men, and was beaten at Sainte-Foy, but Quebec remained in English hands.

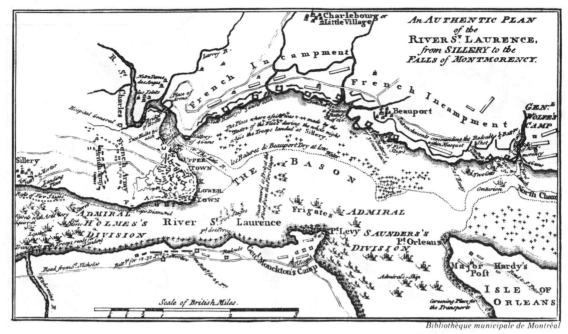

Bibliothèque municipale de Montréal

English map showing the siege of Quebec, in 1759

It was an English fleet that appeared on the river in May. It was part of a huge plan intended to crush French resistance at last. A triple invasion—18,000 men strong—was to converge on Montreal with Murray coming up the river, Haviland along the Richelieu, and Amherst coming down from Lake Ontario.

The progress of these three armies was slow but sure, and they met with very little opposition. While Murray made his way upstream without having to fight, the French forces on the Richelieu (Île-aux-Noix, Saint-Jean, and Chambly) and those on the upper Saint Lawrence yielded easily by the end of August. The three English armies met before Montreal at the beginning of September, and on the 8th, Governor Vaudreuil signed the general capitulation of the country.

Bibliographical Note

Two important works give a general view of this period:

G. Frégault, *La Guerre de la conquête*. Montréal, Fides, 1955.

G. Frégault, *François Bigot, administrateur français*. Montréal, Études de l'Institut d'Histoire de l'Amérique française, 1948. 2 vol.

On some special subjects, we may mention among many others:

Frontiers

M. Savelle, *The Diplomatic History of the Canadian Boundary, 1749-1763*. New Haven, Yale University Press, 1940.

M. Trudel, *L'Affaire Jumonville*. Québec, Université Laval, 1953; also in the *Revue d'Histoire de l'Amérique française*, VI, 3 (Dec. 1952) pp. 331-373; published in English under the title *The Jumonville Affair*, Pennsylvania Historical Association, 1954.

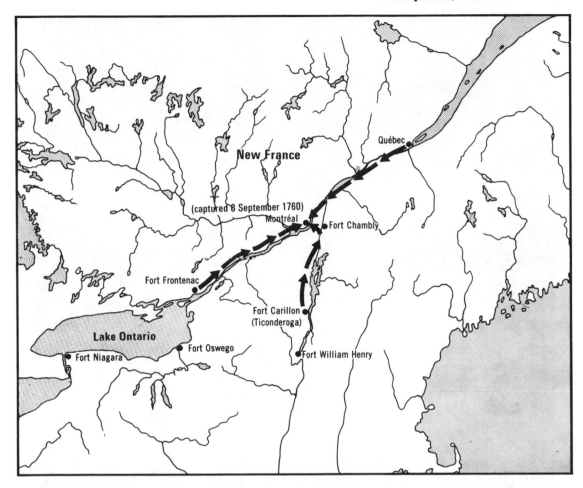

General movement of English troops in the campaign of 1760

Deportation of the Acadians

G. Frégault, *La Guerre de la conquête*. Montréal, Fides, 1955: pp. 223-277.

M. Dumont-Johnson, *Introduction à une étude de la déportation des Acadiens: le rôle politique des missionnaires auprès des sauvages* (thesis for a diplôme d'études supérieures, Laval University, 1964).

The siege of Quebec

C. P. Stacey, *Quebec, 1759. The Siege and the Battle*. Toronto, The Macmillan Co., 1959.

Public Archives of Canada

Sir Jeffrey Amherst, Governor General of the English colonies in America

CHAPTER VIII

Disintegration, 1760-1764

The general capitulation of September 8, 1760, put an end to the war in North America. However, until the conflict ended in Europe and an international treaty decided the fate of New France, this capitulation, in addition to disposing of the defeated army, specified the conditions under which the provisional occupation of the country would take place.

A generous capitulation

The French soldiers found the terms of this capitulation oppressive, because they no longer had anything to do. They were refused the honours of war, that is, the right to serve elsewhere until the end of hostilities. The Canadians, on the other hand, could have expected worse, for their terrible raids had left the bitterest memories in the English colonies. It was known that in New France (at Niagara in particular), a high bounty was paid for English scalps brought back by the Indians. For years, propaganda had demanded the destruction of the "Papists," who were painted in the blackest colours. There had been, in 1755, the massive deportation of the Acadians, which was still going on in 1760. Finally, it was normal practice to treat conquered populations with the utmost harshness, so the inhabitants of New France feared the worst.

General Amherst refused to make a decision on certain requests, because these lay outside his jurisdiction and did not seem essential to a temporary occupation. It was asked that the Canadians be recognized as neutrals for the rest of the war or in any future war between the French and the English. Other suggested terms included the retention of the customary law of Paris, the preservation of religious communities and their privileges, the continued obligation to pay tithes to the curés, and the appointment of a new bishop by the French king.

Although certain stipulations were not agreed to, Governor Vaudreuil obtained, for the Canadians, conditions that appear exceptionally advantageous, considering the custom of the time and the long duration of the Conquest. Amherst promised that the Canadians would not be deported or maltreated and that they would be free to stay in the country, or leave for France with all their possessions. He guaranteed to all laymen, priests, and religious communities, the ownership of all their goods, fixed and moveable, including seigneuries, slaves, and furs. He gave the inhabitants the right to carry on trade in the colony and in the interior, on the same conditions as the English. He also allowed them the free exercise of their religion.

The charter of the military regime

The advantageous conditions of the treaty were in harmony with the way the English took possession of the country, once the capitulation had been signed, and in harmony with the system of government that they imposed while waiting for the final treaty. The new masters would, in certain cases, even permit things not granted by the capitulation.

On September 22, 1760, General Amherst, as commander of the British troops in North America, issued a proclamation from Montreal that was to serve as the basis for the new provisional government.

After announcing that General Thomas Gage was to become head of the Government of Montreal and Colonel Ralph Burton, head of the Government of Trois-Rivières (General Murray himself had been Governor of Quebec since the preceding fall), this proclamation guaranteed the Canadians the same privileges as the English, if they obeyed orders. It exhorted both races to live together "in good harmony and understanding." It stated that, contrary to what usually happened in many conquests, the occupation troops would be fed at the expense of England. This term meant everything bought from the inhabitants would be paid for in cash and in "coin." All conveyance of soldiers would be paid for in the same way. The commissions, which militia officers had received under the French regime, would be renewed. These militia officers were allowed to keep their weapons. They were given the responsibility of maintaining "good order and control," and of judging any cases that arose among the inhabitants, with "the proper fairness and justice." If they were unable to decide on a matter themselves, they were to refer it to the English commander, unless it needed to be submitted to the governor. One item concerning trade was completely new to the country: "trade will be free" and carry no taxes. As before, it was necessary to obtain passports to trade beyond the frontier, but these passports would be "dispatched free of charge." Finally, Amherst solved the problem of supplying food for the colony. This was a problem that had led to unbridled speculation when food was scarce. He invited the merchants of the English colonies to come to Canada with their goods. Also, the local inhabitants were able to go hunting again because their guns would be returned when they obtained a permit signed by the governor.

By virtue of this proclamation, the Occupation Government (and this was expected) was to take the form of a military regime. The entire country was to be supervised by the English army under the supreme authority of the commander, General Amherst, and the military governors. The military treasury paid the expenses of the administration. The militia officers even dispensed justice of the first instance, but appeal could be made against their decisions to a tribunal composed of English officers.

No change in the structure of society as a whole

Since Canada was only a British possession temporarily, the military regime respected the structure of the French regime as much as it could.

Archives de la province de Québec

James Murray, Governor of Quebec

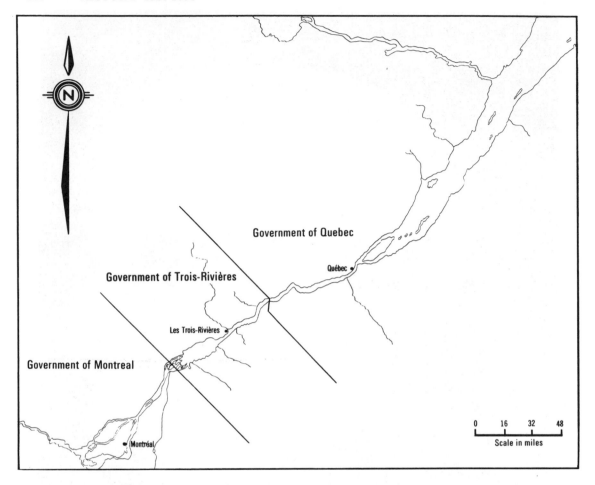

The three Governments of the military regime established in 1760, under the command of Amherst

a) *The administration*

Before 1760, Canada had been divided into three Governments (Quebec, Trois-Rivières, and Montreal), and this administrative structure remained unchanged. Because Montreal and Trois-Rivières no longer depended, as before, on an authority centred in Quebec, passports were required for travelling from one Government's jurisdiction to another. But this regulation was not observed any more strictly than it had sometimes been (under Frontenac, for example). As in the French period, the governors were soldiers, assisted by a general staff. On the parish level, it was still the captain of militia who served as the intermediary between the authorities and the people, as he had during the French regime. He continued to make sure that orders, from both the military and the civil administrations, were carried out.

The civil administration remained similar to the one under the French regime. Admittedly, there was no longer an intendant, and because of the Occupation Government, his three areas of jurisdiction (justice, *police* (that is, the internal government of the country), and finances), had been placed under the single jurisdiction of the governors. This had happened under Frontenac and also before 1665. However, the civil administration still remained the same as before 1760. In matters concerning the protection of agriculture, the highways, and the regulation of trade and hunting, the governors remained true to the letter of the intendants' ordinances. Although the capitulation of 1760 had made no reference to the use of French, orders from the authorities were transmitted in French. Each Government had a French-speaking secretary, and at Trois-Rivières, for almost two years, there was even a French-speaking Governor, Haldimand.

b) *The Law*

The administration of justice was not upset as much as one might at first think, although a council of English military officers replaced the Conseil Supérieur as the court of appeal and judges of the first instance were forced to yield their positions to officers of the militia. In fact, the customary law of Paris was still in force, though Amherst had refused to recognize it officially. Since they were not familiar with any other law, the officers of militia dispensed justice based on the customary law. These officers were improvised judges, but most of the members of the Conseil Supérieur had judged cases of appeal without any better preparation. The legal auxiliaries, notaries, recorders, and surveyors, were the same as before 1760. Curés were still authorized to be substitute notaries under certain conditions.

c) *The seigneurial regime*

The seigneurial regime remained untouched, for it was protected by property rights guaranteed in the capitulation. When the Governor of Montreal intervened at the request of the seigneurs, he ordered the *censitaires* to keep "hearth and home" and pay their rents. He also declared that they would forfeit their rights if they refused to do so. This action was just what the intendant had previously done. Before it was known whether Canada would be an English possession, the Governor of Quebec granted two seigneuries, one to John Nairne (Murray Bay), and the other to Malcolm Fraser (Mount Murray). He carved these seigneuries out of the domain of the King's Posts and made these two grants according to the usual conditions of the country.

d) *Economic life*

In the spring of 1761, economic life returned to its normal course. It was still based principally on the fur trade, the difference being that the furs no longer had to be sent to France but to the English markets and that everybody could participate in this trade. Conditions were the same as before 1760. The traders were provided with a permit (now free) and upon leaving gave a statement of the merchandise they were transporting, the number of their canoes, and a list of their men. As before, brandy could be taken for personal needs, but its use was still forbidden when trading with the natives. The fishing stations, which had been granted before 1760 on the Gulf of Saint Lawrence, still belonged to their original owners. In 1743, the State had taken over the Saint-Maurice ironworks.

The Governor of Trois-Rivières started them operating again at State expense, and he watched over their management like an intendant. There were no changes in weights and measurements, and French coins were still accepted and circulated with English coins. These coins made accounting complicated because of the different rates existing between Halifax and Quebec, between New York and Montreal, and between both these towns and Trois-Rivières. However, this had the good effect of stirring up the economy. Speculation during the war had caused prices to soar; so the military authorities brought them down to the pre-war level by strict control and regulation of supplies.

Bibliothèque municipale de Montréal

**Jean-Olivier Briand, grand-vicaire of Quebec,
later first bishop of Quebec during the English regime**

e) *The Church*

The military regime did not upset the religious arrangements either. When these were modified, it was usually the result of circumstances unconnected with the military regime. When the Bishop died in June, 1760, before the capitulation, it was not possible to replace him before the fate of the colony had been decided. Even if there had been no conquest, it is probable that the appointment of a new bishop would have been delayed until after the end of the war. With the bishop's death, the Chapter took over the administration of the Church in New France, but it does not seem to have appointed a capitular vicar. Authority remained divided between the *grands-vicaires*, so that the *grand-vicaire* of Quebec had merely honorary precedence over his colleagues.

In any case, the terms of the capitulation allowed the Chapter to meet in complete freedom and the *grands-vicaires* to exercise their normal jurisdiction. The curés continued to carry out their functions freely, and the religious communities kept possession of their property.

Under the military regime, the Church in New France continued to act like a State Church, as under the French regime. It carried out the same duties for the English king that it had performed for the French king. From the English governors, it obtained the very same consideration, and the Governor of Quebec even served as its secular arm. Furthermore, it was in the Government of Quebec, where the Episcopal See was located, that the Church became even more closely connected with the State. Murray thoroughly understood how to strengthen the power of the Church for the benefit of the State. When he supported *grand-vicaire* Briand so persistently, it was in order to make him more obedient to English interests. That is why, in September, 1763, Murray intervened with London to have the election of the Sulpician Montgolfier rejected (he had been secretly elected as bishop by the Chapter). The Chapter then proposed Briand, and the latter was accepted.

By the end of the military regime, the Church had lost one third of its priests, through emigration and death. It, therefore, became weak and ineffective. There was a movement to stop the recruitment of Jesuits and Récollets because these orders depended on a Roman superior and were obstacles to the program that the State had conceived for the Church in the colony. The Church was much more under the authority of the governor than it had ever been during the French regime. However, since it had become the most powerful intermediary between the English Government and the people, its political role was assured for a long time to come.

The recruitment of volunteers against Pontiac

A war that broke out upcountry posed a delicate problem for the English authorities: recruiting Canadians for the English armed forces.

The capitulation of the French on the Great Lakes, in 1760, had caused much discontent among the natives of that region, for the Conquest destroyed the important commercial network held by the Ottawas. Only the return of the French could restore this trade, but in February, 1763, any such hope was dashed by the Treaty of Paris. The revolt broke out in the following May, at the instigation of Chief Pontiac, and the natives occupied or destroyed the forts on lakes Michigan and Erie. Soon, Fort Detroit was the only post remaining west of Niagara to hold out. Although Pontiac surrendered in the fall, he continued to be a danger.

To aid the regular troops in their operations, it was necessary to use the militia. If Canadians were enrolled, the natives would understand that they could no longer expect any support from the French. The quickest and most efficient method of enrolling Canadians was conscription, a method to which they had become accustomed under the French regime. This was the first proposal considered until an important objection was raised. By the Treaty of 1763, the Canadians were given eighteen months to emigrate in complete freedom; they could not, therefore, be forced to serve outside their country. The final decision was in favour of voluntary service.

The Canadians were, at first, mistrustful of the unexpected conditions offered to them (pay, food, weapons, clothes), for they were accustomed to serving in the militia without receiving anything. They showed little enthusiasm and only a small number enrolled. They were formed into a battalion of five companies. When the volunteers arrived at Niagara, in the spring of 1764, hostilities had ended on the Great Lakes, and they returned home at the end of November without fighting a battle. But this peaceful campaign had at least been a profitable one for the Canadians.

The inventory of paper money

The problem of paper money was a very serious one. Speculation during the war years had put into circulation an enormous amount of paper money (cards, certificates, orders for payment, and bills of exchange on the Treasury). From the beginning of the military regime, the authorities had forbidden the use of this money as currency. It was generally called "dead money." However, England demanded action from France, since it was her duty to intervene and protect her new subjects from disaster. So, in February, 1763, France undertook to liquidate, as soon as was conveniently possible, "the bills of exchange and notes which have been delivered to Canadians for supplies provided for French troops."

After the summer of 1763, work was begun on a general inventory. Then, because English merchants started speculating in this paper money, which they bought at a discount (sometimes as high as 90 percent), the British Government, in 1764, demanded a detailed inventory. Every person possessing paper money was obliged to state how he had acquired it.

Disregarding what had already been sent to France or England, there was found, in Canada, about 16,782,500 *livres* in paper money, of which only 3.8 percent was in card money, and this was held by institutions: France owed the Hôpital-Général of Quebec more than 130,000 *livres*, and ninety-five parochial vestries together held 293,000 *livres*. Paper money was also held by curés, seigneurs, merchants (Godefroy de Tonnancour had 150,000 *livres*), and people in the humblest circumstances. For these people, sometimes the sum they declared constituted all their savings. Despite English protests, France reduced these demands by about three quarters of their value; in certain cases, the possessors of paper money could only recover one fifth of their value: for example, the 130,000 *livres* of the Hôpital-Général of Quebec yielded only 27,000. The liquidation of paper money was an economic disaster that affected the entire population and helped to alienate France still further from her former subjects.

Society begins to change during the military regime

The Canadian community, isolated by distance from France and closed until the Conquest to the other European settlements in North America, now began to undergo changes. While it lost some elements (officers, high officials, members of the Conseil Supérieur, seigneurs, and merchants), whose importance has not yet been measured, the Canadian community became accessible to a world largely unknown until that time except through smuggling and military raids. From now on, merchant ships arrived to be loaded with furs for the English market, and English merchandise and currency entered the country on an imposing scale.

Even before the final surrender, English elements were mixing on an increasing scale with the existing population that had never possessed more than a very small number of individuals of English origin. English officers and soldiers left the armed forces to settle on the land, acquiring holdings and even seigneuries. After the autumn of 1759, English Protestants married Canadian Catholic girls from the best-known families: Martel de Brouague, Montesson, and Picoté de Belestre.

Furthermore, Protestantism regained its regular position in this society. It had been officially excluded from New France ever since 1627. Not only did Anglican ministers grant the solemn benediction (refused by Catholic clergy) to marriages between Englishmen and Canadian girls (we know of about fourteen of these marriages between 1759 and 1764), but they performed their religious services in Catholic chapels. The Catholics were forced to share, first the chapel of the Ursulines with the Protestants, then that of the Récollets in Quebec and the chapel of the Hôtel-Dieu in Montreal. Protestants were even buried in holy ground reserved for Catholics. The Huguenots, who had settled in Canada in small numbers before the Conquest, had not been able to assemble for prayer and had had no schools, churches, or cemeteries. With the beginning of the military regime, they took their revenge. They openly practised their religion with the English Protestants in Catholic chapels, became intermediaries between the Canadians and the English, and obtained the business of the religious communities. The Huguenot Mounier soon became the only representative of the French population in Murray's Council. Canadian society, until then exclusively Catholic, now had to adapt to the presence of a victorious Protestantism.

The disappearance of New France

In 1712, New France included the immense lowlands of Hudson Bay, Labrador, Newfoundland, the Acadian islands and peninsula, the Saint Lawrence, the Great Lakes, and down the Mississippi, as far as the Gulf of Mexico. The Treaty of 1713 deprived her of Hudson Bay, Newfoundland, and peninsular Acadia. After a long period of resistance, from 1755 onwards, New France was gradually occupied by the English. She first lost the islands of Acadia, then the Saint Lawrence valley, and finally, the Great Lakes.

International agreements confirmed the disappearance of New France. In 1762, by a secret pact, France ceded the whole of Louisiana to Spain. In fact, if one refers to article 7 of the treaty of 1763, Spain kept only the western part, since the eastern part became an English possession. In addition, France gave up all claim to Acadia, including Cape Breton, Île Saint-Jean and the other islands in the Gulf, and retained only the small islands of Saint-Pierre and Miquelon. Finally, she gave up Canada, "with all its dependencies," after obtaining for the French population two privileges in addition to the conditions that Amherst had granted. These privileges allowed the French to practise their religion to the extent that the laws of Great Britain permitted, and to emigrate in the ensuing eighteen months.

The royal proclamation of October 7, 1763, rearranged the conquered territories before reorganizing the institutions. The islands and mainland portion of Acadia (that is,

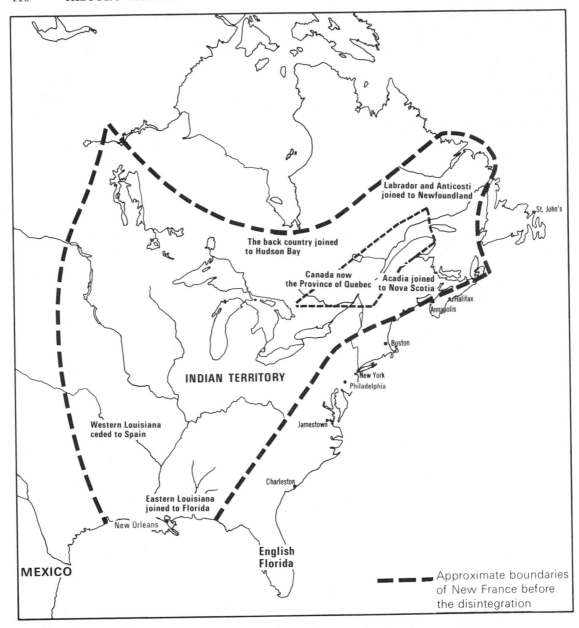

Labrador and Anticosti
joined to Newfoundland

St. John's

The back country joined
to Hudson Bay

Canada now
the Province of Quebec

Acadia joined
to Nova Scotia

Halifax

Annapolis

Boston

New York
Philadelphia

INDIAN TERRITORY

Jamestown

Western Louisiana
ceded to Spain

Charleston

Eastern Louisiana
joined to Florida

New Orleans

English
Florida

MEXICO

— — — Approximate boundaries
of New France before
the disintegration

The disintegration of New France
Nothing further remained of continental New France; from Canada, the area along the Saint Lawrence,
the small province of Quebec was created.

present-day New Brunswick) were attached to Nova Scotia (the former peninsular Acadia); Labrador and Anticosti Island were annexed to Newfoundland; and the Great Lakes now came under the direct authority of the Crown. Because of pressure from the English colonies and the Hudson's Bay Company, the King restricted the valley of the Saint Lawrence, where most of the Canadians lived, to within the following limits. The northern boundary was to cross Lake Saint John and stop at Lake Nipissing; the western boundary was to extend from there to the 45th parallel, which for some time formed the southern frontier; lastly, the eastern boundary was to follow the watershed as far as Chaleur Bay. Thus, Newfoundland received the fisheries in the Gulf. New York, with the Hudson's Bay Company, took over most of the fur trade. It was hoped that these restraints would induce the Canadians to develop their agriculture, which now had an outlet in the vast English market. The name *Canada*, which was two centuries old, disappeared. A new name, *Province of Quebec*, now designated the area of the Saint Lawrence.

On August 10, 1764, an imposing ceremony in Quebec put an end to the temporary government and officially opened what is generally called the *English regime*.

Bibligraphical Note

In general histories, little attention is given to the important period of the military regime. Up to now, it has been the subject of only rare, special studies. We may mention three works here. The first shows how the military regime functioned in a given environment; the second, in two volumes, is devoted to the history of the Canadian Church from 1759 to 1764; the third gives an account of the war with Pontiac:

M. TRUDEL, *Le Régime militaire dans le Gouvernement des Trois-Rivières, 1760-1764*. Trois-Rivières, le Bien public, 1952.

M. TRUDEL, *L'Église canadienne sous le régime militaire, 1759-1764*. Volume I: *Les problèmes*. Montréal, Études de l'Institut d'Histoire de l'Amérique française, 1956. Volume II: *Les institutions*. Québec, Université Laval, 1957.

H. H. PECKHAM, *Pontiac and the Indian Uprising*. Princeton, Princeton University Press, 1947.

PART TWO

INSTITUTIONS

Introduction

After 1713, the features of New France seemed permanently established. Because this had not been the case during the seventeenth century, institutions had come into conflict with one another. Sufficient evidence for this conflict is provided by the disputes on jurisdiction between the governor and the intendant, and between the governor and the bishop. In the eighteenth century, there were still disagreements, but these appear to be largely personality clashes, which no longer affected the institutions themselves. After 1713, the institutions were complete; they had, in fact, finished their evolution and now occupied their normal position in the total plan of New France. This period has been chosen as the most convenient one for studying New France from the inside.

After a general description of New France, we will, therefore, examine the elements making up the population, the method of government, the seigneurial system that enclosed it, the judicial system that maintained social order, the military organization, social security and assistance, economic life (agriculture, industry, and trade), religious life, and finally intellectual life.

Bibliographical Note

There is still no general study of the institutions of New France. There is, of course, the recent work by Raymond DOUVILLE and Jacques-Donat CASANOVA, *La Vie quotidienne en Nouvelle-France* (Paris, Hachette, 1964), a work that is extremely rich in detail, but the authors did not intend to carry out an organic study of society. As far as it goes, however, this volume forms a very useful complement to this *Introduction*.

As in the first part, the reader will find at the end of each chapter a bibliographical note that will indicate to him the principal studies to be consulted on each respective subject. By referring to this note, the reader will generally find it easy to return to the sources.

Also useful are certain works describing French society (from which our institutions are borrowed): such works as the *Introduction à la France moderne: Essai de psychologie historique* (Paris, Albin Michel, 1961), by Robert MANDROU; *La France aux XVIIᵉ et XVIIIᵉ siècles*, by Robert MANDROU, in *Nouvelle Clio* (Presses universitaires de France, 1967); and *Le XVIIIᵉ Siècle* (Paris, Presses universitaires de France, 1963), by Roland MOUSNIER and Ernest LABROUSSE, in the series *Histoire générale des civilisations*. These works contain bibliographies that may lead to more specialized studies.

CHAPTER I

Description of New France

New France in the eighteenth century (after 1713) was composed of the following regions: French Acadia (islands and mainland); Labrador; the *Postes du Roi*; Canada, subdivided into three Governments (Quebec, Trois-Rivières, and Montreal); the *Pays d'en Haut* or interior; the "Western Sea"; and Louisiana.

French Acadia

Having lost the Acadian peninsula by the Treaty of Utrecht, France retained only the islands and coast of Acadia. Her attempts to persuade her former subjects to emigrate to this area met with little success. To compensate for the loss of the peninsula, France became firmly established on the two islands of Île Royale (Cape Breton) and Île Saint-Jean (today called Prince Edward Island).

The most important centre on Île Royale was Louisbourg on the east coast. Construction of this fortified town was begun in 1714, and at that time, it had less than one thousand inhabitants. The people of Île Royale worked mainly in the fishing industry, and their numbers, in 1752, have been estimated at about twenty-six hundred. This area had its own Government headed by a governor and a *commissaire-ordonnateur* (commissar) who acted as the intendant's local deputy. These officials were, in theory, subordinate to the governor general and the intendant of New France. Appeals could be made from courts of the first instance (called *bailliages*) to a Superior Council which, in turn, depended on the Conseil Supérieur of Quebec. Maritime affairs were judged in Louisbourg by an Amirauté. Lastly, a *grand-vicaire* represented the bishop of Quebec on the island.

Île Saint-Jean, also founded after 1713 in order to attract the Acadians from the peninsula, had a much more stable population. There were twenty-two hundred people in 1752, mostly engaged in agriculture. Île Saint-Jean possessed few institutions, for it came under the authority of the governor and commissar of Île Royale.

In the mainland Acadia, there were only scattered settlements: one on the Bay of Chaleur at Restigouche; forts Beauséjour and Gaspareau on the isthmus of Chignecto, cutting off English access to the coast; and some small trading posts on the Saint John River.

116

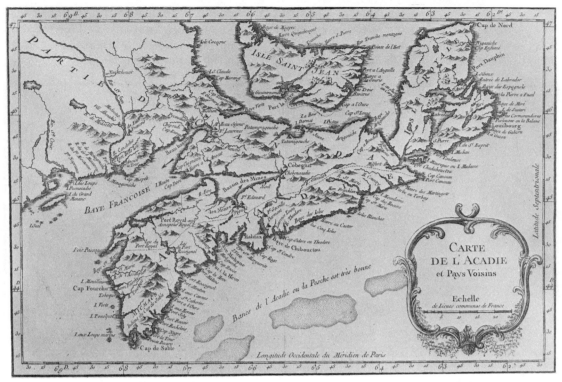

Public Archives of Canada

French Acadia in the eighteenth century according to Bellin

The Acadians, on the island as well as on the mainland, were primarily fishermen and traders for whom farming was only a secondary occupation necessary to support the colony. Spiritual ministrations were provided at Louisbourg by the Récollets (the regular chaplains of the Army). Elsewhere, there were Jesuits and Récollets, as well as priests from the Quebec Seminary and from the Seminary of the Holy Spirit (called Spiritains). Among the latter was the celebrated Abbé Le Loutre.

Acadia continued to live in isolation from Canada. Contact between the two colonies was rare. Civil, military, and religious authorities corresponded more frequently with the mother country than with Canada. Thus, the history of Acadia developed outside the mainstream of Canadian history.

Labrador

Labrador was not organized as a Government, but was administered by an official called the *commandant de Labrador*. The area extended from Eskimo Bay (at the mouth of the Hamilton River) along the Atlantic coastline and the north shore of the Gulf as far as, but not including, Sept-Îles. There had been no entry into the interior partly because of Eskimo hostility, but mainly because there was no economic interest in exploring the region.

Along this coast, there was a continuous succession of seasonal posts used for trade and fishing by merchants from Quebec. These concessions were granted for nine to twelve years and could be renewed. The largest was that of Baie des Esquimaux, managed first by Jean-Louis Fornel and then by his widow, Marie-Anne Barbel.

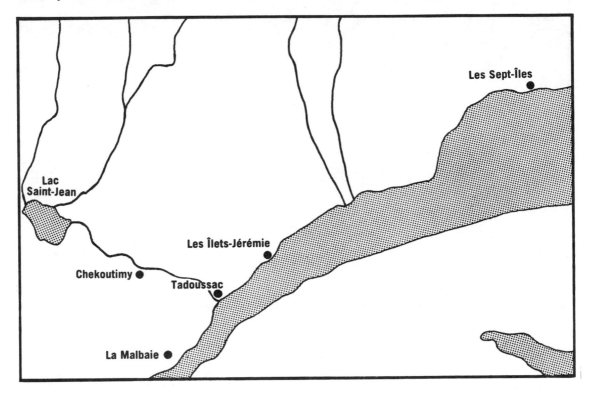

Map of the Postes du Roi

The Postes du Roi

The area from Sept-Îles to the eastern limit of the seigneury of Les Éboulements, including the entire basin of Lake Saint John, was not open to colonization. The State leased it for the fur trade. This *Domaine du Roi* included five posts called the *Postes du Roi*. These were La Malbaie, Tadoussac, the Îslets-Jérémie, Sept-Îles (on the Saint Lawrence), and "Chekoutimy," upstream from the Saguenay.

Canada

During the French regime, Canada was only a small area of New France, but it had the highest population density (with a total of about 76,000 inhabitants) in 1760. Canada included the entire inhabited area from Vaudreuil (upriver from Montreal) to as far as Les Éboulements on the north shore, and from Châteauguay to Rimouski on the south shore. It corresponded to the seigneurial domain and was divided up into three Governments.

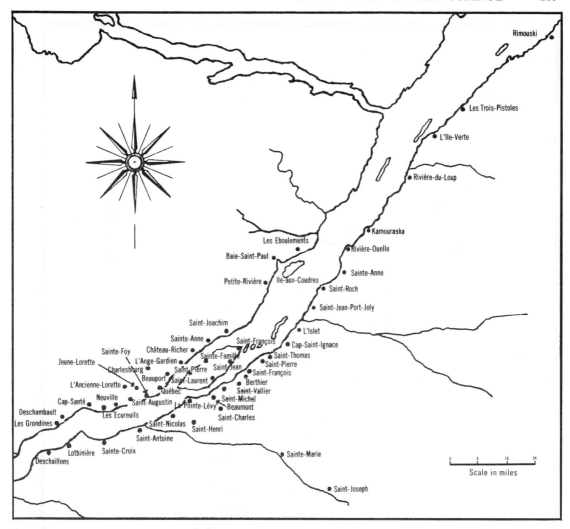

Parishes in the Government of Quebec

a) *The Government of Quebec*

Quebec was the most important of the three Governments because of its size, its population, and its social importance. Its population in 1760 may be estimated at forty thousand inhabitants. The Quebec area extended from Les Éboulements to Grondines and from Deschaillons to Rimouski, including the area of recent colonization in the Beauce.

The capital at Quebec was also the capital of New France. The higher authorities and the institutions administering the French colonies in North America—the governor general, the intendant, the Conseil Supérieur and the Amirauté—were located here. Here also were found the religious authorities: the bishop, the Chapter, the Officialité,

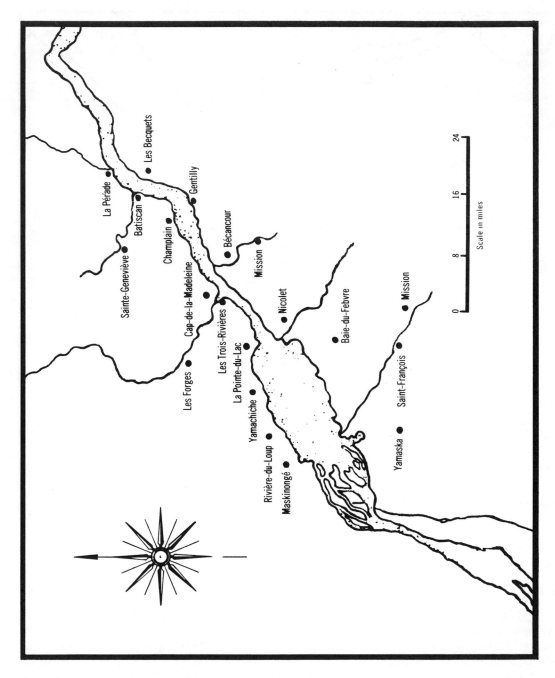

Parishes in the Government of Trois-Rivières

and the Quebec Seminary (a community of priests whose duty it was to train the secular clergy). In the intellectual field, Quebec had the Jesuit College (the only college in New France), and in the field of economic activity, Quebec had the main office of the Compagnie des Indes, the only body allowed to export beaver fur.

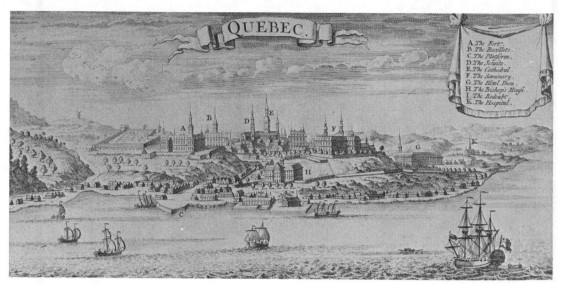

Public Archives of Canada

Quebec at the end of the French regime
(engraving by Richard Short)

Although Quebec was the centre of New France, the Government of Quebec had its own administration. The governor general of the colony had a second function, that of governor of Quebec. He was assisted in this office by a king's lieutenant. Royal justice of the first instance was dispensed by the *Prévôté de Quebec*. The clergy was directly supervised by a *grand-vicaire*. Four nunneries fulfilled important social functions. The Hôtel-Dieu provided a hospital for the sick; the Hôpital-Général took in the old, the disabled, and the insane; the Ursulines educated young girls, in the Upper Town; and the Sisters of the Congregation of Notre-Dame ran a school in the Lower Town.

In Quebec, there were plenty of artisans, soldiers, civil servants, and merchants. The latter usually lived in the Lower Town and were interested in the exploitation of the Gulf. However, there was no industry of any importance at the end of the French regime.

b) *The Government of Trois-Rivières*

This area extended, on the north shore, from Sainte-Anne-de-la Pérade to Maskinongé, and on the south shore, from Saint-Pierre-les Becquets to Yamaska. With its six thousand inhabitants, it was therefore the smallest of the three Governments of Canada.

The town of Trois-Rivières, with a population of 586 inhabitants in 1760, possessed the name but none of the attributes of a capital. Nonetheless, it was the main stopover on

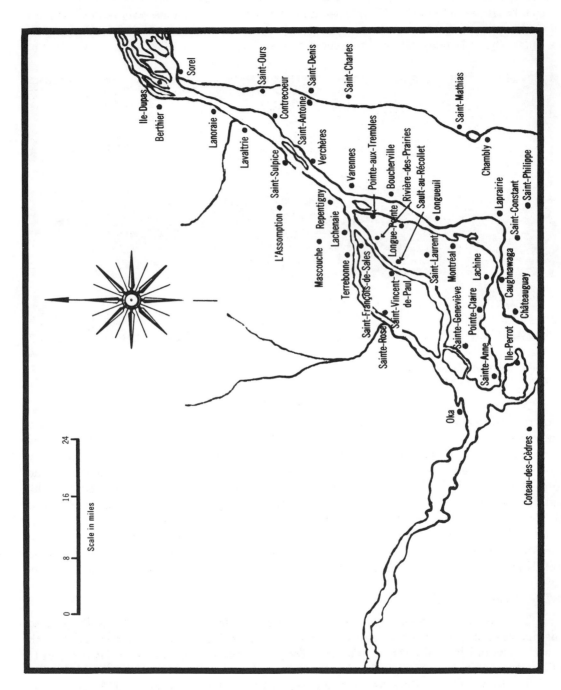

Parishes in the Government of Montreal

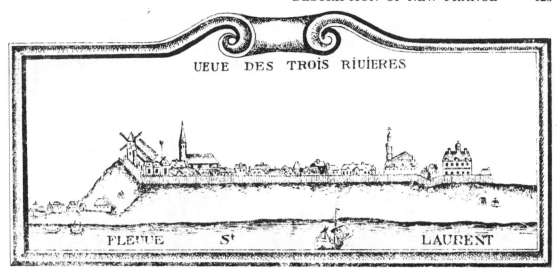

UEUE DES TROIS RIUIERES

FLEUUE   St   LAURENT

Trois-Rivières at the beginning of the eighteenth century
(from a map by Gédéon de Catalogne)

the four-day journey between Quebec and Montreal. For historical rather than practical reasons, the Government of Trois-Rivières had a complete administrative organization: a governor, a king's lieutenant, an adjutant, a court of royal jurisdiction (of the first instance), and a *grand-vicaire*. In the town, the Ursulines ran a hospital and a girls' convent, while the Sisters of the Congregation of Notre-Dame had a school at Champlain.

There were two small industries: the making of canoes and the Saint-Maurice ironworks. Taken over by the State, the ironworks produced ammunition and stoves in limited quantities. New France had no other heavy industry.

c) *The Government of Montreal*

The Government of Montreal controlled a region beginning west of Maskinongé and Yamaska and ending at Fort Saint-Jean, Châteauguay, and Vaudreuil, the limits of the inhabited area.

Here, the population, which was about thirty thousand inhabitants in 1760, had not followed the usual practice of settling only on the banks of the Saint Lawrence. Settlers could be found on both banks of the Richelieu, on the edges of Montreal Island and Ile Jésus, on the banks of the Mille-Îsles, the Assomption, and Des Prairies rivers, as well as at the mouth of the Ottawa River. Although the people were farmers, each year a good number of them worked for the merchant traders.

The Government of Montreal had the same civil and military institutions as the other Governments, with the addition of a *Commissaire de la Marine*, who represented the intendant. This post was made necessary by the economic importance of Montreal, which was an indispensable base for voyages upcountry, a supply centre for traders, and the site of the spring fur-trading fair. Being the capital of the area, Montreal had an Hôtel-Dieu

Montreal in 1760
(reproduced from Sulte's *Histoire des Canadiens français*)

Public Archives of Canada

and an Hôpital-Général. The Congregation of Notre-Dame devoted itself to the education of girls, while the Sulpicians, the seigneurs of Montreal Island, ran *petites écoles* for boys.

The Pays d'en haut

Setting out from Lachine—the point of embarkation from Montreal—the traveller reached another area, the *pays d'en haut,* so-called because it was above (*en haut*) the Saint Lawrence. This area, in fact, corresponds to the Great Lakes basin, and it could be reached by two routes.

One route, which had been known since the beginning and was used for a long time, was the Ottawa River. This route led to the post of the Temiskamings and the region of the Abitibis, or it could lead, along the Mataouan River, to lakes Nipissing and Huron. It was uninhabited, because the authorities were opposed to settling colonists there, since they could not resist the temptation of becoming traders. The other route, that of the upper Saint Lawrence, was broken by a great number of rapids, and remained mainly a military route. It was guarded by several forts: La Présentation, Frontenac, Rouillé (or Toronto), Niagara, and on Lake Erie, Fort Presqu'Île, where portages led to the Ohio.

Detroit, a small capital with six hundred inhabitants in 1751, was the centre of the *pays d'en haut*. It possessed two religious foundations: Sainte-Anne-du-Détroit—where the Récollets ministered, protected by a fort—and on the east bank, Pointe-de-Montréal or Assomption-du-Détroit—a mission served by the Jesuits. Detroit was an indispensable stopping-point on the journey to the West and an important trading post where a very mixed population with many half-breeds had gathered.

The *pays d'en haut* was not made into a separate Government, although this had been proposed, and the commandant of Detroit exercised civil and military authority in the area.

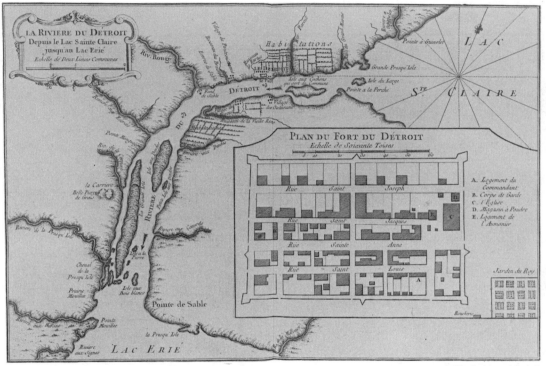

Public Archives of Canada

Detroit, at the end of the French regime, according to Bellin

Beyond Detroit, at the entrance to Lake Michigan, lay Michilimackinac, an important trading post and the ecclesiastical capital of the *pays d'en haut*. From here, past the bay of the Nipissings (Green Bay) and up to the portage of Chicago, lay the route to the Illinois and Mississippi rivers. To the north of Michilimackinac, another narrows (that of Sault Sainte-Marie) was used as the entrance to Lake Superior. On this lake, at least four important posts had been established: Chagouamigon, on the south shore; Kaministigoya, on the western shore; the post of the Nipigons; and Michipicoten, on the north shore.

The "Western Sea"

This name was usually given to the territory situated to the west of the Great Lakes, and it explains the purpose behind the explorations of La Vérendrye and his sons.

Kaministigoya, on Lake Superior, was the gateway to this area and the first link in a chain of posts leading to the Rockies along Rainy Lake, Lake of the Woods, Lake Winnipeg, and the two branches of the Saskatchewan. In spite of what has been said on this subject, Fort La Jonquière, built in 1751 and marking the limit of the French advance, was not situated in the area of Calgary. It cannot have been farther west than the middle of the present-day province of Saskatchewan.

The "Western Sea" was a vast area uninhabited by Europeans. The La Vérendrye family were employed there in gathering furs, which they tried to direct to Montreal. They were also engaged in the slave trade.

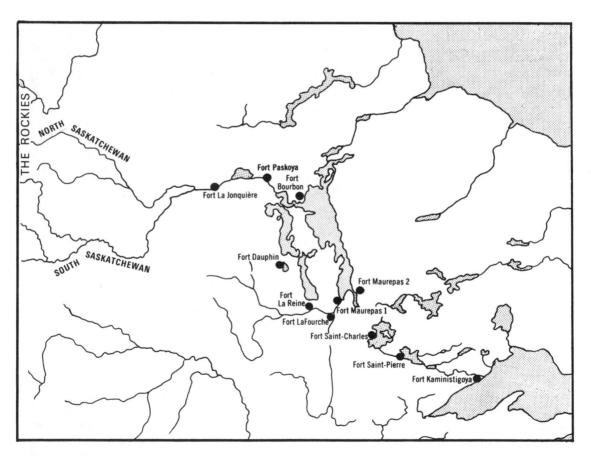

The trading posts of the "Western Sea"

Louisiana

To the south of the Great Lakes, the Government of Louisiana included the entire Mississippi valley with all the land drained by the rivers flowing into it. It was divided into two regions: Upper Louisiana (or the country of the Illinois), and Lower Louisiana.

The country of the Illinois was inhabited mainly by Canadians, ministered to by the Jesuits and priests from the Quebec Seminary. It had some important centres, such as Vincennes on the Wabash, Cahokia, Nouvelle-Chartres, and Kaskaskia on the Mississippi. Apart from a few posts guarding the lines of communication, there was a large empty space between the country of the Illinois and the second settled area, Lower Louisiana, or New Orleans, which was six hundred miles further south.

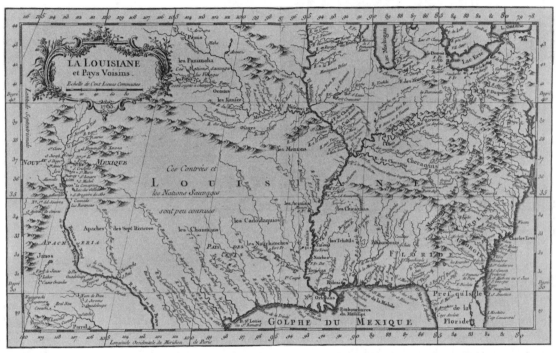

Public Archives of Canada

Louisiana, according to Bellin

New Orleans was the seat of military, civil, and religious institutions for Louisiana. The governor, the commissar, the superior council and the *grand-vicaire* were all, in theory, subordinate to Quebec. It was a small town of about one thousand inhabitants, already rich in slaves. The Jesuits and the Capuchins ministered to the people, while the Ursulines ran a girls' school as well as a hospital.

The colony of Louisiana was far behind Canada in development, since it was not founded until the eighteenth century. At the end of the French regime, it had only two small settlements, which were very far from each other, and possessed a total population of only about four thousand inhabitants.

Public Archives of Canada

New Orleans, according to Bellin

An illusion of territorial power

If one wished to indicate on a large-scale map the territory actively held by New France, three pencil strokes would be sufficient. The first line would start at Cape Breton and join another drawn from Labrador to the Rockies, passing through the Saint Lawrence and the Great Lakes. A third line would go from the Great Lakes down to the Gulf of Mexico. These lines would cover a distance of four thousand miles.

In reality, however, this size was only an illusion of territorial power. Throughout this area of four thousand miles, there lived a numerically insignificant French population of eighty-five thousand inhabitants, while in a smaller area—a strip along the Atlantic—the English had settled a population fourteen times greater. What is more, 90 percent of the French population was crowded along the Saint Lawrence, over a distance of 300 miles, which left no more than ten thousand inhabitants spread over the remaining 3,700 miles.

Without a population of millions, it was impossible to set up an effective network of defence for such a vast area. If one link were to yield, the entire network would be destroyed.

Dispersal and isolation

These different population groups were, of course, under the authority of the same governor, intendant, and bishop, located in Quebec. However, this was a purely artificial unity, since the authorities of Acadia and Louisiana found it more convenient to communicate directly with France than with Quebec. All that the Acadians and the people of Louisiana had in common with the Canadians, was the same French origin and the same dependence on the mother country.

New France developed by a process of dispersal. This process had begun in 1608, when the colonists, already weak in numbers, split into groups. One group continued to maintain Acadia, while another went up the Saint Lawrence to settle at Quebec. They were further subdivided in 1613, when Madame de Guercheville broke with Poutrincourt in Acadia and founded her own colony at Saint-Sauveur. In 1642, when Quebec was still only a small settlement and Trois-Rivières a little fort, a new group went to settle at Ville-Marie. Later on, from this meagre Laurentian settlement, men set out to develop the distant post of Detroit. Upper Louisiana was also settled by Canadians.

But even more striking was the fact of isolation in New France. First, this isolation was internal: a journey between Acadia and the Saint Lawrence across the wilderness took about two weeks. A man from Montreal wishing to go to New Orleans had to travel five hundred miles before coming to the first settlement at Detroit, then four hundred miles to find a second one, Illinois. Finally, it was only after a further six hundred miles that he reached the third settlement of Lower Louisiana.

The colony of the Saint Lawrence remained for months in two isolated halves, divided by a wide river that could be crossed only with great difficulty during the winter. Furthermore, the two centres of social activity (Quebec and Montreal) lay at the two extremities of the country and were separated by a distance of at least four days' journey. The result was that, during the French regime and for a long time afterwards, these two towns formed two distinct societies. Each developed its own way of life, its own mentality, and its own linguistic variations.

The French colonies were also isolated from the other European settlements in America. Quebec, for instance, was one month's travel by sea from Boston. There was no land route to the English colonies, and in any case, New France was forbidden to carry on any regular trade with them.

Lastly, while the English colonies were in constant contact with Europe, the colony of the Saint Lawrence was cut off for half the year, because of the winter. During the other half, communications with Europe were extremely slow. The journey from Paris to La Rochelle (the port of embarkation in the eighteenth century) took a week or two, and if one missed the boat, one had to wait until the next year. The crossing from La Rochelle to Quebec was considered extraordinarily fast if made in one month; normally, one had to reckon on two months, and very often, three. And what dangers had to be faced! Storms blew the ship off course (Talon's ship in 1669 was driven back to the Spanish coast, and the Intendant was unable to start his voyage again until 1670). There was sickness. There were corsairs and pirates, who looked for booty in time of peace as well as in time of war. But the Gulf and river were even more dangerous than the Atlantic, because of the sudden squalls, the fogs, and the reefs. Since the ship usually arrived very late at Quebec and had to start back immediately, there was little time to reply to the only mail of the year.

Under these conditions, cut off from frequent communication not only with Europe, but even with the neighbouring settlements, the French colony retired within itself and maintained a mentality of isolation that was to be marked for a long time to come.

Bibliographical Note

Elsewhere we have given a more detailed description of New France.

M. TRUDEL, "La Nouvelle France," *Cahiers de l'Académie canadienne-française*, No. 2, pp. 25-50.

For Louisbourg around 1740:

G. FRÉGAULT, *François Bigot*. Montreal, Études de l'Institut d'Histoire de l'Amérique française, 1948, Vol. I, pp. 73-101.

For the area of Trois-Rivières in 1760:

M. TRUDEL, *Le Régime militaire dans le Gouvernement des Trois-Rivières*. Trois-Rivières, Éditions du Bien public, 1952, pp. 1-31.

For Louisiana around 1740:

G. FRÉGAULT, *Le Grand Marquis*. Montréal, Éditions Fides, 1952, pp. 121-142.

CHAPTER II

Population

In this general survey of New France for the period near the end of the French regime, we have calculated the population at about 85,000 inhabitants, distributed as follows: 4,000 in Acadia (islands and mainland); 76,000 in Canada (the Saint Lawrence area); 600 in the *Pays d'en haut* (Great Lakes); and 4,000 in Louisiana.

Still an insignificant number

What is immediately surprising about this population is its numerical insignificance at all times in its history. French settlement in North America came late and consisted of only a small group. In the autumn of 1608, there were only 28 people in Quebec. In 1641, a century after Cartier, the population did not exceed 500. Thirty years later, there were only 2,500 inhabitants. The rate of increase then accelerated, but there were still only 12,000 people in the whole of New France in 1689. After this, it took three quarters of a century to reach a total of 85,000 people.

This numerical insignificance is even more surprising if one compares the population of New France with that of the other colonies begun by Europeans in North America, the colonies New France wished to displace.

	New France	Other European Colonies
1608	28	500
1641	500	40,000
1689	12,000	250,000
1760	85,000	1,200,000

The small number of immigrants

French immigration to New France was always small, not only in proportion to the immense territory that was claimed, but also in number. From 1608 to 1627, the annual total of arrivals scarcely passed thirty, and we must subtract from this total those who decided to return to France. In 1627, the Cent-Associés undertook to send 4,000 colonists in fifteen years, but in 1641, the population was only 500! It has been estimated that, from 1608 to 1660, only 1,260 immigrants arrived, an annual average of about twenty.

The port of La Rochelle
Present-day view of the old port, from where the colonists of the eighteenth century embarked. In the background are the towers that guard the exit.

Immigration increased in the time of Talon. From 1660 to 1680, New France received 2,542 colonists, but this rate was not maintained. From 1680 to 1700, the total was only 1,092. From 1700 to 1720, it fell to 659, while between 1720 and 1740, it climbed back up to 1,008. It was only in the last twenty years of the French regime that an important increase took place. From 1740 to 1760, the highest rate of immigration occurred in the history of New France: 3,565 people. New France probably received only about 10,000 immigrants altogether.

Why so few came to New France

In order to explain the numerical weakness of this immigration, it is usually claimed that the French do not emigrate. But this claim ignores the fact that, in the seventeenth and eighteenth centuries, the French emigrated en masse to Spain and the West Indies. The agricultural wealth of France does not provide a more satisfactory answer because England in the seventeenth century was also a rich agricultural country. To fall back on the reason that the French Government was slow or indifferent in applying a policy of settlement only confirms that there was no natural movement of population to New France.

The essential reason must be looked for in the colony's economy itself. In order to attract immigrants, a country must offer excellent prospects for agriculture as well as industry and commerce, but New France offered nothing of the kind. In fact, since any outlet to European countries other than France was forbidden and the only American colonies with which she could trade were those of the very distant West Indies, New France could really only export her agricultural products to France. France, however, had no need to import agricultural products. Nor were there any prospects, from the industrial point of view, since the mother country opposed any industry in competition with French manufacturers. New France existed only to provide raw materials. Even the fur trade, the only important venture in the colony, was little more than a shipping business in which furs were received from the natives and were loaded on ships bound for France.

New France had no economic activity requiring considerable manpower, unlike Virginia with its tobacco production.

French recruiting sources

According to the genealogist Godbout, the following regions provided the greatest number of colonists (2,816 have been identified) in the seventeenth century.

Normandy	547
Île-de-France and Paris	508
Poitou	352
Aunis, Îles de Ré and d'Oléron	332
Brittany	117

For the eighteenth century, the following table gives a total of 3,347 colonists.

Île-de-France and Paris	516
Normandy	464
Brittany	346
Poitou	255
Guyenne and Artois	244
Aunis and Île de Ré	238
Saintonge	232
Languedoc	219

Île-de-France and the provinces of the west contributed most to the settlement of the colony. Île-de-France was the administrative centre as well as an area having a problem of overpopulation, so it naturally comes at the top of the list. The western provinces, being close to the sea, possessed the ports of embarkation for America. The most important of these was La Rochelle, in Aunis. The Mediterranean contribution, always small, did not appear until the eighteenth century.

Former provinces of France
(map of 1758)

Public Archives of Canada

However, it must not be hastily assumed that the French Canadians of today are descended mainly from Parisians, Normans, Bretons, and Poitevins. One must first take into account the families founded by these immigrants. Thus, the Perche area, on the borders of Normandy and the province of Maine, was thirteenth on the list for the seventeenth century and does not appear on the table for the eighteenth century. Nevertheless, the most impressive number of families in French Canada came from there.

Foreign sources

The French-Canadian ethnic group does not have the absolute purity of origin that is normally ascribed to it. Foreign elements mingled with it from the very beginning of the French regime. No systematic list has yet been drawn up, but documents often indicate a variety of immigrants. There were Englishmen (coming mainly from New England, as

An eighteenth-century flûte: a merchantman armed with guns

prisoners or refugees), Irishmen (who were admitted without difficulty because they were persecuted Catholics), Scotsmen (the allies of France), and others, such as Spaniards, Portuguese, Italians, and Germans. Some record of their numbers is also available. It is known, for example, that from 1710 to 1730, 127 English and Irish were naturalized. From 1717 onwards, the king excused European Catholics from naturalization. Many marriages are recorded between Canadians and English women, but again, the important consideration here is the number of descendants.

Intermarriage

Among these foreign newcomers, the contribution of the Amerinds must not be forgotten. There has been no systematic list made in this area either, but it is possible that this contribution was large. France, indeed, worked for a long time to turn the Amerinds into Frenchmen. It was Colbert's policy in 1667 that Canadians and natives should form *un mesme peuple et un mesme sang* ("one people and one blood"). In 1679, the King encouraged Intendant Duchesneau to settle natives among the French. The Jesuit Charlevoix wrote of the Canadians' passion for the *"sauvagesses."* There was certainly intermarriage. In the outlying regions, the official records mention marriages between Canadians and Amerindian women and the births of several halfbreeds. The presence of Indian slaves contributed to this mixture. Between Canadians and native female slaves alone, some thirty marriages have been noted. These relations, within the law or not, were sufficiently numerous for the authorities to forbid them in an attempt to reduce their number because they were disappointed by the poor quality of the children they produced.

The elements of immigration

It has been estimated that of the 10,000 immigrants who settled in New France, 3,900 were tradesmen, 3,500 were military recruits, 1,100 were marriageable girls, and 1,000 were deported people.

a) *Tradesmen*

These men constituted the most important element of immigration in the seventeenth century. The charter of the Cent-Associés stated that those tradesmen who practised their trade for six years in New France would be considered masters on their return to France and would be able to open shops. Furthermore, ships' captains were obliged to carry three contracted settlers for every sixty tons of cargo, and six for every one hundred tons; however, tradesmen counted as two people. Since the rank of master had become almost impossible to obtain in France, and since the future seemed uncertain for them, tradesmen emigrated in a body. The recruitment of 1653 (about 100 colonists) was composed of only tradesmen; of the 1,344 inhabitants listed in the census of 1666, about one half professed a trade, even if they were settled on the land. However, 90 percent of the immigrants who claimed a particular trade when they embarked had no real experience of a trade. Some were too young to have done scarcely more than serve their apprenticeship.

Assured of a passage and board at the expense of the person who had recruited them, these tradesmen normally contracted for a period of three years; thus, they were nicknamed *trente-six mois*. They generally received an annual salary of seventy-five

Poop of a French warship in the eighteenth century

livres. When their service was finished, they settled, in theory, on land granted to them in the seigneuries and tried their hands at farming.

b) *Military recruits*

After the tradesmen, the most important group is that of the military recruits. The first body of these recruits to settle in the country was about four hundred officers and men who left the Carignan-Salières regiment, instead of going back to France with the others in 1668. Afterwards, the intendants saw to it, as far as possible, that the soldiers who were sent to the country by France were tradesmen, in order that they could work for the *habitants* and the merchants when they were not on military campaigns. It seems certain that these military recruits included only a few qualified workmen. In any case, once their period of service was over, many of these soldiers did the same as the tradesmen and settled on the land to try their hands at farming. They at least had the advantage of being trained for the defence of the country.

c) *Marriageable girls*

It was a long time before women arrived in New France. In the period before 1627, not a single one came to Acadia, and in Canada, in 1627, there were only five adult women. They arrived in greater numbers after 1634, and at that time, the immigration of women began to be organized.

First, there were the girls brought by the women founders, such as Madame de La Peltrie, Marie de l'Incarnation, Jeanne Mance, and Marguerite Bourgeoys. These girls were chosen with care and some 220 arrived between 1634 and 1661. Then, there were the selected orphans, as healthy and sturdy as possible, who were sent by the Government. They were called *filles du roi* (king's daughters) and had been raised by the nuns at State expense. The State, which took the place of their fathers, assumed responsibility for them in the same way that fathers assumed responsibility for their daughters at that time. Between 1665 and 1673, about 900 of them landed, after being brought over under close supervision.

When these female newcomers arrived, they were housed in convents, where the colonists presented themselves to choose wives from among them. If the bachelors hesitated about making a choice, an order from the intendant obliged them to marry within two weeks of the arrival of the vessels. In general, the girls did not remain "wall-flowers" for long. In 1669, out of 165 girls who arrived, 135 were married in the course of the summer; in 1673, 50 of the 60 girls found husbands immediately. After 1673, the numbers of marriageable girls declined and the State soon stopped dispatching women to the colonies.

d) *Those sent into exile*

New France was not a penal colony, but nonetheless, it served in some cases as an outlet for undesirable elements from the mother country. Thus, young men, called *fils de famille,* were sent to the colony. These men had incurred paternal wrath because of their disobedience or their dissipated way of life. The parents obtained *lettres de cachet* from the King, and the guilty sons had to take the road to New France. From 1722 to 1749, sixty-eight were sent out, but only about ten seem to have settled in the country and to have left descendants.

The mother country went as far as sending out convicts, who came to serve as volunteers. This group was mainly composed of poachers and salt smugglers, men who were guilty of infringing the hunting laws or the salt trade, and New France received 648 of them between 1730 and 1749. About thirty other criminals arrived in 1723, but the protests of the colony's authorities immediately put a stop to this method of colonization.

Kitchen of a well-to-do home, in the eighteenth century

e) *The Huguenots*

The Huguenots, who had played an important role in the founding of New France, had lost official permission to settle there in 1627. They still came, however, and until the Revocation of the Edict of Nantes, they were permitted to spend the summer, and sometimes the winter in the country. After 1685, they were treated with great severity. Unless they became converted they were refused permission. Then, gradually, in the time of Louis XV, a tolerant attitude was adopted. Huguenots came to live in New France in such numbers that they caused concern to the bishop. But they were forbidden to assemble for prayer, to have ministers, meeting-houses, or cemeteries, and they could only engage in trade.

After the Conquest, they served as intermediaries for the English. The Test Act assured them of a glorious revenge. Protestantism became the only official religion and the required one for government posts. One of the Huguenots became the only representative of the French population in Murray's Council.

An extraordinary birth rate

Although immigration was not considerable, the population reproduced itself at a surprising rate. Furthermore, after 1666, the State encouraged early marriages with financial subsidies. For a long time, it gave an annual pension of 300 *livres* to fathers having ten children and 400 *livres* to fathers having twelve. In Canada, this system of encouragement, along with other reasons that have not yet been properly studied, raised the marriage rate: it varied between 17.5 and 23.5 per 1000 (22 per 1000 is considered a peak). The birth rate was even higher. When the highest rate in the world reached 55 per 1000, it has been shown that in New France this rate was constantly equalled or exceeded and that in the period 1751-1760 the rate reached 61.8. It even went to 65.2 in the following ten years.

This prodigious birth rate was checked by the death rate (23.6 average, rising to 39.6 in the years 1700-1770), and it has been calculated that of 1000 children born, 246 died within their first year.

The fact remains, nevertheless, that this remarkable birth rate enabled New France, in spite of nominal immigration, to reach a total population of 85,000 inhabitants by 1760.

Social groups

In eighteenth-century France, the traditional divisions (clergy, nobility, and third estate) no longer corresponded to their legal definition. The nobility, for its part, had lost its social function. The third estate, on the other hand, had obtained an increasingly larger share in what used to be the exclusive role of the nobility. This group, which included tradesmen and peasants, had a most active element in the bourgeoisie. Outside these legal institutions, social classes had formed, that is, groups within society that presented a certain economic uniformity, maintained a distinctive standard of living and cultural level, and were conscious of their common goals. With their common source of income, their cultural traditions and their self-awareness, the French nobles behaved like a social class. The merchant bourgeoisie was a second social class. Bound together against the nobility as against the other groups of the third estate, it corresponded, as much as the nobility, to the definition of a class. The same cannot be said of the tradesmen, who scarcely had a corporate sense, or of the peasants, who lacked economic uniformity and a common consciousness. Finally, outside these classes, we must mention (still in France) those who were called *métis sociaux* (social halfbreeds). This was the case of the law nobility, called *robins,* who held office in the judicature. They came from the bourgeoisie, to which they no longer wished to belong, but were not yet recognized by the nobility.

What became of this social division in New France? In 1672, Frontenac wanted to establish three divisions (clergy, nobility, and third estate) based on wealth, and to bring them together in something like the Estates General. Louis XIV put an end to this system and the three divisions never had any legal existence in the colony. But were there at least social classes in New France?

a) *The nobility*

In New France, there was no nobility of office or people who had bought letters patent of nobility. The nobles in the colony came either from the French nobility or from former commoners recently elevated by patents of nobility. The old nobility was conscious of its cultural traditions, and the new nobility tried to become a part of this tradition, although superficially at first. From the first generation, they adopted the *de*, although it was not essential and did not constitute a proof of nobility. They also took a second family name; so we find Giffard de Fargy (by simple inversion, as would occur with Bourdon de Dombourg), Lemoyne de Longueuil, and Boucher de Grosbois. In these ways they tried to behave like the old nobility.

The members of the Canadian nobility were essentially hard-working and had really only one privilege, a non-lucrative one, that of carrying a sword and bearing the title of knight *(écuyer)*. This situation was in great contrast to the nobles of France who were idle and laden with privileges. Furthermore, the Canadian nobility was small in number, some twenty families in the seventeenth century. They had no economic uniformity, and their standard of living and cultural level hardly distinguished them from the other social groups. What is more, at no time did they have any awareness of a common goal. The Canadian nobles did not constitute a social class but only an ill-assorted group of individuals who were noble. In their mentality, in their preoccupations, in their participation in the fur trade, and in their way of life, the nobles could easily have been mistaken for commoners. This similarity became even greater as a result of the seigneurial system. The possession of a seigneury did not confer nobility, but because the title of seigneur and the ownership of land were attached to it, the seigneur was bound to carry out the ceremonies of the old nobility (fealty and homage, the setting up of a maypole). Because he occupied a rank above that of the majority of people, the commoner seigneur was on the same level as the nobility. The word *dit*, which coupled a surname to a family name, sometimes ended by becoming the particle *de* (this happened in the case of the Gadois dit Mogé). In addition, important people like the Decouagne family took pleasure in letting themselves be known as the de Couagne family.

b) *The bourgeoisie*

The bourgeoisie in New France was even less well defined than the nobility. It did not even have any distinctive privilege. The only recorded case was in 1676 when the Lieutenant General of the Prévôté confirmed a merchant of Quebec in his privileges as a *bourgeois*. How did one become a member of the bourgeoisie in the colony? It seems that it was through one's standing in business (in terms of the numbers of employees) and by conspicuous signs of prosperity (such as the ownership of slaves which, in Canada, were simply a luxury expense).

In any case, for individuals themselves, the notion of the bourgeoisie seems to have been as confused as that of the nobility, no doubt because the French legal status of the bourgeoisie did not apply in the cities. Thus one person could, at different times, call himself a merchant-bourgeois, a merchant, and a businessman. From this, it may be concluded that the activity was more important than the legal status.

New France had a wide range of businessmen—merchants, traders and entrepreneurs—whose careers began with the Communauté des Habitants in 1645. Well known examples are Le Moyne, Le Ber, Aubert de Lachenaye, Pachot, Hazeur, Dupré, and Cugnet. There were also women like Madame Boüat, the widow Fornel, and Madame d'Youville. Represented by an elected official, these bourgeois were often consulted by the intendant about the trade regulations and prices. As in France, a number of them held high administrative or judicial functions. Through marriage with the military nobility, they had access to aristocratic society.

However, although one finds certain bourgeois habits—like ostentation—and a certain cultural continuity transferred from the mother country, the Canadian bourgeoisie generally had no class feeling to separate it from the other classes. There was no capitalistic mentality and very little of the level-headedness and thrift that distinguishes the French bourgeoisie. The bourgeoisie in Canada looked for short-term profits and lost its fortunes in unsound undertakings. Its members were constantly short of capital. They were not rich enough altogether, according to the testimony of an intendant, to support the iron-working industry of Saint-Maurice. They lived beyond their means and created the general impression, by their way of life and their marriages, that they sought (above all) to join aristocratic society. They did not form a class. They were a group without uniformity, desiring to be promoted to a higher position. Taking into account the institutions of France, what we have here is not a bourgeois class but only individual bourgeois, and even this word must be interpreted in a different way from its European counterpart.

Although Canada, at the end of the French regime, possessed about forty people whose fortunes had reached or passed a million *livres*, we cannot speak of an "upper middle class." In fact, these millionaires were rich in paper but not in gold. This makes it clear that they did not have the bourgeois spirit. They were civil servants who had made their fortunes mainly by speculating in army supplies. In short, they were individuals who owed their accidental wealth to an activity that was not part of the normal economic life of the colony.

It has been maintained that the Conquest of 1760 put an end to the existence of what is called the "upper middle class", by replacing them with English merchants. A closer examination of the facts makes it clear that some businessmen from before the Conquest were still engaged in the fur trade after 1763, and they dominated trading ventures until the American Revolution. The disappearance of these French-Canadian businessmen, upon the arrival of the English merchant class, was probably not due to the Conquest, but to the loss of their traditional area of exploitation—the lower region of lakes Erie and Michigan—in 1783. There was also a decline in the beaver trade, and these men refused to adapt to the new economic structure. They may have been attracted by high public office which, in this monarchical society, was one way of reaching an aristo-cratic level or way of life. Before a satisfactory answer can be found, the behaviour of businessmen, both before and after 1760, remains to be studied.

Dress of the ordinary people
(according to Richard Short)

Public Archives of Canada

c) *The working classes*

Of all the groups making up society in New France in the eighteenth century, only the nobility (through its military function) and the *marchands-bourgeois* (through their connection with the fur trade) were clearly above the mass of the people.

The working classes included small merchants, traders in the service of the entrepreneurs, and minor civil servants. They also included tradesmen who did not form a class or even a socio-professional group, in spite of the importance of their associations in the preceding century. It seems that they no longer had even a corporate sense, although, like the tradesmen of France, they sometimes took on apprentices and con-tracted to teach them the secrets of their art. However, except in rare cases, these appren-tices do not appear to have gone beyond the level of apprenticeship. It is surprising that tradesmen were unable to become a powerful socio-professional group in a colony that was inhabited at its beginning by so many tradesmen, and in which the rank of master could be acquired by a six-year apprenticeship.

In these lower classes, the *habitants* or peasants as a whole did not form a group that was better organized or more active than the other groups. They were simply a large group of *censitaires* bound to the seigneur by voluntary contract, just as in the towns groups of workmen could be found who also placed themselves in the service of the entrepreneurs by voluntary contract.

A black slave owned by the Canadian painter François Beaucourt

There was no division between these social groups, according to the role each group played, but rather, according to the easy circumstances or initiative of the individual. However, there remained a large gap between these groups and domestic servants, as in Europe. Servants bound by a contract, or in bondservice, held a much lower position than those mentioned above; but it must be added that their conditions were better than they would have been in Europe. They received higher wages, and it seems, they "held their heads up" because they were in short supply.

d) *The slaves*

The group placed at the very lowest level of society was the slaves because it was composed of individuals who were bought and sold. Their number has been estimated at more than 4,000 over a period of 125 years (apart from those in Louisiana). 2,400 Amerindian slaves entered Canada alone. Three quarters of these were mainly Panis taken from the Mississippi Valley and some 1,200 Negroes imported from the English colonies or the West Indies.

Montreal, Quebec, and Detroit (in order of importance) were the principal slave centres, but slaves were found more or less everywhere in the countryside.

There was no economic necessity for slaves, but the possession of a slave or two (especially a negro) amounted to visible proof of high social status. For this reason, slave owners included a wide cross section of colonial society: governors, intendants, army officers, high ranking civil servants, bishops, curés, religious communities, seigneurs, merchants (who possessed the most), professional men, and small tradespeople.

Apart from the fact that they were bought and sold, it seems that slaves were considered to be like servants or even adopted children. Since they were few in number and most were very young (Amerindian slaves died on an average at 17.7 years), they posed scarcely any problems for Canadian society.

An American society

An attempt had been made to transport a monarchical European society to New France, but once in place, this society rapidly lost its European character and became American, although it remained highly stratified. The apparently rigid framework and the still powerful hierarchy should not hide the social confusion that reigned in New France, as it did in every European colony. Moreover, it was impossible to transplant the power and the traditional privileges of the classes in France in their original state, because the immigrants during the French regime did not represent French society in its entirety. The lack of men brought about a large number of social functions that could only be found in a colony.

In fact, if one considers that the nobles were almost without privileges, that their social duties were the same as everyone else's and that they were as hard-working as people at any level of society, they cannot be distinguished from the other classes. Unlike the situation in Europe, where the lower classes were condemned to remain the lower classes, in the colony they could easily reach the higher levels. A man went from one level to the other according to his ability or his success, and a small trader could suddenly become an influential businessman. By the end of the French regime, most of the seigneurs came from the common people. Men of small means, such as Charles Le Moyne and Cavelier de La Salle, rapidly reached the nobility. Pierre Boucher, as a young man, started out as a servant and then became judge, seigneur, governor, and nobleman. In the face of adventure, all men were equal.

Although this society was essentially different because of the elements that formed it, it was also different in national origins to an extent that has not yet been exactly determined. It integrated many other Europeans, besides the French, and a large number of Amerinds. These groups, as well as the new environment in which he was developing, left a deep impression on the American Frenchman. He emerged as a new kind of French-man characterized by independence, instability, a habit of immediately spending what he had worked so hard to earn, a taste for danger and risks, a facility for adapting to new conditions, surprising endurance, and considerable generosity in helping others.

It has usually been stated that, as early as 1760, the French in America felt separate from the French in France; in fact, the whole society had already become conscious of no longer being European.

Public Archives of Canada

Signature of Louis XV
Notice that in most cases the signature is that of a *secrétaire de la main*.

Bibliographical Note

The following are some general studies on the origins and evolutions of the population:

E. SALONE, *La Colonisation de la Nouvelle-France. Étude sur les origines de la nation canadienne-française.* Paris, Guilmoto, 1906.

G. LANGLOIS, *Histoire de la population canadienne-française.* Montréal, Lévesque, 1935.

A. GODBOUT, "Nos hérédités provinciales", in the *Archives de Folklore*, Vol. I, pp. 26-40.

J. HENRIPIN, *La Population canadienne au début du XVIIIe siècle. Nuptialité, fécondité, mortalité infantile.* Paris, Presses universitaires de France, 1954.

Society has been the subject of some general studies:

G. FRÉGAULT, *La Civilisation de la Nouvelle-France.* Montréal, Pascal, 1944.

G. FRÉGAULT, *La Société canadienne sous le régime français,* pamphlet no. 3 in the Publications of the Canadian Historical Society, Ottawa, 1954; translated into English under the title *Canadian Society in the French Regime.*

W. J. ECCLES, *Canadian Society During the French Regime*. Montreal, Harvest House Ltd., 1968.

J. HAMELIN, *Économie et société en Nouvelle-France*. Québec, Université Laval, 1960.

A. G. REID, "The Nature of Quebec Society During the French Regime" in the *Report of the Canadian Historical Society for 1951*, pp. 26-35.

These other studies give information on various social groups.

The Nobility

C. E. LART, "The Noblesse of Canada," in *Canadian Historical Review*, Vol. III, 3 (Sept. 1922), pp. 222-232.

The Bourgeoisie

The following are not special studies but material that may serve as a basis for discussion.

M. BRUNET, *La présence anglaise et les Canadiens*. Montréal, Beauchemin, 1958.

M. BRUNET, *Les Canadiens et les débuts de la domination britannique, 1760-1791*, pamphlet no. 13 in the Publications of the Canadian Historical Society, Ottawa, 1962.

C. NISH, "La Bourgeoisie et les mariages,1729-1748" in the *Revue d'histoire de l'Amérique française*, XIX, 4 (March 1966), pp. 585-605.

F. OUELLET, *Histoire économique et sociale du Québec, 1760-1850. Structures et conjunctures*. Montréal, Fides, 1966. See in particular the Introduction and the first part.

Slavery

M. TRUDEL, *L'Esclavage au Canada français, Histoire et conditions de l'esclavage*. Québec, Université Laval, 1960.

Immigrants

G. DEBIEN, "Engagés pour le Canada au XVIIᵉ siècle, vus de La Rochelle," in the *Revue d'histoire de l'Amérique française*, VI, 2 (Sept. 1952), pp. 177-220. An important study on the engagement contracts.

G. MALCHELOSSE, "L'Immigration des filles de la Nouvelle-France au XVIIᵉ siècle" in the *Cahiers des Dix*, XV, 1950, pp. 55-80.

G. LANCTÔT, *Filles de joie ou filles du roi. Étude sur l'immigration féminine en Nouvelle-France*. Montréal, Chanteclerc, 1952.

G. MALCHELOSSE, "Faux-sauniers, prisonniers et fils de famille en Nouvelle-France au XVIIIᵉ siècle," in the *Cahiers des Dix*, IX, 1944, pp. 161-197.

G. MALCHELOSSE, *Les Fils de famille en Nouvelle-France*, ibid., XI, 1946, pp. 261-311.

P. A. LECLERC, *L'Émigration féminine vers l'Amérique française aux XVIIᵉ et XVIIIᵉ siècles*. Doctoral thesis, manuscript.

CHAPTER III

Government

The administrative system of New France varied greatly during the seventeenth century. Until 1674, the colony was a dependency of one trading company after another. The functions of the governor and the intendant were still poorly defined. The Conseil Souverain served as an executive council as well as a court of justice. In short, the cadres of society were not yet firmly fixed. Any complications that arose almost always placed institutions in danger. However, about 1715, the administrative system was at last firmly established and enjoyed a stability that lasted until 1760.

Kings and viceroys

Louis XV succeeded to the throne in 1715 and came of age in 1723. With the end of the regency, he personally presided over the destinies of New France. His presence was felt everywhere as that of his predecessor and great-grandfather Louis XIV had been. He named men to high offices. All authority and honour stemmed from him, and it was to him that final appeal could always be made, above the heads of those who represented him or wielded power.

Viceroys were still appointed. Until the resignation of Lévy de Vantadour, in 1627, the colony had been the responsibility of a viceroy who actively presided over the administration. Viceroys are listed again in 1644 and continue until 1737. But the later ones were ineffective, and none of them, in their official capacity, played an important role in the history of New France.

The Minister

At first, the colony was under the authority of the Amirauté. After 1627, the Ministère de la Marine (Navy Department) was in charge except for a brief period from 1715 to 1723 when it was replaced by a *Conseil de Marine* (Marine Council). The Navy Department first appeared in 1669, when the King created the post of Secretary of State for the Navy and gave it to Colbert. Other holders of the office were Seignelay, the son of Colbert, from 1683 to 1690; and Phélypeaux de Pontchartrain, who was succeeded by his son in 1699, and his grandson Maurepas, from 1723 to 1749. The holder of the Navy office was called *le Ministre* (the Minister) in official correspondence.

Although the King possessed the final authority, the Minister had complete power in New France. He was assisted by chief clerks who looked through dispatches and extracted the essential points from them, but left important decisions (indicated by notes in the margins of the documents) to the Minister. If there was some very important business, a summary was made for the King. When replying to the governor and the intendant, the Minister spoke in the name of the King.

Public Archives of Canada

Château Saint-Louis, in Quebec, at the beginning of the eighteenth century

The Governor General

Even in New France, the higher administration was divided between two individuals, the Governor General and the Intendant. The Governor General was appointed by the King and was liable to be recalled by him. He was the highest dignitary in New France since he was the King's personal representative. He had precedence over everyone and was given the title *Monseigneur*. His authority covered the whole of New France, although for practical reasons, his subordinates in Acadia and Louisiana found it more convenient to correspond directly with the mother country.

The Governor General had exclusive and sovereign jurisdiction over the military administration. He was usually a regular soldier, and along with the title Governor General, he held that of Lieutenant General of the King's Armies, and was often called *M. le général*. He commanded all the troops of New France and decided on plans of campaign and fortifications, in co-operation with the intendant who was responsible for expenditure. In the same way, he had sovereign jurisdiction over external affairs (that is, relations with the English colonies), permits to leave the country, and the government of the "savages." In other phases of administration, such as the writing of annual reports, the granting of seigneuries, and the allocation of trading permits, he worked closely with the intendant.

The Governor General's personal influence was, nevertheless, limited (the only offices nominated by him were those of the militia), yet he could recommend candidates for different positions in the army. From the revenues of trading posts under State control he had 10,000 *livres* at his disposal, to distribute as gratuities.

The privileges of his position included the Château Saint-Louis in Quebec and a garrison. He received a salary of 12,000 *livres*, plus 3,000 *livres* as head of the Government of Quebec. To this was added 25,000 *livres*, from various sources (including 6,000 *livres* as a gift from the *Compagnie des Indes* and some 4,000 *livres* as his share of the income from the canteen). So the Governor General received some 40,000 *livres* a year and was strictly forbidden to engage in trade of any kind.

Pierre de Rigaud de Vaudreuil-Cavagnial, the first Canadian to become Governor General of New France

The following people presided over the government of New France, with the title of Lieutenant to the Viceroy, or Richelieu's Lieutenant (like Champlain), and the title of Governor, or Interim Governor.

1608-1635   **Samuel de Champlain,** *navy captain. Lieutenant to Lieutenants General de Monts and Soissons; then Lieutenant to Viceroys Condé, Thémines, Montmorency, Vantadour; lastly, Richelieu's Lieutenant. Died at Quebec in 1635; also buried there.*

Marc-Antoine Brasdefer de Châteaufort. *Knight of Malta. Interim Commander from 1635 to 1636.*

1636-1648   **Charles Huault de Montmagny.** *Knight of Malta. Appointed Governor at about 53 years of age.*

1648-1651   **Louis d'Ailleboust de Coulonge et d'Argentenay.** *Appointed at 36 years of age.*

1651-1656   **Jean de Lauson.** *Appointed at about 67 years of age. Returned to France before the end of his period of office.*

Charles de Lauson de Charny, *son of the above. First appointed administrator in 1656, at the age of 27; then, Interim Governor in 1657, while awaiting d'Argenson. Returned to France in the same year to prepare himself for the priesthood. Came back to take up ministry in Canada.*

Louis d'Ailleboust de Coulonge et d'Argentenay, *former Governor. Became Interim Governor in 1657, while awaiting the arrival of d'Argenson. Died in Montreal.*

1657-1661   **Pierre Voyer d'Argenson.** *Viscount. Appointed in 1657 at 32 years of age; did not arrive until 1658.*

1661-1663   **Pierre Dubois Davaugour.** *Baron. Appointed at about 50 years of age.*

1663-1665   **Augustin Saffray de Mézy.** *Knight. Died in Quebec during his period of office.*

1665-1672*   **Daniel de Rémy de Courcelle.** *Appointed at 39 years of age.*

1672-1682   **Louis de Buade de Frontenac.** *Count. Appointed at 50 years of age. Recalled to France in 1682.*

1682-1685   **Joseph-Antoine LeFebvre de LaBarre.** *Appointed at 60 years of age.*

1685-1689   **Jacques-René de Brisay de Denonville.** *Marquis. Appointed at 43 years of age.*

1689-1698   **Louis de Buade de Frontenac.** *Count. Again appointed Governor at 67 years of age. Died in Quebec in 1698.*

Louis-Hector de Callières. *Knight. Interim Governor from 1698 to 1699.*

1699-1703   **Louis-Hector de Callières.** *Knight. Promoted Governor at 53 years of age. Died in Quebec, in 1703.*

1703-1725   **Philippe de Rigaud de Vaudreuil.** *Marquis. Appointed at 60 years of age. Died in Quebec, in 1725.*

Charles Le Moyne de Longueuil. *Baron. Interim Governor from 1725 to 1726. The first Canadian to occupy this high position.*

1726-1746   **Charles de La Boische de Beauharnois.** *Marquis. Appointed at 56 years of age. Brother of Intendant François de La Boische de Beauharnois. Period of office ended in 1746, but he had to wait for his successor. Did not leave until 1747.*

Roland-Michel Barrin de La Galissonière. *Appointed Interim Governor while awaiting La Jonquière. Governed from 1747 to 1749. Brother-in-law of Intendant Bégon.*

---

*It will be noted that in 1666-1667 the supreme command at Quebec was in the hands of the Marquis Prouville de Tracy: as Lieutenant General of French America (New France and the West Indies), he was above Governor Courcelle.

1749-1752	**Jacques-Pierre de Taffanel de La Jonquière.** *Marquis. Appointed Governor in 1746, at 61 years of age. Did not arrive until 1749. Died in Quebec, in 1752.*
	Charles Le Moyne de Longueuil. *Baron. Son of the Baron de Longueuil, mentioned above. Interim Governor in 1752. The second Canadian to occupy this high position.*
1752-1755	**Ange de Menneville Duquesne.** *Marquis. Appointed at 50 years of age.*
1755-1760	**Pierre de Rigaud de Vaudreuil-Cavagnial.** *Son of the Rigaud de Vaudreuil, mentioned above. Appointed at 57 years of age. The first Canadian to become Governor of New France.*

The Intendant

By far the most important individual in New France was the Intendant although, in order of precedence, he came after the Governor General and the Bishop. He was called *Monseigneur* and was honoured by having a retinue of archers, or carabineers. His jurisdiction covered three extensive areas: justice, *police* (that is, internal administration), and finance. In Bigot's time, the administration of internal shipping was added to these three areas.

As the arbiter of justice, the Intendant presided over the sessions of the Conseil Supérieur, watched over the courts of justice, interpreted the customary law, and received the fealty and homage of the seigneurs. He recommended candidates to positions in the judicature, and named notaries and land surveyors. As the intendant of *police*, he directed the entire internal administration (including highways, health, morality, and security). Finally, as the intendant of finance, he was the chief treasurer and the director of the country's economic life. He had authority over the colony's budget, military expenses, taxes, rate of exchange, prices, fisheries, agriculture, shipbuilding, industry, regulation of trade, and the trades and professions. The Intendant was connected with all fields of human activity within the country. Admittedly, his powers were, in practice, limited to Canada alone, but this was by far the most densely populated part of New France.

Like the Governor General, the Intendant was appointed by the King and was liable to be recalled by him. He resided in Quebec (at the Palais de l'Intendance), but as part of his duty, like the governor general, he had to spend several months each year in Montreal, preparing the many departures for the *pays d'en haut*. He received a salary of 12,000 *livres*, in addition to some 10,000 *livres* from various sources (one of these was 4,500 *livres* presented by the Compagnie des Indes), which gave him a total annual income of about 22,000 *livres*.

The office of Intendant, established in 1663, was occupied by the following people:

1663	**Louis Robert de Fortel.** *Appointed Intendant in 1663. Never came to New France.*
1665-1668	**Jean Talon.** *Appointed at 40 years of age. Returned to France in 1668.*
1668-1670	**Claude de Boutroue d'Aubigny.** *Knight. Appointed at 43 years of age.*
1670-1672	**Jean Talon.** *Went back to France in 1672, never to return.*
1675-1682	**Jacques Duchesneau de La Doussinière et d'Ambault.** *Knight.*
1682-1686	**Jacques Demeulle de La Source.** *Died in France.*

Public Archives of Canada

Palais de l'Intendance, in Quebec
(engraving by Richard Short)

1686-1702   **Jean Bochart-Champigny.** *His wife was a cousin of Mgr de Laval. Almost obtained the position of Governor on the death of Frontenac.*

1702-1705   **François de La Boische de Beauharnois.** *Elder brother of Governor Beauharnois. Appointed at 36 years of age.*

1705-1710   **Jacques Raudot.** *Appointed at 58 years of age.*

Antoine-Denis Raudot, *son of the above. Appointed Deputy Intendant in 1705, at 26 years of age. Returned to France in 1710.*

Jacques Raudot. *Period of office ended in 1710. Continued his functions while awaiting a successor. Returned to France in 1711.*

Francois Clairambault d'Aigremont. *Interim Intendant from 1711 to 1712, while awaiting the arrival of Bégon who had been appointed in 1710.*

1712-1724   **Michel Bégon.** *Knight. Appointed in 1710 at 36 years of age. Did not arrive until 1712. Nephew of the former intendant Beauharnois and brother-in-law of the celebrated letter-writer Elisabeth Bégon.*

1724   **Edme-Nicolas Robert.** *Died on board the* Chameau *on the way to New France.*
Michel Bégon. *Substituted for the above. Continued his function as Intendant.*

1725   **Guillaume de Chazelles.** *Died at sea on board the* Chameau.
Michel Bégon *continued as substitute Intendant until 1726.*

1726-1728   **Claude-Thomas Dupuy.** *Appointed at 39 years of age, in 1725. Arrived in 1726.*
François Clairambault d'Aigremont. *Interim Intendant from 1728 to 1729.*
Gilles Hocquart. *Commissary General in the absence of an Intendant, from 1729 to 1731. Appointed at 35 years of age.*

1731-1748   **Gilles Hocquart.** *Intendant.*

1748-1760   **François Bigot.** *Appointed at 45 years of age.*

Public Archives of Canada

Intendant Gilles Hocquart

Public Archives of Canada

Château de Vaudreuil in Montreal, residence of the governors

The Conseil Supérieur

The Conseil Souverain was instituted in 1663 to take the place of an executive council and a court of appeal, but since the first years of the eighteenth century, it has been called the *Conseil Supérieur*. It was originally composed of the governor and the bishop, as well as five other members appointed by them. In the eighteenth century, the governor rarely attended the sessions, and the bishop sent an ecclesiastic substitute. By the end of the French regime, the Conseil Supérieur (with the intendant as president) was composed of sixteen members appointed by the King, and a number of Councillor-Assessors (young gentlemen who were destined for positions in the judicature).

Although, in theory, it was above the superior councils of Acadia and Louisiana, the Conseil Supérieur of New France really had jurisdiction only in Canada. It became little more than a free court of appeal for any court of justice (lay or ecclesiastical, royal or seigneurial). However, it retained a very important right. Since it took the place of a provincial "Parlement" (high judicial court), the King's decrees were considered invalid if the Council had not recorded them.

Councillors had to be content with the honours paid to them in church and with the prestige of their office, for remuneration was poor and they sat in the Palais de l'Intendance in ordinary street clothes. Nevertheless, for the tradesmen who made up the great majority of the Council, such distinction was the fulfilment of their dreams of social climbing.

The Governments of local areas

Under the authority of the governor general, the intendant, and the Conseil Supérieur, New France was subdivided into several local Governments: Louisiana, Acadia, Quebec, Trois-Rivières, and Montreal.

At the head of each of these Governments was a local governor (at Quebec, it was the Governor General who assumed his functions) who was assisted by a king's lieutenant.

For civil affairs, the Intendant was represented in each Government by a sub-delegate: this was the Commissary-director (in Acadia or Louisiana), the Naval Commissary in Montreal, or the Surveyor-in-chief, or even a storekeeper.

This double authority, civil and military, on the parish level, was united in the hands of the captain of militia, who represented both the governor and the intendant to the settlers.

The following table illustrates briefly the transmission of power.

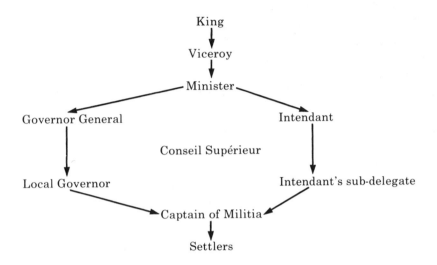

An overabundance of officials

If a complete list were made of the civil servants in the general administration, in the courts of justice, and in army affairs, a whole host of minor clerks would be found drawing salaries from the State budget.

Admittedly, one must take into consideration the distances separating the various sections of New France. While the population of the entire colony did not exceed eighty-five thousand, it was necessary to set up a complex system of administration in Acadia, an equally complex one on the Saint Lawrence, and another in Louisiana. Furthermore, on the Saint Lawrence alone, within a distance of scarcely two hundred miles, serving only some seventy-six thousand inhabitants, there were three complete Governments: Quebec, Trois-Rivières, and Montreal. Each had a governor, king's lieutenant, general staff, and the entire administrative structure that that involved. Two Governments would have been sufficient. So, it is not surprising that, in 1764, the English abolished the administration of Trois-Rivières and were satisfied with two districts, doing away with the Governments of local areas.

Civil servants, then, existed in great numbers, and both the employees of the administration and the soldiers were poorly paid. While the Governor General of New France received some 40,000 *livres* a year, the Governor of Trois-Rivières received only 4,300 *livres*; his deputy (the King's Lieutenant) received only 1,800 *livres*. In the civil administration, officials were rarely paid more than 1,000 *livres* per annum: the Naval Commissary, who represented the Intendant in Montreal, received only 1,800 *livres*, while the Intendant received some 22,000. The civil and criminal Lieutenant General (or Chief Judge) of the Government of Quebec received 1,000 *livres*, but his colleagues in Montreal and Trois-Rivières were paid only 450. (This was little more than the executioner, who was paid 330 *livres*.) The crown prosecutor in Montreal and Trois-Rivières was given only 250 *livres* per annum. It is understandable that civil servants were accused of neglecting their duties and that they continued to defraud and speculate. Thus, it was common for minor clerks to profit by their positions and rapidly build up a fortune. This was part and parcel of the system.

These officials were all practising Catholics, since only they had access to public positions. In fact, nomination (even for an ecclesiastic) was preceded by an "inquiry as to the way of life, morals, suitable age, conversation, and Catholic, Apostolic, and Roman religion." With his papers, the candidate had to include a "certificate of Catholicism" signed by his curé. It was a French version of the Test Act!

The type of government: a relaxed absolutism

In this monarchical society, with its features of absolutism, it is useless to look for democracy; the people, as such, were satisfied with the type of government they had, and their voices could be heard (provided that they were respectful) through the regular channels of the hierarchy. Any assembly, however, that had not previously received the permission of the authorities was considered as being in the nature of a riot. It was the same with any delegation or any petition. Before taking any steps, approval of the authorities had to be obtained. A very simple principle was followed: every man spoke for himself; no one spoke for a group. The merchants, it is true, had received the privilege of designating officials (syndics) to speak on their behalf, but the election was carried out in the presence of the intendant and the fortunate person chosen then had to be approved by the authorities. Churchwardens were also elected, but they administered only the small worldly possessions of the church and the presbytery.

A completely hierarchical society would naturally assume that authority came from above. In France during the same period, men were generally convinced absolute monarchy remained the best form of government, so that absolute monarchy was accepted in New France as a necessary state of affairs. This explains the French-Canadians' early indifference towards parliamentary institutions. Members of the ruling class also exhibited strong dislike for such institutions.

This absolutism sometimes presented milder aspects. It was an absolutism of institutions and not of men. New France was, in fact, composed mainly of officials whose positions carried little security. Venality of office did not exist here, and neither did hereditary office. A civil or military position was obtained only by nomination and was subject to "the king's pleasure," even where someone succeeded his father. Taken individually, the governor general and the intendant appear all-powerful, but in fact, they were appointed subject to "the king's pleasure," and both positions lacked security (they possessed only a shared authority, one counterbalancing and keeping watch over the other). In certain matters, they made decisions as a result of common agreement. Throughout the hierarchy, there existed this insecurity of the subordinate with respect to his superior. Whatever position a man occupied, he was under a superior to whom he had to submit accurate reports. Institutions, then, much more than people, oppressed the individual.

The absolutism of this regime was lessened by paternalism. The king was sincerely convinced that he represented God on earth for the common good, and thus he did his best to reign as a "good father of the family." Such paternalism was exercised in many areas. For example, the king (that is, the State) was invested with the power that a father had over the marriages of his children. He could prevent a professional soldier from making an unsuitable marriage, or send orphan girls for whom he had accepted responsibility to New France where they would find husbands. This same paternalism existed in the seigneurial regime, when the State protected both the *seigneurs* and the *censitaires*, or when for example, it made the seigneur construct and maintain the essential flour mill. It existed, too, in the administration of justice since anyone could appeal to the intendant personally, or even to the king. Any appeal to the Conseil Supérieur was free of charge, the choice of an appropriate punishment being left to the discretion of the judge. Lastly, the husband, as the administrator of the common possessions, was subject to only one rule: that of acting as a "good father of the family." Paternalism was present everywhere in society, and like the insecurity of officials, it helped to reduce the severity of absolutism.

Bibliographical Note

Four important general studies describe the mechanism of government in New France:

W. J. ECCLES, *The Government of New France* (Ottawa, 1965), pamphlet No. 18 of the Canadian Historical Society.

G. FRÉGAULT, "Politique et politiciens au début du XVIIIᵉ siècle," in Vol. XI of the *Écrits du Canada français* pp. 91-208.

G. LANCTÔT, *L'Administration de la Nouvelle-France. L'administration générale.* Paris, Champion, 1929.

R. LA ROQUE DE ROQUEBRUNE, "La Direction de la Nouvelle-France par le Ministère de la Marine," in the *Revue d'histoire de l'Amérique française*, VI, 4 (March 1963), pp. 470-488.

The following two studies deal with particular problems:

H. M. THOMAS, "The Relations of Governor and Intendant in the Old Regime," in *Canadian Historical Review*, XVI, 1 (March 1935), pp. 27-40.

A. G. REID, "Representative Assemblies in New France," *Ibid.* XXVII, 1 (March 1946), pp. 19-26.

CHAPTER IV

Military organization

Seen from the outside, New France must have resembled a military camp. The governor general was normally a professional soldier, and one of his duties was to command the colony's troops. The regional governors and their assistants were also soldiers, and their military general staff acted as a council. A captain of militia in every parish represented the governor and the intendant, and the entire male population was divided into companies of militia. (The censuses of the eighteenth century were made in order to replenish this militia.) Trading posts also served as defence posts. Lastly, once the nobility had become unattainable, the only important honour within reach was the *Croix de Saint Louis* reserved exclusively for soldiers.

The military high command

The supreme commander of all the different troops in the country was the Governor General. He was responsible for defence and decisions concerning the campaigns to be undertaken and the strategy to be followed. He also nominated the officers of militia. Although he was in charge of promotions, he had no power to nominate the officers of the regular troops.

His general staff, which acted as his military council, was composed of the general staffs of the three governments. Each of these included the regional governor, the king's lieutenant, a major, and a major's aide. In addition, there was a major-general inspector of troops, and an engineer-in-chief, who was in charge of fortifications.

This military high command directed the regular troops and the militia. New France did not possess a navy, and neither did the English colonies.

Regular troops

Among the regular troops composed of professional soldiers, we must make a distinction between the troops who were here for only a certain time and the permanent troops.

a) *Temporary troops*

Before 1663, the companies who were landowners and held the trade monopoly had maintained the minimum number of soldiers necessary to keep order. If the colonists had

Public Archives of Canada

**Officer of the
Carignan-Salières Regiment**
(from a sketch by H. Beau)

**Officer of the Berry
Regiment, 1757**
(from a sketch by H. Beau)

Militiaman going to fight
(reproduced from
Bacqueville de la Potherie's
*Histoire de l'Amérique
septentrionale,* 1722 edition)

not taken over the defence of the country themselves, they would have been completely unprotected against the enemy.

It was not until 1665 that the first body of troops—the *Carignan-Salières* regiment—arrived, the only complete regiment to come to Canada during the French regime. It was composed of twenty companies of fifty men each and their superior officers. The men wore grey and brown uniforms with black hats on their powdered hair. The officers carried pistols and swords, while the men carried matchlocks, armed with bayonets. This regiment stayed only a short time in the colony, and it re-embarked in 1667 and in 1668, leaving behind about four hundred men as colonists.

The only temporary troops that New France received were those that came in the very last years, after 1755. These were *Troupes de Terre,* under the authority of the War Department. In France, in 1750, these Troupes de Terre formed an infantry of eighty-two regiments and a cavalry also divided into regiments. From these effective forces, France sent only three groups of infantry troops, which were always limited to battalions or to sections of regiments, and no cavalry contingents.* In 1755, the first group arrived under

*In theory, a company included fifty men. There were thirteen companies to a battalion and two, three, or four
  battalions normally formed a regiment.

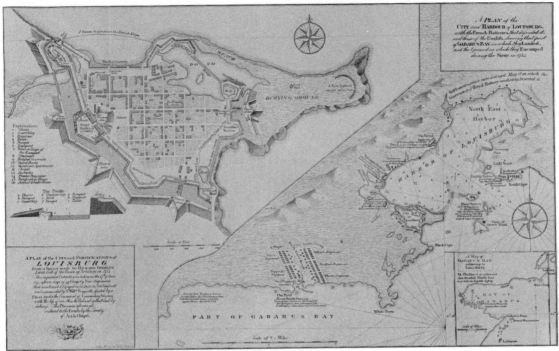

The fortress of Louisbourg   *Public Archives of Canada*

the command of Dieskau, comprising battalions from the regiments of *Guyenne, La Reine, Béarn, Languedoc, Bourgogne, Artois,* and *Cambrésis.* In 1756, under the command of Montcalm and Lévis, battalions from the regiments. of *La Sarre* and *Royal-Roussillon* came. Lastly, in 1757, there was a battalion from the *Berry* regiment.

These temporary troops, arriving between 1755 and 1757, re-embarked for France after the capitulation of 1760.

b) *Permanent troops*

Between the return to France of the Carignan-Salières regiment and the arrival of the first Troupes de Terre, France sent out some other regular troops, who this time settled permanently in the country. They were the *Troupes de la Marine*, infantry troops under the authority of the Navy Department.

The first contingent, composed of three companies, arrived in 1683. By 1688, these Troupes de la Marine numbered thirty companies. The reform of 1690, and particularly the special regulations adopted for Canada in 1695 (replacements were to be made from among the colonists), gave this army a Canadian character, and they were soon referred to only as the *Troupes de la Colonie.*

By 1757, these troops included forty companies of infantry, with sixty-five men each, and two companies of gunner-grenadiers, with fifty men each. In a land where horses were so numerous that the intendant had to limit the breeding of them, there was no cavalry until the very end of the French regime (June 1759). This was formed with two hundred men from the militia, and lasted for one year.

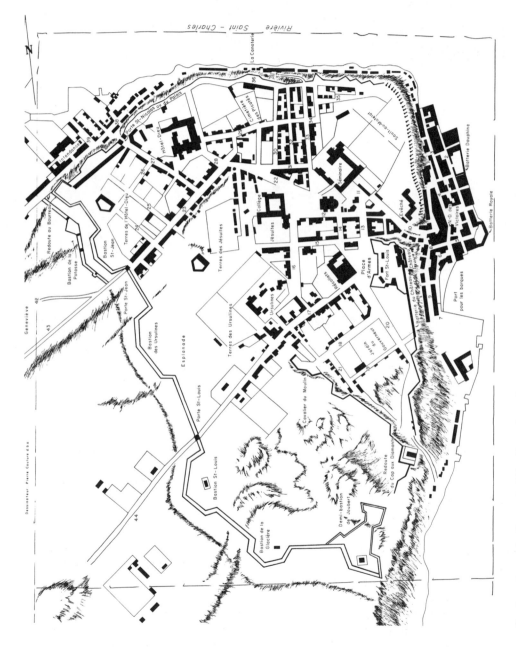

Quebec, towards the end of the French regime
(drawn by Marcel Trudel, based on contemporary maps)

Among the men in an infantry company, one would normally find a captain (who commanded the company), a lieutenant, an active ensign (as opposed to the discharged or retired ensign), two *cadets a l'aiguillette* (young gentlemen in training, until they were made officers), two sergeants (who had just abandoned the halberd for the musket), three corporals, three lance corporals (called *anspessades* in the seventeenth century), one or two drummers, a fifer, and lastly, the soldiers. It should be observed that when the officers of a company are mentioned, this term refers to those who were above the rank of sergeant.

The regular soldiers were dressed, armed, fed, lodged, and paid by the State. Where there were no barracks, they were billeted with the local residents by means of *billets de logement*, and the people were reimbursed for the food that they supplied. These troops, who were under the authority of the general staff of the Government in which they were stationed, were scattered across the country. They were administered by the *Commissaire de la Marine* (naval commissary), who was, as well, the intendant's sub-delegate in Montreal, and by a *Contrôleur de la Marine* who looked after military storehouses, assisted by a chief clerk, storehouse-keepers, and regular clerks and employees.

A staff-surgeon, accompanied by *fraters* or surgeon's boys (one per company), was responsible for the surgery and care of the wounded. When they were sick or wounded, the soldiers could be hospitalized (in return for their pay) in the Hôtel-Dieu of Quebec or Montreal, and in the hospital of the Ursulines at Trois-Rivières. The fate of the disabled soldiers was pitiful. Some were lucky enough to find shelter in the Hôpital-Général of Quebec or Montreal; others considered themselves very fortunate to receive a meagre half-pay. Those who got nothing had to be content with the honour of having served their country.

After 1692, the Récollets served as regular chaplains to the army and in the forts. (Jesuits became army chaplains only by chance.)

The militia

The militia was created to supply a need for defence, at a time when the country had no army. In 1651, Pierre Boucher in Trois-Rivières, and in 1663, Maisonneuve in Montreal brought the *habitants* together in a militia corps, but it was not until 1669 that Louis XIV commanded the Governor to organize a militia for the whole country.

The militia of the eighteenth century recruited all men from sixteen to sixty years of age who were capable of bearing arms. Commanded by the governor general and divided among the three Governments, the militia was centred around the parish. Each parish had at least one company of fifty to eighty men, while certain larger parishes had two or even three companies.

The parish leader was a captain of militia, who held a commission from the governor general. In addition to making sure that orders from the higher military and civil authorities were carried out (in this, he was placed above the seigneur), he had to supervise the training of the men and to command them during campaigns. His position allowed him to wear a sword and a high gold collar and to sit in a specially reserved pew in the church, a place of honour next to that of the seigneur.

The members of the militia had to go on campaign whenever they were required. Their service was not paid for, however long it might last, and in theory, they provided

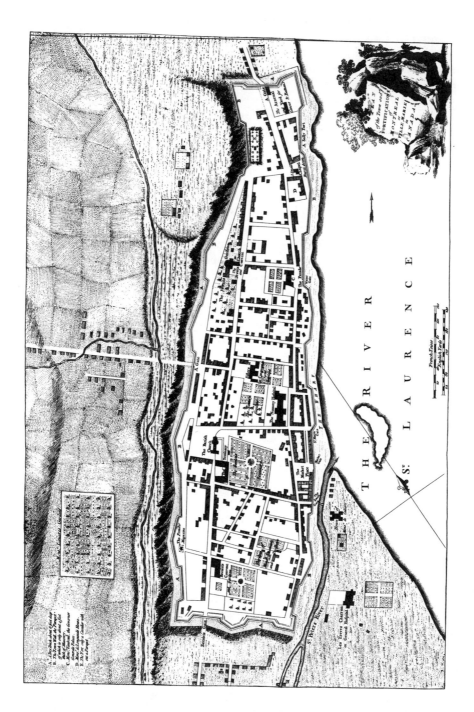

Fortifications of Montreal in 1760

their own weapons, clothing, and even food. Although they were very useful in skirmishes (like the English colonists, they were hunters through habit and necessity, and were excellent marksmen), the men of the militia were poor recruits for battles of the classical type. Since making war was not their career, they were despised by the "regulars" and were assigned mainly to the unpleasant task of transportation. They had no interest in carrying on long campaigns, and they deserted in a body during the course of the Seven Years' War, to go home and take care of the harvest.

During the military regime, the militia rose from this subordinate position to take, temporarily, a role of the first importance. Because the authorities wished the English troops to have as little contact as possible with the people, it was the militia that then constituted the new forces of order. The militia officers even took the place of judges in the royal tribunals of primary jurisdiction.

Fortifications

The military defence of New France rested upon a whole network of fortifications, which included three fortified towns and some forts, a few of which were capable of resisting a siege for a long time.

a) *Fortified towns*

The three fortified towns, Louisbourg, Quebec, and Montreal, met different fates. The first was completely razed after its capture. The second, in spite of repeated sieges and changes in society, kept its citadel and its ramparts. The third, which never underwent a siege, was demolished to create space.

The fortress of Louisbourg was founded immediately after the Treaty of Utrecht, in an area of Cape Breton known until that time by the name of *Havre-à-l'Anglais*. It was designed according to classical rules, with a moat, a rampart with protected gates, and bastions (the most important being the *bastion du Roi*). In addition, it was also a complete town, with the Château Saint-Louis, the hospital of the Brothers of Charity, the convent and school of the Sisters of the Congregation, a market, stores, and straight, well-made streets. This fortress, which was believed to be impregnable, was captured twice by the English. It was first captured in 1745, and then after being restored to France, in 1748, it was again invaded in 1758. It later served as a naval base for the invasion of 1759. During the year 1760, the English totally demolished the fort and transported the stones to Halifax.

Quebec had the benefits of natural defences because most of the town was situated on the heights of Cap-aux-Diamants. However, since the construction of the first fort in 1620, an attempt had been made to render its position more secure by setting up batteries at the weaker points and by placing cannons on the east side—the direction from which the enemy was expected to attack. Nevertheless, Quebec was still not enclosed on the west side in 1685. At the end of the seventeenth century, regular fortification in the style of Vauban was undertaken. In 1720, at the suggestion of the engineer Chaussegros de Léry, a new plan was adopted, but it was not completely carried out until about 1749. This plan saw the addition of a rampart on the west side, which gave strong protection to the town from north to south. It was built with bastions, curtain walls, and gates, and was

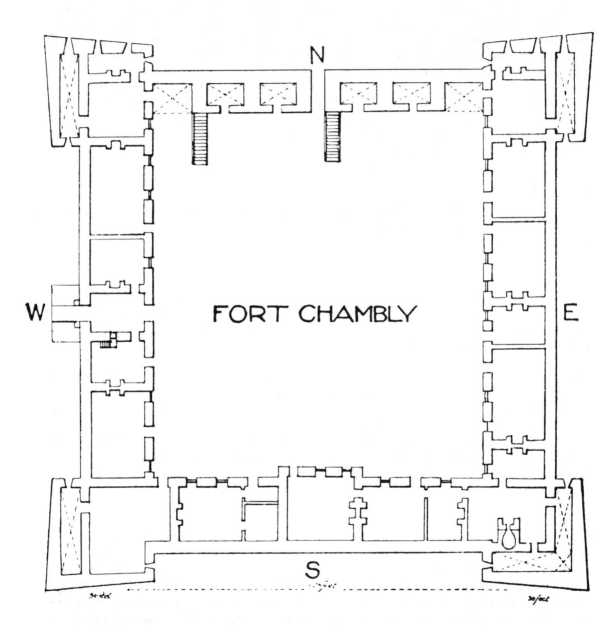

Plan of Fort Chambly
(from *Guide du fort Chambly*)

supported by redoubts and a cavalier. Quebec survived sieges in 1759, 1760, and later in 1775 and 1776. Between 1820 and 1832, it underwent a renovation of its system of defence. Then, at the end of the nineteenth century, some of its military gates were demolished and others remodelled in a discordant style, which completely altered the whole appearance of the fortifications.

Montreal, unlike Quebec, did not have the advantage of natural defences, but it was protected throughout the seventeenth century by a wooden stockade. In 1716, a rampart of stone was begun around the town but was only finished in 1741. To this rampart was added a battery constructed on a natural hillock fifty feet high, which did duty as a citadel. Montreal was never besieged, and consequently, it kept its fortifications intact; but at the beginning of the nineteenth century, the citadel was levelled in order to make use of the land, and the ramparts eventually disappeared.

The other towns of New France were unfortified. Until 1752, Trois-Rivières was surrounded by a wooden palisade, but when a fire destroyed this sole fortification, nobody bothered to restore it. Detroit relied on a small fort. New Orleans was defended only by a wet moat which, in any case, did not surround the town completely.

b) *Forts*

To supplement the natural barriers protecting the colony of the Saint Lawrence, it had been necessary to set up a long barrier of forts and posts against the English colonies. Among the most important of these were the Gaspareau and Beauséjour forts in mainland Acadia, which kept the English in the peninsula. The other important forts were forts Chambly, Saint-Jean, and Ile-aux-Noix, on the Richelieu, and forts Saint-Frédéric and Carillon, on Lake Champlain. On the route of the upper Saint Lawrence were forts La Présentation, Frontenac (at the end of Lake Ontario), Niagara (at the mouth of the river of the same name); on the Ohio, there was the Duquesne fortress, which was never completed through lack of time.

Certain of these forts (like Carillon, Niagara, Duquesne) were real fortresses. Care was taken to clear a wide surrounding area in order to prevent any surprise attack. Inside the garrison, there was considerable space. There were officers' quarters (many officers had had their wives and children with them), a chapel, wells, kitchens, a bakery, a forge, and stores, so that the fortress was self-sufficient in time of siege.

The Croix de Saint Louis

At the end of the seventeenth century, when the King no longer allowed Canadians to become nobles, only one important honour remained: the *Ordre royal et militaire de Saint Louis*. Founded in 1693, and divided into eight *grand-croix*, twenty-four commanders, and an unlimited number of *chevaliers*, it was the only military order in which New France had the honour of taking part. Its insignia was a golden cross with eight points, enamelled in white, and edged with golden fleur-de-lis. The *grand-croix* and commanders wore this insignia on a sash; *chevaliers* wore it on the chest attached to a small red ribbon. When the owner died, it had to be returned to the king.

To obtain this decoration one had to be an officer in the regular army (which immediately eliminated the entire militia and the other ranks), and one could serve no prince other than the King of France, except in cases of written authorization.

Public Archives of Canada

The Croix de Saint Louis

The first person to receive this decoration in Canada was Callières, in 1694. On this occasion, Frontenac, who was constantly being reprimanded by the King, could not conceal his displeasure. He received the honour only in 1697. The first Canadian *chevalier* was Iberville, in 1699. From 1693 to 1760, some 145 men were decorated in Canada. After the Conquest, about a dozen of these *chevaliers de Saint Louis* remained in the country, despite the wishes of Haldimand. He quite rightly mistrusted these soldiers whose decoration prevented them from taking the oath of allegiance to the English. Finally, an understanding permitted them to take the oath in 1767, and six of them became members of the Council of 1775.

In France itself, the *Croix de Saint Louis* rapidly lost its value because it was too easily obtained (from 1814 to 1830, 12,180 of these decorations were given out), but in Canada, this decoration retained its glory and prestige for a long time, precisely because it was rare. One may still hear the common people, although they know nothing about the history of this medal, say about someone who is not very highly regarded or at any rate is not worthy of much respect: «*Ce n'est pas une croix de Saint Louis.*» ("He's no Cross of St. Louis"), just as one might say: «*Ce n'est pas la tête à Papineau*» ("He's certainly no Papineau").

Bibliographical Note

Two important studies describe the military organization of New France:

G. LANCTÔT, "Les Troupes de la Nouvelle-France," in the report of the *Canadian Historical Association* for the year 1926, pp. 40-60.

G. MALCHELOSSE, "Milice et troupes de la Marine," in the *Cahiers des Dix*, XIV, 1949, pp. 115-147.

On the officers of the militia, a lengthy list has been published.

C. DE BONNAULT, "Le Canada militaire. État provisoire des officiers de milice, de 1641 a 1760," in the *Rapport de l'Archiviste de la province de Québec, 1949-1951*, pp. 261-527.

On the *chevaliers de Saint Louis*, see

A. FAUTEUX, *Les Chevaliers de Saint Louis en Canada*. Montréal, les Dix, 1940.

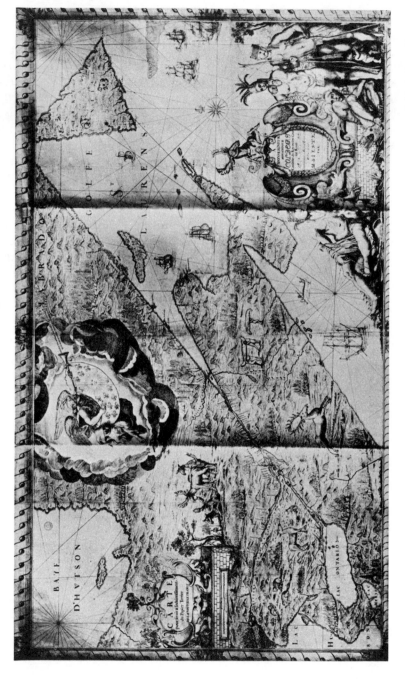

Public Archives of Canada

The Saint Lawrence and the Northeast
(map by Franquelin, 1678)
In this map stylized so that it could be used as a register of landed property, Franquelin wanted to show how the general orientation of the river brought about the orientation of the seigneurial frontage.

CHAPTER V

The seigneurial system

After a long succession of vain attempts, it was finally realized that the surplus population of France would not, of its own accord, emigrate to New France. Something had to be done to stimulate this immigration as well as provide newcomers with at least the bare necessities. Arrangements had to be made to prevent a haphazard distribution of the land and to get the large landowners to settle as many people as possible on their domains.

The arrangement selected was the seigneurial system. This system can be defined by the way in which it was applied. The entrepreneurs, who were called *seigneurs*, were granted tracts of land of varying sizes on which they had to establish settlers. Reciprocal rights and duties were specified in advance, and their performance was closely supervised by the State.

A country divided into narrow rectangles

There were seigneuries almost everywhere in New France, but the only area where a methodical and lasting record of the seigneurial system can be found is in Canada, that is, in the region of the Saint Lawrence. It is this region alone that we will have in mind as the seigneurial system is examined.

Two factors had to be taken into consideration. First, in a country completely dependent on the river, settlement should not be limited to the river banks; secondly, the shape of the seigneuries was never to be left simply to chance. The river flowing towards the northeast, through a large valley, provided a natural dividing line. But, since the river was the only means of communication between different points in the country, all the landowners had to have access to it. Therefore, the seigneuries could only have limited frontage on the river. However, they were allowed to extend far inland. (This arrangement was to encourage penetration into the interior of the country.) Two parallel lines were drawn northwest to southeast (that is, at right angles to the frontage along the Saint Lawrence, which flows from the southwest to the northeast). In this manner, a seigneurial area was divided into long, narrow rectangles that ran in a northwest and southeast direction along the river valley.

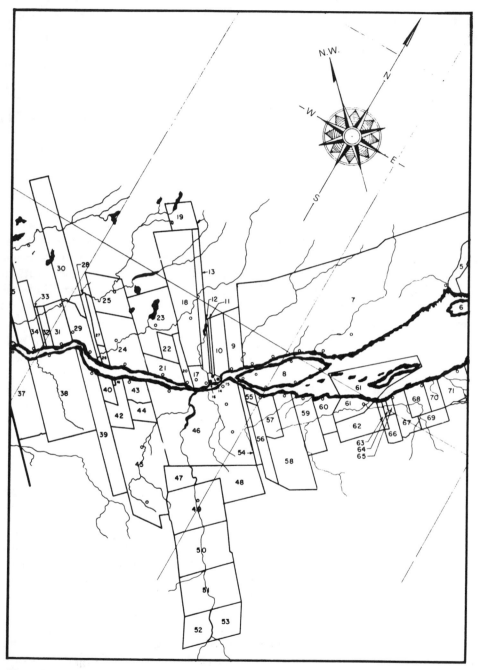

Plan of the seigneuries in the Government of Quebec
The seigneuries trend in a northwest southeast direction.

There were many exceptions to this pattern, almost always the result of physical geography. Large islands escaped this geometrical plan and the Ottawa River, the Richelieu River, and Lake Champlain introduced a different orientation. Many exceptions were also found beyond the seigneuries, on the riverbanks. Nevertheless, the fact remains that the seigneurial area of the Saint Lawrence has, in general, kept the appearance of a mosaic composed of narrow rectangles orientated in the direction northwest to southeast. The counties (political divisions) were created in 1791, on the basis of the seigneurial borders. A simple glance at a map of the present-day province of Quebec enables one to rediscover—for example, in the region of Joliette or in the Bas-du-fleuve—the broad, geometrical plan of the seigneurial regime.

Inside the seigneury

This plan is found again, on a more modest scale, within the seigneury. The seigneury was also subdivided into rectangular lots, much longer than they were wide. This division was done to obtain uniformity and because it was important for the first settlers to have frontage on the waterway. Although at first sight the Saint Lawrence valley appears like a mosaic of long parallel rectangles, a closer examination shows it to be composed of a vast number of narrow, parallel rectangles having the same northwest to southeast orientation as the whole of the seigneurial area.

The most important part of a typical seigneury, from the hierarchical point of view, was the personal domain of the seigneur, a piece of land that he was not obliged to grant. Its size varied from one seigneury to another. For example, the seigneur of Port-Joly, who possessed a fief of 168 *arpents* of frontage by 2 leagues deep, reserved for himself a personal domain of 12 *arpents* by 2 leagues.

Normally, we also find some land called the *terre de la Fabrique*, not far from the manor, which the seigneur reserved for a church and a presbytery, and for the support of the curé. In many seigneuries, the seigneur granted common land as grazing land for the *habitants'* animals. The long and narrow grants of land, which followed the orientation of the seigneury, generally measured 3 *arpents* of frontage by 30 deep. These were grouped in rows, the first row having the land directly on the riverbank. The remaining land had to be left untouched until the seigneur granted it.

In theory, there was no village in the seigneury. (The village must not be confused with the parish.) To allow the *habitants* to occupy as much land as possible, the State forbade the construction of buildings on an area of land that measured less than 1½ *arpents* by 30. It is possible that these restrictions limited the development of village life. Seigneurial society, nevertheless, needed a village community where the tradesmen necessary for material progress could settle. In the seventeenth century, with the full sanction of the authorities, there appeared five or six villages and a few hamlets. After 1745, ordinances from the intendant sanctioned and regulated the formation of new villages.

The duties of the seigneur

The State relied on entrepreneurs to settle the country, and when granting a large portion of land, it put the seigneur under certain precise obligations. The owner was

Extract from a map by Gédéon de Catalogne, 1709
In the area of Île d'Orléans, the arrangement of the seigneuries appears not to vary at all.

Archives de la province de Québec

accountable to the State for his fief, and as soon as he took possession, he had to perform an act of fealty and homage before the intendant in the governor's château. This ceremony, although originating in feudalism, was merely a solemn occasion to allow the seigneur to affirm his desire to carry out his duties. Furthermore, upon request by the intendant, the seigneur had to submit an *aveu et dénombrement*, which was a description of the condition of the seigneury, with the sums that were received from the tenants. Oak wood was reserved for the King (for the construction of ships), as well as mines and ore, because the subsoil or substratum was still the property of the State. The seigneur only possessed the ground. Lastly, the purchaser of a seigneury had to pay to the State *le droit de quint*, that is, a tax equivalent to the fifth part of the value of the fief. This tax was intended to discourage the selling of fiefs.

The seigneur also had duties towards the tenants in his seigneury. He had to own a *manoir habité* (settled manor), for it was here and nowhere else that the settlers had to pay their *cens* and *rentes*. An essential duty was the granting of land. It was on this fundamental condition that the seigneury had been granted. The seigneur was obliged to grant sufficient land to every settler whom he recruited or who presented himself. This grant, attested by a *billet de concession* (certificate of cession) was at first only provisional. When the settler proved that he was serious in his plans to take up residence, he obtained from the seigneur a *contrat de concession* (cession contract) signed in the presence of a notary. If the seigneur neglected this duty of granting land, the intendant could replace him, or even add the fief to the King's Domain, which left the seigneur exactly where he started (this happened in eighteen seigneuries in 1741). The seigneur was also required to construct and maintain a communal flour mill, where the *censitaires* of the seigneury ground their wheat. When the seigneur had the right to administer justice, he had to assume the expenses of a seigneurial court. In the eighteenth century, the State reserved major cases for itself, and the seigneurial magistrates were left only the minor cases (those referred to as *moyenne* and *basse justice*). Finally, in addition to these duties, the seigneur had to contribute taxes for the upkeep of the church and presbytery (like everyone else), and to take part in the forced labour (*corvée*) on the highways.

The privileges of the seigneur

The seigneur was well compensated for these duties by rights conferring both honour and responsibility. «*A tout seigneur, tout honneur*» ("To every seigneur, every honour"). Since the people met together regularly only for religious ceremonies, it was in religious assemblies, that is, in church, that the seigneur received most of the honours due to him: a free pew in the position of honour; prayers during the sermon for himself and his family; precedence over the people in ceremonies; and burial beneath the seigneurial pew. The seigneur's civil rights included the collection of *cens* (the source of the name *censitaires* given to the inhabitants of the seigneury). This nominal tax, of little value (two, four, or six *sols* per year for an entire holding), was a symbolic payment by which the *censitaire* acknowledged his dependence on the seigneur. If the seigneur had granted secondary fiefs in his seigneury (a rare action), he received fealty and homage from their owners. A traditional event was the planting of the maypole (a fir tree that had been stripped of its branches) in front of the manor on the first of May.

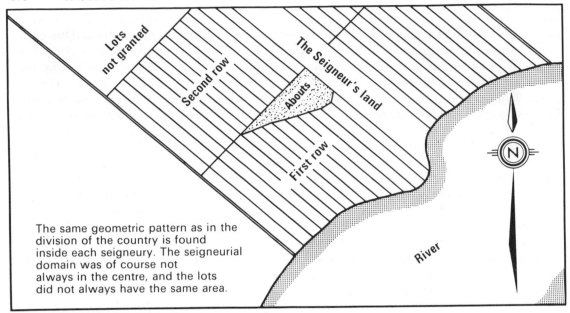

The same geometric pattern as in the division of the country is found inside each seigneury. The seigneurial domain was of course not always in the centre, and the lots did not always have the same area.

The theoretical subdivision of a seigneury

These honours were important for the dignity of the seigneur, but it was the onerous and profitable rights that guaranteed the owner of the fief the income he needed to fulfil his role and lead the kind of life that befitted his rank.

In the first place, he collected rents. The amount was definitely fixed in the cession contract. They were usually estimated as being twenty *sols* per *arpent* of frontage, so that a lot with three *arpents* of frontage produced an annual rent of sixty *sols* or three *livres*. The seigneur also had the right of *lods et ventes*, a tax which had to be paid by the purchaser of land already granted (it was normally the twelfth part of the value of the land). He had the *droit de retrait* (when a *censitaire* sold land at too low a price or when the buyer offered no genuine guarantee). In this case, the seigneur paid the sale price and kept the land. The *droit de mouture* related to the fourteenth measure of grain the *censitaire* had to leave when he ground his grain at the common mill. The *droit de pêche* was a portion of the fish caught along the frontage of the seigneury (either the twentieth or the eleventh fish). There was also the *redevance de commune* (rent on the common land) which, at Boucherville, was seven *livres* per annum. The *droit de coupe de bois* permitted the seigneur to gather wood on the land of his *censitaires*. The *droit de corvée* (right to forced labour) consisted of a number of statutory days (three per annum, rarely four) determined in the cession contract. Finally, with the permission of the intendant, the seigneur could take back land already granted when the copyholder did not fulfil his obligations.

The censitaire's rights and privileges

When the State granted rights to the seigneur and imposed duties upon him, it followed that his duties towards the *censitaires* became rights for the latter: such rights as the *manoir habité*, the obtaining of land, the use of the flour mill, justice of primary jurisdiction within the fief, and the help of the seigneur in public contributions.

Archives de la province de Québec

Livingroom of the seigneurial manor belonging to the Sulpicians

In his turn, the *censitaire* had to fulfil the duties he owed to the seigneur. Thus, he was obliged to remain resident on his land, to go to the manor and pay his dues, to produce his papers when these were required, to clear the land as necessary, and to pay *lods et ventes* on land he had bought. (As mentioned before, his land could be confiscated if he failed to fulfil his obligations.)

The seigneurial system was not feudal

The seigneurial system practised in New France was a modified version of the seigneurial system that had existed in France since feudal times and that still maintained its heavy traditional obligations. Admittedly, the Canadian seigneurial system, like that of France, preserved some feudal ceremonies (such as the act of fealty and homage), and particularly, a good part of its vocabulary; but under this system, the seigneur was nothing like a feudal seigneur.

In transplanting this system to New France, the State was careful to do away with some of the requirements which, from time immemorial, had demonstrated the power of the feudal lord over the peasant. Certain rights were also removed that would have made the *censitaire* destitute in America. The *droit de chasse* (hunting rights), which in France were reserved for the seigneurs and were denied to the peasants, did not apply in New France. The *banalité du four* (common oven) and the *droit de fouage* (hearth-tax, or right of the seigneur over the peasant's hearth) were absent. Other rights missing were the *champart*, collected by the seigneur on the number of sheaves, and the arbitrary *corvées*, which the seigneur could require from those who resided on the land of the seigneury without being *censitaires*. Even the *droit de coupe de bois* (right to cut wood), which was applied here in the seventeenth century, was considered odious, and the intendant did all he could to restrict it.

The general terms of the system demonstrate how far removed it was from feudalism. A man might become owner of a fief and be given the title of seigneur; but this man, in fact, was no more than a state official. He was guaranteed certain definite privileges that he used, under the intendant's supervision. Duties towards the State and his *censitaires* were imposed on him, and he was not free to neglect them. His relationship with his *censitaires* was determined in a contract drawn up by a notary. Nowhere could he be both judge and party to the case. He came under the law and the intervention of the State as much as any *censitaire*. The seigneur was in the same position as his tenants in the matter of common taxes. Appearances must not lead us into error: the society was not a feudal one.

A fairer distribution of the land

In a new world, it can be easy for powerful men to seize all the land. In the beginning, New France did not entirely escape this danger. Before the seigneurial regime took on its definitive form, members of the Compagnie des Cent-Associés were granted enormous estates but did not develop them. Most of these vast seigneuries soon fell into disuse, and in 1663, the King took back his ownership of them.

Some of these very large seigneuries that the owners had not neglected still remained: Côte de Beaupré, Montreal Island, Batiscan, and Cap-de-la-Madeleine

Archives de la province de Québec

Bedroom in the seigneurial manor belonging to the Sulpicians

(the latter two penetrated as much as twenty leagues inland). After 1695, Louis XIV forbade huge grants. In contrast to the immensity of the Laurentian territory, the seigneuries very often covered a rather small area (numerous seigneuries covered two, four, or six leagues). Consequently, the settling of the valley was entrusted to a larger number of entrepreneurs.

There was also the possible danger that the seigneuries would pass into the hands of a single group of men or institutions. In the beginning, the State—which left education and hospitalization to the religious communities—had generously distributed seigneuries and land to them to enable them to fulfil their role in society. The Jesuits held 11.2 percent of these seigneuries, and the bishop and Seminary of Quebec held 8.7 percent. At the end of the seventeenth century, the Church, including the religious communities, already possessed one quarter of all seigneurial lands, and to make things easier, these had been carved out of the best parts. However, in the eighteenth century, the State forbade any further distribution of the land to religious communities. When they needed land, they had to buy it, and their lands no longer fell into mortmain.

During the eighteenth century, the period when other institutions were becoming firmly established, the seigneurial system was putting right the errors of the founding period. New seigneurs received domains corresponding to their capacity to develop them, and laymen were favoured in proportion to their numbers and the progress they made.

How the seigneurial domains increased

By the end of the French regime, the seigneurial domains occupied an area that corresponded to the limit of its expansion. Along the north bank of the river, from La Malbaie as far as the Vaudreuil-Soulanges peninsula, and on the south bank, from Beauharnois to Pointe-au-Père, the seigneuries stretched without a break. Inland, the valleys of the Beauce, the Richelieu River, and Lake Champlain were also covered with seigneuries.

It had taken more than a century to reach this point. At first, from 1623 to 1653, about forty seigneuries appeared around the small centres of Quebec, Trois-Rivières, and Montreal; from 1653 to 1663, less than ten had been granted because of the low rate of immigration. The Iroquois wars had also prevented any further expansion. The reorganization of 1663 saw new progress in seigneurial expansion. In 1672, the largest number of grants (forty-six) was made. Ten of these grants were on the Richelieu, where the veterans of the Carignan-Salières regiment finally blocked the Iroquois invasion route.

The seigneurial area continued to expand. The occupation of the riverbanks was completed, and a second row of seigneuries was begun behind the land grants on the riverside. From 1673 to 1732, the State gave ninety grants, and between 1732 and 1739, it gave twenty-eight. During this period, men were moving into the Beauce and the Lake Champlain region. However, in spite of a very sharp increase in immigration (the rate reached its highest point for the whole of the French regime), the last twenty years did not see an extension of the seigneurial domains. The concession of a score of seigneuries was cancelled because the owners had neglected them, and the last grants made by the State numbered only about twenty.

A limited success for the seigneurial system

The seigneurial system made sure that the riverbanks became occupied. This gave the traveller the illusion of going past an endless village. But, behind the banks, there was generally a huge wilderness known only to Amerindian hunters. Important routes to the interior were still unoccupied by Europeans: the Saguenay River, the Saint-Maurice, Saint-François and Yamaska rivers, and the Ottawa River. There was no settlement on the shores of Lake Champlain. This was not necessarily the fault of the seigneurial system. The Ottawa valley could have been settled rapidly, if the State had not forbidden it through fear that on this great route the colonists would become traders rather than farmers.

The seigneurs were relied on as the vehicle of settlement, but the seigneurial system itself did not bring in immigrants. At the very most, it could guarantee that immigrants would be established when they arrived, but agriculture, industry, and trade did not attract great numbers of them. It is very significant that, during the period when New France was receiving its highest immigration (1740-1760), the seigneurial domain was not expanding to any great extent.

Archives de la province de Québec

The manor of a small country seigneur: Aubert de Gaspé

A system of mutual social aid

The seigneurial regime may be termed "mutual social aid raised to the dignity of a system." This help was essential, at least in the beginning, in a new country isolated from Europe for six months of the year. To the colonist who wished to cross to New France, the seigneur guaranteed passage and keep during the arrival period, and the seigneur gave him a certain amount of land. The new *censitaire* settled in surroundings that had been organized for him. He lived close to a settled manor (*manoir habité*) with a flour mill in operation. The church had been provided with land, and someone had built the necessary roads in the seigneury. Sometimes pasture land was reserved for the common use of the settlers. In return, the *censitaire* had to contribute to the support of the seigneur with rents and some days of service. He also contributed to the maintenance of the common mill and to the supplies of the community. Both seigneur and *censitaire* had to share certain duties, such as the repair or construction of the church and presbytery, and the upkeep of the highways. Thus, in the difficult period of colonization, the immigrant came, not to try his luck in the wilderness, but to become part of a previously organized society that took care of his immediate needs, a society that he, in his turn, maintained by his contribution.

However, it is interesting to note, no doubt due to the absence of a village grouped around the manor, that it was not the residence of the seigneur that became the centre of social life. It was the church that filled this role. The society thus formed was much more typical of a parish than of a seigneurial society.

A world closed to the outside

As the country became settled, these conditions of mutual social aid became less and less necessary. The system gradually became an obstacle to progress because of its closed-off economy.

The settler remained in a state of complete dependence on the seigneur, for the settler held his land from him and continued to pay rents. The exchange of land was controlled by the seigneur through the *lods et ventes* and the *droit de retrait*. He owned everything that brought in a good income; he alone could possess a flour mill, which all *censitaires* had to use; the fishing rights belonged to him; and since he also owned the important streams, the seigneur was, in fact, the only one to possess a sawmill. The settlers were under such pressure from the seigneur, who owned the flour mill, and the curé, because of the tithe, that they could hardly grow anything other than wheat. The seigneur himself, because rights were exclusive to each seigneury, remained isolated from economic development. The seigneurial regime closed the door to any sizeable enterprise that would reach outside the limits of the seigneury.

This system ended by producing, on the one hand a society composed of seigneurs who had been left far behind by the rapid economic development of the eighteenth and nineteenth centuries, and on the other hand, *censitaires* who by tradition completely lacked the spirit of initiative that was found among the colonists in the English system of tenure. Lord Durham wrote that the *censitaires* had been provided with material comforts, far beyond their former means, and that because of the bounty lavished upon them by the land they had made no further progress beyond the initial occupation. Besides, this system, which impeded the mobility of property, could not help an economy of the capitalist type. Because this system did not provide for a village, agricultural development was less efficient.

The French Canadians, stifled in overpopulated seigneuries, nevertheless refused to go and settle in "townships" during the first third of the nineteenth century. An inquiry in 1821 proved they did not find there the advantages of the seigneurial system to which they were accustomed.

However, since the parish could not exclude foreign immigrants, it seems to have been the seigneurial system that helped preserve the distinct French-Canadian character of the population during the English regime by forming a closed, interdependent society. Despite the continual stream of foreign immigrants, French Canadians preserved their integrity.

The slow disappearance of the system

Although it provided a fortunate solution to the problems the colony had to face at the beginning, the seigneurial system was soon outdated. The careful watch that the intendant had kept over it ceased with the Conquest. Basing their claims on the increased value of the land, the seigneurs demanded more than was provided for in the old contracts. They granted the small amount of remaining land at excessively high rates. Sometimes, they refused to part with it at all. They forgot their duties and thought only of their rights. However, it was not these exorbitant demands—although they were fairly numerous—that brought about the end of the seigneurial system, it was the fact that this system no longer suited a society that had left the first stage of colonization behind. But it was even less suited to an economic life based increasingly on industry.

On December 18, 1854, the Parliament of a United Canada finally abolished the titles of *seigneur* and *censitaire*, and thus brought the seigneurial system to an end.

The abolition of the system was carried out to the advantage of the owners of fiefs. The 242 seigneurs were generously compensated for the lucrative rights they had lost and were allowed to keep their personal domains and the ungranted land. The settlers, however, were obliged to buy their grants of land and pay the seigneurs for them.

Ignoring the settlers on fiefs in mortmain (fiefs belonging to religious communities), who were not able to buy their land back and who still continue to pay rent today, in 1854, the majority of the other *censitaires* were unable to buy their land back; they therefore continued to pay rent to the old seigneurial families until 1945. The Government of Quebec then decided that the money owing to the former seigneurs would be paid off by the municipalities and the settlers would now have to deal with them. In this way, relations between ex-seigneurs and *ex-censitaires* came to an end. But, even today, more than a century after the abolition of the system, when landowners go to pay their taxes to the town treasurer, the latter still writes on the official receipt: «*pour rentes seigneuriales.*»

Bibliographical Note

In the following pamphlet, I have published a somewhat more detailed description of the seigneurial system.

M. TRUDEL, *Le Régime seigneurial*. Ottawa, 1956, pamphlet no. 6 of the Canadian Historical Association; translated into English under the title *The Seigneurial Regime*. A complete bibliography will be found on page 20.

A recent work, although primarily of a geographic nature, provides much new insight for the study of the seigneurial regime.

R. C. HARRIS, *The Seigneurial System in Early Canada*. Madison and Quebec, 1966.

The following study will be useful too.

C. NISH, "La bourgeoisie et le système seigneurial," in *L'actualité économique*, (Oct.-Dec. 1967), pp. 507-535.

CHAPTER VI

Economic life

Champlain and Talon had dreamed of a New France in which every resource would be developed so that the country could provide for its own needs. They wanted a prosperous agriculture, a variety of industry, and "infallible" trade, but in the eighteenth century, these ideals were not even approached. Agriculture was poor in quality and only just provided the settlers with the basic necessities. The mother country only tolerated industries that were completely essential. In the matter of trade, New France was merely a place of transit for beaver fur.

Introduction

Before observing how trade, industry, and agriculture were carried on in the eighteenth century, we must examine the monetary system, the financial system, and internal communications.

a) *The monetary system*

The monetary system was based on the *livre*, which was a purely artificial unit since no coin with the face value of a *livre* existed. The *livre* was subdivided into *sols* and *deniers*, so that one *livre* was worth twenty *sols* and one *sol* was worth twelve *deniers*.

Sums of money were often expressed as follows: *5.8.9.* which meant *5 livres 8 sols 9 deniers*. Abbreviations were also used: $5^{ll}.8^s.9^d$. The abbreviation ^{ll} often looks like ^{lt}, but it definitely refers to *livres*. For long additions, they made use of counters arranged in a box with three compartments.

i. Coins: The same confusion as in weights and measures is found in the monetary system. There were various kinds of coins of French or foreign origin. *Deniers*, *liards* (worth three *deniers*), and *sols* were made of copper. *Sols marqués* were coins made of billon (an alloy of copper and silver) and worth more than twelve *deniers*. Silver coins included the *petit louis*, *petit écu*, or *écu blanc* (worth 3 *livres* 6 *sols*), *gros écu a couronne* (worth 6 *livres* 12 *sols*), and the *piastre espagnole*, or dollar. The *louis*, *pistole* and *guinée portugaise* were made of gold.

The écu worth 6 livres
(Marcel Trudel's collection)

In practice, it was necessary to consult a table of equivalence and use an assay balance in order to differentiate between many of these coins. Most of them were not stamped with the amount they were worth.

To calculate the contents of a cash box, the procedure was as follows.

	livres	sols	deniers
10 *portugaises*	480.	0.	0.
1 *louis d'or*	24.	0.	0.
1 *écu à couronne*	6.	12.	0.
2 *petits écus* @ 3.6.0.	6.	12.	0.
1 *sol marqué* 6 *liards*	0.	0.	18.
1 *sol*	0.	0.	12.
1 *pistole d'Espagne*	21.	10.	0.
	537.	34.	30.

The resulting total is 538 *livres*, 16 *sols*, 6 *deniers*.

Until 1717, a distinction was made between *argent de France* or *livres tournois* (minted at Tours) and *argent du Canada* or "local money." A statute explained this in the following way—*argent de France* was the money of Canada "lessened and reduced by the extra one quarter with which it had been inflated and given value in Canada." So, in 1690, the *louis d'or* was worth 11 *livres* 12 *sols* in France, but in Canada, 15 *livres* 9 *sols* 4 *deniers*. In 1717, the King fixed the two currencies at the same level, making an exception for longstanding debts and old contracts in which it was stated that repayment would be made in *monnaie du Canada*.

With the Conquest, the addition of the English monetary system further complicated matters. In Quebec, the English adopted the currency of Halifax; in Montreal, they used the currency of New York. From 1765 onwards, New York currency was accepted everywhere until it was replaced, in 1777, by the currency of Halifax and French coins began to disappear from circulation. One denomination, the *louis*, remained in use for a long time. Since the French *louis d'or* had the same value as the English "pound," the word *louis* was retained as a translation for "pound."

ii. Paper money: No coins were struck in New France. The administration counted on the arrival of cash in the *vaisseau du roi* (King's Ship) in order to pay civil servants, suppliers, soldiers, and clerks. There was confusion if the ship did not arrive until the end of the season, and even more if it did not come at all. In that case, the Government borrowed from the merchants.

Intendant Demeulle invented a type of paper money in 1685, with the purpose of meeting the expenses authorized by the King, but this measure was not intended to increase the amount of money in circulation. He printed various face values on playing cards and affixed his seal to them. In this way, he put into circulation a total of 39,000 *livres*. When the *vaisseau du roi* arrived, he redeemed this first "card money" in cash.

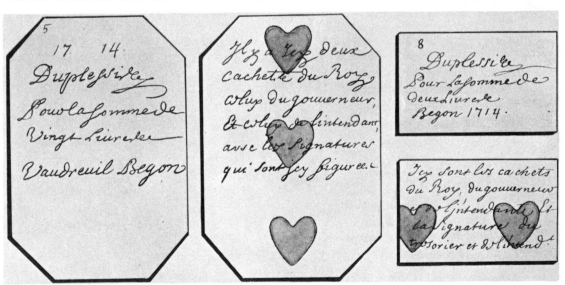

Card money from 1714
The intendant still had to resort to playing cards.

This system was brought to an end after 1686, but it was necessary, however, to return to these card games during the period 1689-1719. In 1714, card money to a value of two million *livres* was in circulation, some cards being worth as much as one hundred *livres*. The crash after the Treaty of Utrecht reduced their value by three quarters. The King later returned to using card money in 1729 because the merchants themselves demanded it.

Public Archives of Canada

Card money from the last period
The intendant used unprinted cards, which were cut according to a fixed value.

This time, the Government used white cards without colours, which were cut or had their corners removed according to a fixed table. The whole card was worth 24 *livres* (which was the highest sum in card money); with the corners cut off, it was worth 12 *livres*; with a quarter cut off, it was worth 6 *livres*; in this form, and with the corners cut off, it was worth 3 *livres*; the value of the half-card was worth 7 *sols* 6 *deniers*. Playing cards duly signed and sealed were also still in use.

It must not be forgotten that, in the eighteenth century, card money was not the most important form of paper money. There was the *certificat* (certificate), a certified sum given to the supplier by the storekeeper, which had the monetary value of the sum written on it. The *ordonnance* (order), a promissory note, was signed by the intendant on a printed form, and like cards and certificates, was redeemable by a *lettre de change* (bill of exchange) on the Naval Treasury and thus became a receipt for the Government. Finally, there was the *lettre de change*, or *traite* (draft), used between private citizens to avoid a cash transfer, which the State also used, particularly to redeem paper money. The disastrous liquidation of bills of exchange at the time of the Conquest, refers only to bills of exchange on the State.

A thorough inquiry during the military regime revealed that Canadians still held some 16,782,500 *livres* in paper money. Of this total, only 3.8 percent was in card money; 4.7 percent in certificates; 13.1 percent in bills of exchange on the State; the rest, 78.4 percent was in orders. Certain bills of exchange were redeemed in full, others at half their value, while all the other forms of currency were accepted in France at only one quarter of their value. This is the reason that, ten years later, the French Canadians did not want the paper money offered by the Congressional Army.

b) *Finances*

Between 1632 and 1645, the Cent-Associés assumed the costs of administration in New France. Afterwards they unloaded these costs on to the Communauté des Habitants, the new holders of the trade monopoly. In the eighteenth century, the State defrayed the cost of the administration by counting for part of it on the Compagnie des Indes Occidentales, which had the export monopoly on beaver fur.

It was part of the intendant's duty to send the "financial plan" for the next year by the fall ship. The Conseil de Marine discussed it the following spring, and then composed an *arrêt du roi* (royal decree), divided into various sections: administration and safety; justice and religion; public works and relief to the poor. Expenses were met by taking money from two sources. The first one was the royal treasury, *l'état du roi* (King's Return) that provided the greater part through the intermediary of the navy treasurer. The second source was the tax farming area of the Western Domain, to which was attached the Compagnie des Indes. The *état du Domaine* (Return of the Domain) accepted responsibility for certain expenses, which did not change very much from year to year: gratuities to the governors, emoluments for civil and legal officials, and subsidies to Church institutions. At about 1740 the total averaged 115,000 *livres* per year. This total was paid off in Canada from the income of the Domain so that the tax farmer did not have to send away any money, and those who were paid from the budget of the Domain did not suffer.

After the budget had been approved, the sum requested in the King's Return was sent in the form of cash to Canada, where the intendant distributed it to pay overdue accounts, or to redeem the paper money that he had had to give out while waiting for the *vaisseau du roi* to arrive.

In comparison to the cost incurred, Canada brought the intendant's treasury only a small income. In this land of colonization, where there was no *taille* (a tax on landed property and on income "from industry") revenue came from several sources. There were the customs duties on imports and exports, as well as the profits from the King's stores and the royal *censive* (lands belonging to the State, on which were paid rent and *lods et ventes*). The leasing of the Tadoussac trade (also called the *Postes du Roi*), and occasional taxes (certain fines, taxes collected on wrecks and on goods in escheat) also provided some income. In addition, there were special taxes, such as the one collected in Quebec for the upkeep of barracks, and in Montreal for the construction of ramparts. In 1740, for example, income was put down as 120,000 *livres*, but expenses mounted to 220,000 *livres* in that year. Most of the time, actual expenditure was greater than the sum called for in the King's Return. The intendant then carried the deficit forward to the next budget and satisfied creditors with bills of exchange, redeemable the following year or over a period of years.

During the war years, the budget was completely upset by very heavy military expenses and speculation, so that the deficit sometimes became very considerable.

In 1747, the deficit was 960,000 *livres* and during the following year it reached catastrophic proportions. In 1757, with a revenue of only 335,000 *livres*, an official budget was presented with expenditure amounting to 1,600,000 *livres*. The intendant, in fact, spent 19,270,000 *livres*, twelve times the original sum. The deficit continued to increase. By 1758, expenditure reached 28,000,000, and in 1759, it was 30,000,000.

Since the greater part of the funds from the royal treasury was used to purchase supplies for the army, the State became a very important and generous customer. A widespread system of extortion helped contractors to accumulate unheard-of fortunes at the expense of the public treasury. This war economy could only be temporary, but it lasted thirteen years and ended only at the Conquest. Canada always cost more than it yielded, but for some years, the costs were unbelievable. At the end of this period of frantic speculation, it is not surprising that the King had the chief officials of New France, including the intendant and the governor general, sent to the Bastille to be arraigned before a court of law.

c) *Internal communications*

Until the eighteenth century, the Saint Lawrence waterway was the only important route across Canada. From Quebec to Montreal, reefs, particularly in the region of Portneuf and Grondines, presented certain difficulties to navigation although there were no waterfalls. From Montreal three routes gave access to the interior: the Saint Lawrence, the Rivière des Prairies, and the Mille-Iles River. These all contained rapids, but a cart track made the portage easier from Montreal to Lachine. In 1700, utilizing the small Saint-Pierre River, the Sulpicians dug a canal 12 feet wide and 24 *arpents* long, at a cost of more than twenty thousand *livres*. But this canal at Lachine was abandoned when it was three-quarters finished. Solid rock was the cause of the standstill, and no further work was done on it during the French regime, despite attempts made by the engineer Chaussegros de Léry.

Various types of boats were used on this waterway. The fastest means of travel was the canoe, which made the voyage between Montreal and Quebec in three or four days. The sailing ship was the cheapest method of transportation, because it made use of the wind, but it was very slow, taking as long as two or three weeks to go downstream from Montreal to Quebec. The *barque* used both sails and oars (the oarsmen were called *nageurs de barque*) and made the voyage between Montreal and Quebec in just a few days. Lastly, for transporting heavy goods, there was the *cajeux*. This vessel was a raft made of pieces of wood tied together, to which a sail could be attached.

Land routes appeared during the last quarter of the seventeenth century. At first, there were only the seigneurial paths that ran alongside the river, between the farms of a single seigneury. Then, when a surveyor-in-chief was appointed, a small network of *chemins du roi* (royal roads) was developed in sections. A systematic effort was made, after 1706, to join together the seigneurial paths running along the north bank of the river, in order to build the *grand chemin du roi* (King's Highway: twenty-four feet wide) from Quebec to Montreal. This route was finished in the summer of 1737, and from then on, it was possible to go from one town to the other by carriage in four days. After 1733, the King's Highway was extended in various directions: on the south bank, towards

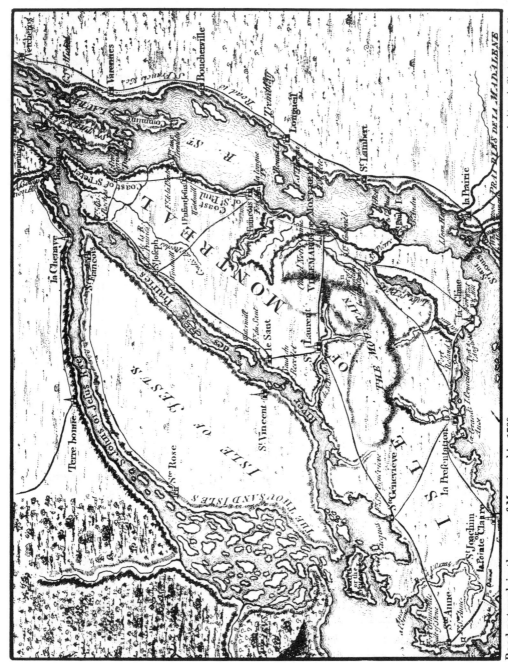

Road network in the area of Montreal in 1760
(from an English map)

Archives du Séminaire de Québec

Kamouraska; in the Montreal area, towards Île Jésus and Terrebonne; and from Laprairie, towards the Richelieu.

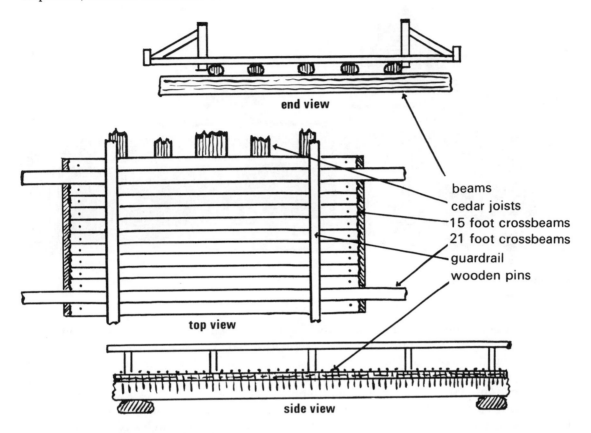

end view

beams
cedar joists
15 foot crossbeams
21 foot crossbeams
guardrail
wooden pins

top view

side view

The bridge, during the French regime

Bridges were 15 feet wide with a maximum length of about 40 feet. They were rarely used to span anything larger than a stream. A ferry service was considered sufficient wherever there was a sizeable river. This ferry service was a monopoly granted by the intendant, and the ferryman collected a passage fee according to a predetermined list of fares that allowed for both men and beasts. Along the north bank, for example, one had to rely on a ferry to cross such important rivers as Rivière des Prairies, the Saint-Maurice, Batiscan, La Pérade, and Jacques-Cartier, as well as streams that today seem unimportant (the Berthier and Maskinongé, Rivière du Loup [today the Louiseville], the Yamachiche and the Champlain, and even the little Cap-Rouge River).

A surveyor-in-chief appointed by the intendant headed the highways administration. He chose his own deputy chief surveyors, or local surveyors, to assist him in the towns. The local surveyor was in charge of the streets in the town. He had to see that the houses were aligned along the streets and that the streets were kept cleared according to the highway regulations.

Public Archives of Canada

Calèches
(from an engraving by Richard Short)

The construction and maintenance of the highways made no inroads into the State budget. Roads were built by public *corvées* directed by the captain of militia. Bridges were also built by *corvées*. The wood for this purpose was taken, without payment, from the nearest properties, because it was maintained that the owners of the nearby land got the most use out of these bridges. The maintenance of highways and streets was also carried out without cost to the State by means of *corvées*, if a good deal of work was required. Otherwise, every settler was obliged to take care of the section of highway that passed by his land or in front of his house in the town. In the seventeenth century, townspeople were even forced to pay for their section of the street. In the countryside, summer maintenance was limited to digging the necessary drainage ditches and to filling up holes. Winter maintenance became a little more complicated because each settler had to plant poles at intervals of 24 feet along the section of road that went past his land. These poles were to indicate the roadway, and after each snowfall, the settler walked his animals up and down to level it.

Speed limits for carriages were established everywhere. In the countryside, horses were not allowed to trot or to gallop within ten *arpents* of the church, while in town streets, they were not allowed "to gallop or trot fast."

A private cartage service existed, and after 1727, carters in the towns had to register with the intendant and put numbers on their carts. They had a predetermined price list for journeys and a specially elected official (syndic) who looked after their interests.

In 1721, an official postal service (a public stagecoach and cartage service) was introduced. The first holder of the concession was Lanouiller de Boiscler, the future surveyor-in-chief, who had to guarantee the transportation of travellers and letters

Public Archives of Canada

Cart
(from an engraving by Richard Short)

between Quebec and Montreal. Along the route, inns and hostelries served as stage-stops, while simple taverns displayed a sign or a picture of a green bush. Inns displayed signs without the bush. Innkeepers had to obtain permits from the intendant and keep a register of the persons to whom they gave lodging. The inn had a lower room, where drinks were served (but not after ten o'clock in the evening), and furnished rooms. Drinking, playing cards, or shooting craps was forbidden in the rooms. Where there were no inns, travellers lodged with the settlers at a price agreed to between them.

Trade

a) *The fur trade*

Fur was still by far the most important article of trade, and the trading company holding the export monopoly had its head office located in France.

Since 1612, New France had been controlled by a monopolist company. The Compagnie des Cent-Associés, owner of the country from 1627 to 1663, followed various small trading societies. This company was, in turn, replaced by the Compagnie des Indes Occidentales, after 1663. Monopolist companies no longer played any part in administration after 1674; they were simply concerned with the general monopoly on the trade and export of beaver fur. The State curtailed this monopoly in 1717, when trade in the interior of New France was opened to everyone. Of the trading companies appointed after 1674, the most powerful and the most stable was a new Compagnie des Indes Occidentales (1718 to 1760). This Company assumed the costs of administration, an amount totalling some 115,000 *livres* per annum, which included gratuities to the authorities. The governor general received 2 percent of the beaver fur exported (an annual average of 6,000 *livres*) and the governor of Montreal, one half of 1 percent (an average of 1,500 *livres*).

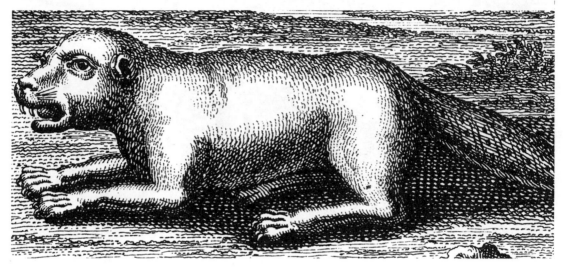

Public Archives of Canada

Beaver
(from de La Potherie's *Histoire de l'Amérique septentrionale*)

i. *Trade furs:* Trading was carried on in all the commercial furs—beaver, otter, marten, fox, mink, raccoon, muskrat, bear, deer, moose, wolf, and seal—but the fur most in demand and with a well-established market (the one that made the finest hats, muffs, and other articles of clothing) was beaver fur.

There are several kinds of beaver fur, graded according to the quality of the skin and the season in which the beaver is killed. Two kinds were usually distinguished: *castor sec* and *castor gras*. *Castor sec* (dry beaver) was fur "as it came from the animal" with only the flesh removed. The Company rejected the *castor sec* taken in the summer and only accepted *castor sec* taken in the winter. *Castor gras* (greasy fur) was so-called because it had been worn by the natives for two or three years, on both the fur and the skin side. This made the fur greasy and got rid of the long hair. The *castor gras* was normally worth four *livres* per pound in the seventeenth century.

ii. *Trade goods:* In exchange for pelts, the natives accepted a great variety of articles that the traders obtained from suppliers in Montreal. French clothes, blankets, tools, guns, gunpowder, and brandy were popular items. A fortune was often represented in these supplies because large amounts were needed for long voyages. A trader leaving in 1727 for Chagouamigon (on Lake Superior) had to borrow 23,500 *livres* for his supplies. The merchants often demanded interest as high as 40 or 50 percent.

Guns (especially Tulle guns) and gunpowder became very popular with the Amerinds. These items, in any case, had the advantage of making hunting more profitable for the next trading session. The *couvertes* (blankets) called *écarlatines*, were made of white, red or blue cloth edged with black stripes. The natives were very particular about the blackness of these stripes, and since it had been found impossible—after several attempts at imitation—to obtain black stripes as fine as those on English blankets, the French were obliged to get their supplies in England. Every large-scale trader had to have at least 2,000 or 3,000 *livres'* worth of them.

Brandy was the article of trade which gave rise to the most heated debates during the seventeenth century. The natives would easily part with their furs to obtain it, without considering the effect that it had. Afterwards, they were left without the strength for more hunting. The brandy trade was forbidden and tolerated, by turns, but it remained necessary because of English competition. When the natives were refused brandy by the French, they went to the English trading posts with their furs. For this reason, the State authorized Fort Frontenac after 1716, as the only centre where the brandy trade could be carried on, but they naively added that it was to be "in small quantities." Everywhere else, it was forbidden and the Church made it a sin that could be absolved only by the bishop.

iii. *Trading operations:* Trading in the country was not the exclusive privilege of the Compagnie des Indes Occidentales. It was also shared by the State, the smaller trading companies, and private individuals. But whoever the agent of trade might be, beaver fur could only leave the country through the Compagnie des Indes Occidentales.

The Domain of the King's Posts belonged to the State, which leased it out. The area stretched from Sept-Îles to Île aux Coudres and covered the immense lowlands of Lake Saint John. In 1749, the widow Fournel (the last person to hold the lease during the French regime) obtained the trade of the King's Posts for the sum of seven thousand francs per year. The State also leased out the trade at the forts of La Présentation, Frontenac, Toronto, Niagara, Presqu'Île, Machault, and Duquesne. These were the forts on the great military route of the upper Saint Lawrence. The leasing of forts Frontenac and Niagara in 1742 brought in the sum of 10,400 *livres*.

Elsewhere, regions were granted to merchants for periods of six, nine, or twelve years. In the majority of posts, trading was reserved as the right of the commander. Exceptions were made at Detroit and Michilimackinac, where trading permits were sold.

All New France was subdivided into trading areas except in the areas organized into Governments. The region farthest away was the "Western Sea," a leased area that included a chain of posts from Lake Superior to the Rockies. This area was developed by a company of Montreal merchants.

Trading was even carried on in the colony (between settlers who often used furs as money, and by those trading at the spring fairs) and in areas belonging to the natives.

To trade in the native areas, a *congé de traite* (trading permit) was required. These the State granted in limited numbers. They were first established in 1681, then abolished in 1696. 25 permits were restored in 1716. In fact, this number was often exceeded, because

A trading post
(a reconstructed trading post in Old Fort Niagara)

in 1739 there were 81. These permits were granted, in principle, to individuals in needy circumstances (sometimes even to religious communities). They cost 1,000 *livres*, half of this sum going into the coffers of the State, the other half remaining at the disposal of the governor, who gave it out in gratuities and pensions. The holder of a trading permit would later resell it to a trader.

Official permission to leave on a trading trip was granted by the governor, countersigned by the intendant. This permit indicated the exact place in which trading would be carried on, the number of canoes and hired men, the quantity of brandy taken for personal use (8 quarts per person), and the date of return.

Those who went trading in native areas without authorization were called *coureurs de bois*. They were outlaws liable to be condemned to the galleys, or at the very least, to a fine of 1,000 *livres*. They must not be confused with the *engagés* (hired men, otherwise known as *voyageurs* or *canotiers*). These last were men who contracted with an accredited trader before a notary to take a load of merchandise and to return, sometimes the following year, with a cargo of furs. They were normally paid in furs, and their departure and return was carefully supervised.

The spring fairs took place when the natives came down with their furs. During the eighteenth century, these fairs were held only in Montreal, because Trois-Rivières had lost almost all its importance. Various regulations were imposed to avoid disturbances.

No one was allowed to go to meet the canoes on the Ottawa River, and trading outside the fair was forbidden. The natives were guaranteed the right to choose the stores that they wished to enter, free from harassment. In the evenings, they were forced to find accommodation outside the town walls.

iv. *The export of furs:* The Compagnie des Indes Occidentales had a head office in Quebec and local offices in the other Governments. The beaver furs had to be delivered to these offices after a delay no longer than forty-eight hours. They were delivered in bales of one hundred and twenty pounds, but the Company was given five extra pounds in every hundred to "make up the weight . . . because of wastage." Every skin was stamped with the Company's lead seal to prevent fraudulent entry into France. The Company made payments in bills of exchange that remained valid even if the cargo was lost later on.

During the eighteenth century fur was by far the largest export commodity. In 1739, of exports valued at 1,461,675 *livres*, fur accounted for 70 percent, while agricultural produce came to only 18 percent, fishing products to 9 percent, the iron of the Saint-Maurice Ironworks to 1.3 percent, and wood to one half of 1 percent.

b) *The control of internal trade*

The State kept a watchful eye on internal trade in furs (a commodity settlers had been free to sell among themselves since 1717) and in various essential goods. In this area, the economy was strictly controlled.

i. *The merchants:* The State carefully distinguished between *marchands habitués* (regular merchants) and *marchands forains* (itinerant merchants). The *marchands habitués* were resident in the country; they had a family or property there valued at more than two thousand *livres*; and only they were allowed to carry on retail trade. The *marchands forains* came to the country only in the summer months to trade and had no other ties with it. They were restricted to the wholesale trade, although sometimes they ran a retail operation when wholesaling was no longer very profitable. These regulations were made to protect the resident merchants, who were helping to build the country, against the possibly ruinous competition of foreign merchants. However, these provisions were largely ignored. As the eighteenth century progressed, the *marchands forains* took over the market at the expense of the *marchands habitués* whose protests were of no avail.

There were also *coureurs de côtes*, speculators who went into the countryside to purchase farm products, especially wheat, which they later resold at great profit. One ordinance states that they "caused hardship in places where, without them, it would never appear." These men were dealt with severely.

ii. *Markets and stores:* The State decided on the sites for markets and set the days and hours during which they could be open. In Quebec, for example, there was a market place in the Upper Town and another in the Lower Town, with trading taking place on Tuesdays and Fridays. Here again, the citizens were protected against profiteers who attempted to meet the *habitants* before opening time to buy up everything and then resell it at high prices. Both hotel managers and innkeepers were admitted to the markets only after the common people.

The number of stores was sometimes restricted for, in certain areas, not everyone who wanted to could become a merchant. Only authorized bakers could make and sell bread, and inspectors made sure that they offered all grades of bread. The sale of beef was a monopoly. In Quebec in 1706, only four butchers' stalls were authorized after auction bids were made. Later, there were only two. These sold only beef, since the holder of the monopoly was unable to offer chickens, butter, eggs, and other produce for sale. He was obliged to slaughter a certain number of animals every week. Since no meat could be eaten during Lent, the butchers' stores closed for forty days.

iii. *The merchandise:* The colonists in New France were supposed to use only goods made in France. An exception was made for enemy booty, but in this case, a distinctive mark allowed it to be added to stock. However, smuggling was widespread, because of the proximity of the English colonies, the slowness of communications with France, and the advantage in price. The amount of smuggling that went on can only be measured by the large number of prohibitions against it and by the size of the fines imposed. An extensive investigation, made in Montreal in 1741 (in convents and churches as well as in private houses) attests to the fact that English manufactured goods were circulating in extraordinary quantities. 449 of the 506 houses searched contained some smuggled goods, while smuggled articles were found even in the religious communities.

Certain types of merchandise, such as alcohol, were subject to very close inspection. There was no restriction on the trade and manufacture of alcohol, but in this particularly difficult area, an attempt was made to limit its abuse, because brandy was consumed in such great quantities. The most important legislation concerning alcohol was that made by Intendant Dupuy, in 1726. This legislation stated that merchants and storekeepers could only sell alcohol wholesale. A licence from the intendant was required for running a tavern, but these were easily obtained. Drinks could not be served after ten o'clock in the evening, and on Sundays, only from 9 to 11 and from 2 to 4. Soldiers could consume alcohol only with their meals, and personal servants were not served without the written permission of their masters. Whether these regulations were respected or not is another matter.

The making and selling of beer was not restricted either, and it was a very common beverage. When Mgr de Laval proposed a brewery for the Seminary in 1685, he wrote that it was difficult to force the employees of that establishment to drink nothing but river water. The Conseil Souverain declared beer a "nourishing and healthful drink," and it is known that the religious communities themselves brewed it. The Récollets and the Jesuits produced an excellent beer, and Madame d'Youville, who carried on the work of the Brothers Charron, also made and sold beer.

iv. *The regulation of prices:* Because prices played an essential role in economic life, they were subject to even closer supervision. In this regard, the intendant had periodic meetings with the principal merchants and tradesmen to decide on a price scale. The practice of establishing a ceiling for prices existed from the beginning. Such control was necessary to stabilize the economy and to avoid the speculation forced on merchants by the number of possible accidents (the late arrival of the ships, or a complete interruption in the supply system). In 1664, the Conseil Souverain was obliged to limit the profit made by importers to 55 percent on solid merchandise and 100 percent on liquid merchandise. But the merchants immediately exceeded these undeniably generous limits.

The prices of all essential articles were, therefore, regulated. The most important was wheat, the basis of the standard of living. Every time it varied in price, grave repercussions resulted. The intendant fixed the price after an exhaustive inquiry into the last harvest and the *habitants'* reserves. The price of bread was also regulated, and bakers were obliged to have every loaf marked with its weight. Prices for meat—which varied with the seasons—beverages, and firewood (whose quality and length were also determined) were all controlled.

In spite of these provisions, an alarming rise in prices took place, with the connivance of the Government, during the last years of the French regime. This situation was finally brought back to normal by the military regime.

Industry

When Champlain sketched out a program of development in 1618, he had set a value of some 3,600,000 *livres* per year on the possible income from fisheries and mines, and from wood and wood products, hemp, canvas, and rope manufacturing. However, during the first half of the seventeenth century, the mother country was still only interested in furs. Then, under Colbert, nothing was considered "more important for the expansion of this colony than the search for merchandise and the establishing of mills and fisheries." Intendant Talon became the enthusiastic agent of this policy, but unfortunately, the policies of the mother country were soon to restrict industry to the immediate and essential needs of the colony. For example, in 1704, the King prohibited the making of canvas in Canada at the expense of the French product. The theory behind this action was that "nothing that might compete with the manufactured goods of this Kingdom must ever be made in the colonies." The colonies existed solely to supply raw materials and were only being maintained "for the benefit of the countries which founded them and never with the intention of dispensing with those countries." This view was to be the standard French policy. When the manufacture of beaver hats was begun in Montreal and Quebec, the mother country gave strict orders, in 1736, to close down the factories. Hatmaking could have become the starting point for a rich industrial life.

Under these conditions, permission was granted only to industries satisfying the essential needs of the country: shipbuilding and ironworks, fisheries, and the products of small-scale industry.

a) *Shipbuilding*

In a country whose whole life revolved around the sea, and where the forests seemed to offer an abundance of oak and pine, shipbuilding would appear to have been certain of great success. Talon's shipyards, however, were no more than a promising beginning, and in the half-century following his departure, only some ten large hulls were constructed.

Because the State took the initiative, shipbuilding acquired importance after 1729. Hocquart set up his shipyards at Quebec, near the Palais de l'Intendance, and in 1745, another shipyard appeared at Cul-de-sac on the river itself. At first, ships of low tonnage

Windmill on Île aux Coudres

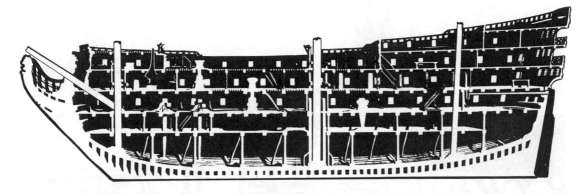

Cross section of a warship

were built. Then, in 1739, the construction of the first *flûte* (merchantman) began. It was a ship of 500 tons, armed with cannon, called the *Canada*, and was launched in 1742. Another merchantman, the ship *Caribou*, came from the yards in 1744; then in 1745, a frigate, the *Castor* with 26 guns; the *Martre*, in 1747, with 22 guns, and the *Saint-Laurent*, in 1748. In 1750, the *Orignal*, with provision for 72 guns, took in water when it was launched and had to be dismantled. Although important for the decade 1739 to 1750, shipbuilding later declined. The *Algonquin*, a frigate with 72 guns, was finished with great difficulty in 1753. The *Abénakise*, with 36 guns, was launched in 1756, but there was never enough time to complete the *Québec*, begun in 1756.

Various factors explain the rapid decline in shipbuilding. Good-quality wood was scarce (sometimes it had to be brought from as far as Lake Champlain) and manufacturing costs were high. Qualified workmen were lacking, and it was very expensive to bring them from France. The absence of secondary industries to back up the yards made it necessary to import essential parts and an enormous quantity of canvas and rope. In the end, a ship built at Quebec from Canadian wood cost a great deal more than a ship built in France from the same wood.

b) *Ironworks*

From very early times, the French were aware of the mineral riches of the country —silver, copper, lead, and particularly iron—but in this area again, the lack of capital and the absence of qualified workmen made large-scale undertakings impossible. Only iron had been worked to any extent. After various attempts, starting as far back as Talon, the State granted the first licence for the processing of iron ore in 1730. The licensee, François Poulin de Francheville, founded a company in 1733 and set up ironworks on the Saint-Maurice River, some nine miles to the north of Trois-Rivières. This enterprise failed in 1741, and since Canadian businessmen were neither numerous nor rich enough to put it back on its feet, the State took over the works in 1743 and ran them at a loss until the Conquest. The Saint-Maurice Ironworks remained a small-scale enterprise, rather badly managed, and employed about one hundred men. As with shipbuilding, the absence of

Eighteenth-century blast furnace

secondary industries, and the impossibility of recruiting specialized workmen on the spot (they had to be brought from Burgundy and Franche-Comté), made processing very costly. The works served their purpose, however, for they supplied local requirements for anvils, pots, tops for brick stoves, stoves, shells, cannonballs, and a small number of cannon.

c) *Fisheries*

New France was rich in possible fisheries, and when Champlain considered the coastal fisheries, he estimated the income that might be obtained from them at one million *livres* per year. While Frenchmen and Basques continued to fish on the Grand Banks and to hunt the whale, Canadians took more than a century to become involved in fishing. It was only in the eighteenth century that the merchants of Quebec were in a position to exploit the wealth of the sea on a modest scale. The merchants were found, from Esqui-maux Bay (the gulf of the Hamilton River) to as far as Sept-Iles, occupying fairly sizeable concessions during the summer. They hunted the seal—whose oil brought a good price and whose fur was as valuable as that of the beaver— the porpoise and other fish. The post of Phélypeaux Bay, for example, was valued at ten thousand *livres* per year. Gros-Mécatina, for a certain period, produced an income of forty thousand *livres* per year.

On the lower part of the river, rich porpoise and eel fisheries were also developed. However, very little cod fishing was carried on.

At no time did the fisheries become a large lucrative enterprise for New France. Capital and trade fisheries were both lacking, and there were no plans to create them. Since attempts to establish saltworks failed, the supply of salt still depended on France. What is more, many of the fishing enterprises were managed from France, for the benefit of French merchants. New France had no part in the large fisheries of the Gulf and the Banks.

d) *The products of small-scale industry*

Small industries geared to supply immediate needs sometimes remained in operation for a fairly long time, but they were usually of short duration. Lady Legardeur de Repentigny, in 1704, founded a small cloth and textile factory in Montreal. This enterprise was run by English prisoners, but she lost her workmen in 1707, and the factory disappeared after a few years. After 1719, there was a stocking factory in the Hôpital-Général in Montreal, but it ceased to exist in 1722 after a good deal of disagreement.

A considerable income could be made from wood because it was readily available. In 1676, Peuvret de Mesnu obtained an exclusive licence to saw planks on the Saint Lawrence, but he was only able to set up one sawmill. In 1690, Hazeur and Grignon had two important sawmills at La Malbaie. Canada, and afterwards Acadia, were counted on to supply masts for the ports of France, but neither of the two colonies managed to organize a profitable export trade. However, the number of sawmills increased rapidly from ten, in 1717, to about fifty, twenty years later. There was even one on Lake Champlain in 1746. The products of this small lumber industry only occasionally reached the European market. Since the merchants were not rich enough to charter and load their own ships, this market was only profitable if the wood could be carried free of charge on board the King's ships. The same was also the history of other enterprises such as brickworks, tileworks, tarworks, and tanneries. They appeared and disappeared, without reaching export level or without supplying even local needs. There was always a lack of capital and experienced workmen. Only the breweries had really long careers because they were sustained by a steady consumption.

Agriculture
a) *Amateur farming*

The principal characteristic of agriculture during the French regime was the lack of professional skill. The classic example of this fact is the man usually hailed as the first farmer in New France: the apothecary from Paris, Louis Hébert. He arrived in 1617, settled on virtually uncultivated high ground, and tried to live off the land. But, in order to survive, he in fact had to work as a civil servant, and it is known that he never ploughed the ground, because he had no plough. This example of a city dweller, or professional man, acting as a farmer was repeated surprisingly often throughout the French regime. Of the ten thousand immigrants who came to New France and settled mainly on the land, one can reckon that 75 percent had no agricultural experience. They were either military recruits or tradesmen. The census of 1666 is very important in this context because it lists

Farmer and wife
(from an engraving by Richard Short)

Public Archives of Canada

a large number of weavers, masons, carpenters, ploughmen (a ploughman at that time was not a farmer), tailors, sailors, and other tradesmen who had been transformed into settlers.

Although these people were ignorant of even elementary techniques and lacked any agricultural background, they began the tradition of farming "in a haphazard manner." As a result, returns remained small, the good land became exhausted, and the choice livestock (which Talon had imported) rapidly degenerated. At the end of the French regime, observers were speaking scornfully of farming methods and the poor livestock.

b) *The absence of agricultural policy*

This amateur method of farming could have been corrected by a positive policy aimed, in the first place, at instructing these tradesmen and military recruits in their new profession. Intendant Talon seems to have been conscious of this problem, but his stay here lasted too short a time. The seigneurial regime itself was only a system for occupying the land.

Apart from the brief administration of Talon, the authorities' only agricultural policy was to protect the products of the land against the ravages of man and beast. Numerous regulations prohibited owners from allowing their animals to wander over unenclosed ground (this was called "neglect of animals") and prevented riding over seeded ground while hunting. Other regulations made the settlers destroy thistles, forbade the gathering of ginseng before the middle of September (this last prohibition was only imposed when the precious plant was already scarce), and attempted to check the excessive number of horse breedings. When the State ordered a grain census from time to time, it was only to prevent famine.

Barns of the French regime
(according to R.-L. Séguin, *Les Granges du Québec*)

Nothing was done to improve seed grain or to preserve the original quality of the livestock. No one was required to fertilize his land (the settlers threw manure into the river) or prevent the soil from becoming exhausted by the repeated growing of wheat and tobacco.

Because of the important part agriculture played in colonization, settlement, and trade, it is surprising that the State did not intervene to settle agricultural problems. Judging from all the evidence, the authorities were not interested in building up an agricultural colony.

c) *The lack of agricultural outlets*

In the seventeenth and eighteenth centuries, France did not need an agricultural colony. She was largely self-sufficient, and even if crops failed unexpectedly in autumn, it was too late to bring in supplies from New France, since ships left France only in the spring and returned the following summer. In any case, a surplus of wheat in the small colonies of Acadia and the Saint Lawrence was uncommon and unforeseeable, and therefore, of little use.

A farm in Château-Richer
Watercolour by Thomas Davies, 1787

Was trade with the West Indies possible? These islands, situated three thousand miles away from Quebec but within reach of the English agricultural colonies, could serve as an outlet only in times of a glut or in difficult circumstances. In fact, wheat was rarely exported from New France, and it was very unlikely to reach the West Indies. Various reasons (the lack of capital, the absence of ships, and running battles at sea) prevented the export of wheat in the years when New France recorded a surplus. The English colonies, of course, were nearby, but all regular trade with them was forbidden.

The only permanent outlet for agricultural products was local consumption, by the *habitant* (who consumed more than he produced) and the town dweller. But only a minority of *habitants* bought food, and the town dwellers were reached only by producers who lived near to the towns. Here again, one must remember that the town dweller of this period often planted a kitchen garden and raised animals for slaughter either at home or in the suburbs. In any case, the small number of important settlements and the distances that had to be covered to reach them kept down the actual number of "trading-farmers."

After 1750, a new outlet—supplying provisions to the troops—appeared. This, however, was only an occasional outlet, and the speculations of people in high places, together with the succession of bad harvests, prevented most of the settlers from making use of this outlet.

d) *The average habitant's farm*

According to contemporary observers, and judging from property lists, the average *habitant's* farm consisted of several buildings and was not constructed as a block or a half-enclosed quadrilateral, as in the western provinces of France. The wooden buildings were made of horizontal logs. The house had a chimney of stone or clay, and was covered with thatch or shingles. Oiled skins, because they are translucent, often served as windows. Usually, there was only one room that had a wooden floor. Heating and cooking facilities were provided by a rudimentary stove made of a metal top-plate on a brick framework. A clay oven was set up near the house. The combined barn and stable had a thatched roof.

The *habitants* raised cattle, and these did duty as draft animals. The cattle pulled with their horns, not with their necks as was done in the English colonies. There were cows, large quantities of pigs (since the settlers were great eaters of bacon), many turkeys, capons, and chickens, but only a few sheep, which is unusual in a country where wool was indispensable. On the other hand, they bred horses, which were expensive to feed and could not be worked hard. Governor Montmagny received a horse in 1647 because he was a knight; after that, a dozen horses arrived in 1665. In 1709, each *habitant* was forbidden to keep more than two horses and a colt, but despite this and other regulations, the number of horses reached 5,063 by 1720. There were 15,000 by the end of the French regime, and the horse had become an external indication (true or false) of wealth.

The *habitant* grew mainly wheat, for it was the staff of life, and being French, he traditionally ate a lot of bread. But the influence of the seigneur, who ran the flour mill, and the curé, who collected a tithe on grain, may also explain the importance of this crop. The *habitant* used a Norwegian wheat that ripened in three months, a necessary condition in this climate. The *habitant* also grew oats, a little barley and rye, a great quantity of

House of a well-to-do habitant

Archives de la province de Québec

peas, some corn (or maize), some flax, and tobacco (which was introduced in 1721). Using the method of the Amerinds, he sowed melon, cucumber, and pumpkin seeds in hotbeds before transplanting them at just the right time. Orchards were rare. In the spring, syrup and sugar were made from the sap of the maple tree.

e) *A poor man living in high style*

Many *habitants*, especially in the Montreal region, attained a certain affluence, thanks to trade, and a good number even managed to acquire seigneuries, but such individuals were the exception and not the rule.

The average *habitant* might, at first sight, appear prosperous. He was not subject to the exactions of the *taille* and the *champart*, as he would have been in France. Seigneurial *corvées* were less rigorous here and were established according to a contract drawn up by a lawyer. He did not see his land regularly devastated by French troops seeking to "live off the land." The Iroquois Wars, which had lasted little more than a half century, were much less terrible than the constant damage inflicted on the French provinces throughout the seventeenth century. The *habitant* possessed a large portion of land and a plentiful supply of firewood. He could also hunt freely. His style of life appeared easy, for he seemed able to spend liberally when the traditional celebrations occurred. At auctions, it was a matter of pride with him to make the highest bid—for goods that he could have bought more cheaply from the merchants. He raised more horses than he needed. All such evidence has led to the erroneous conclusion that the *habitant* of the French regime lived in very easy circumstances. This is similar to the confusion that sometimes arises over the styles of the houses of the *habitants* and those of the seigneurs, or middle class.

A study of the agricultural market, and even more, an examination of inventories made after the owner's death demonstrates that the average *habitant* was poor. His expensive habits did not correspond to the state of his fortune. If he did nothing other than farm, his accommodation remained very modest. He had little furniture, and he lived from one year to the next at the mercy of natural disasters, which frequently reduced him to poverty. He did not manage to save, either because it was too difficult for him to get hold of money (because of the lack of markets) or because he was too extravagant.

This picture may appear gloomy, but the constant exodus of country people to the towns bears witness to the fact that the average *habitant's* situation was precarious. In 1749, this exodus became so considerable that the intendant tried (in vain) to stop it. In 1754, in a country having no large industry, one quarter of the population lived in the towns. It is not until the integration of this colony with the English empire, which opened up vast outlets, that we find the average *habitant* reaching a level of financial freedom.

Bibliographical Note

Although many of the problems of economic life remain to be studied more thoroughly (perhaps using a new approach), there are numerous studies that deserve mention. Here is a list of only a few, and these are rarely in agreement with each other. However, they all have the advantage of opening further horizons for anyone interested in the economy of the French regime.

GENERAL STUDIES

E. SALONE, *La Colonisation de la Nouvelle-France. Étude sur les origines de la nation canadienne-française.* Paris, Guilmoto, 1906.

P.-E. RENAUD, *Les Origines économiques du Canada.* Mamers, Énault, 1928.

G. FRÉGAULT, "La Colonisation du Canada au XVIIIe siècle," in the *Cahiers de l'Académie canadienne-française,* no. 2, pp. 53-81.

M. BRUNET, "Le Rôle des métropoles et des entrepreneurs dans la colonisation de l'Amérique et la mise en valeur de la vallée du Saint-Laurent," in the report of the *Canadian Historical Association* for 1959, pp. 16-21.

J. HAMELIN, *Économie et société en Nouvelle-France.* Québec, Université Laval, 1960.

SPECIAL STUDIES

Trade

R. BILODEAU, "Liberté économique et politique des Canadiens sous le régime français," in the *Revue d'histoire de l'Amérique française,* X, 1 (June 1956), pp. 49-68.

H. A. INNIS, *The Fur Trade in Canada: An Introduction to Canadian Economic History.* Toronto, University of Toronto Press, 1958.

J. E. LUNN, "The Illegal Fur Trade Out of New France, 1713-1760," in the report of the *Canadian Historical Association* for 1939, pp. 61-76.

P. C. PHILLIPS, *The Fur Trade.* University of Oklahoma Press, 1961, 2 vol.

A. G. REID, "General Trade Between Quebec and France During the French Regime," in *Canadian Historical Review,* XXXIV, 1 (March 1953), pp. 18-32.

A. G. REID, "Intercolonial Trade During the French Regime." *Canadian Historical Review,* XXXII, 3 (Sept. 1951), pp. 236-251.

Finances

G. FRÉGAULT, "Essai sur les finances canadiennes (1700-1750)," in the *Revue d'histoire de l'Amérique française,* XII, 3 (Dec. 1958), pp. 307-322; 4 (March 1959), pp. 18-32.

Industry

J.-N. FAUTEUX, *Essai sur l'industrie au Canada sous le régime français.* Québec, Proulx, 1927, 2 vol.

L. GROULX, "Note sur la chapellerie au Canada sous le régime français," in the *Revue d'histoire de l'Amérique française,* III, 3 (Dec. 1949), pp. 38-401.

Agriculture

R.-L. SÉGUIN, *La civilisation traditionelle de l'habitant aux XVIIe et XVIIIe siècles.* Montréal, les Éditions Fides, 1968.

R.-L. SÉGUIN, *L'Équipement de la ferme canadienne au 17e et au 18e siècle.* Montréal, Ducharme, 1959.

R.-L. SÉGUIN, "Le Cheval et ses implications historiques dans l'Amérique française," in the *Revue d'histoire de l'Amérique française,* V, 2 (Sept. 1951), pp. 227-251.

F. OUELLET, "La Mentalité et l'outillage économique de l'habitant canadien (1760): À propos d'un document sur l'encan," in the *Bulletin des recherches historiques,* LXII (1956), pp. 131-136.

R.-L. SÉGUIN, *La Maison en Nouvelle-France.* Ottawa, 1968.

Costume

R.-L. SÉGUIN, *Le Costume civil en Nouvelle-France.* Ottawa, Musée National, 1968.

Highways

R. SANFAÇON, "La Construction du premier chemin Québec-Montréal et le problème des corvées (1706-1737)," in the *Revue d'histoire de l'Amérique française,* XII, (June 1958), pp. 3-29.

CHAPTER VII

Justice

A century was required before the system of justice assumed a permanent form. At first, justice was administered by the governor alone, then by the governor and his council. In 1651, justice became the responsibility of the *Sénéchaussée* (Seneschal's Court), a seigneurial court of the Cent-Associés, which, however, had no jurisdiction over Montreal Island. In 1663, this seigneurial court was replaced by a royal court in Quebec and Trois-Rivières. The Sulpicians still controlled the upper courts (that is, they had the right to impose the death penalty and to inflict corporal punishment), but these were abolished in 1693 and Montreal was integrated into the general administration. Various "reforms" made in 1667, 1678, 1679, and 1685, with the recognition in 1684 of an ecclesiastical court (the Officialité) and the creation of an Admiralty Court in 1717, gradually completed the judicial organization. After 1726, the Conseil Supérieur was little more than a court of appeal.

The higher authorities of justice

In the eighteenth century, after its structure was made permanent, the judicial organization was divided into three sections: the higher courts, courts of the first instance, and seigneurial, or lower courts.

The King, in whom, according to the contemporary maxim, "resided all justice" was head of the judicial system just as he was head of the whole administration. Officials were appointed by him or by his representative, the Intendant, for no judicial office could be bought in New France. In addition, final appeal could always be made to the King no matter which court had pronounced sentence.

The Intendant had complete responsibility for justice throughout New France. He appointed legal auxiliaries (notaries and surveyors), supervised the royal and seigneurial courts, determined the procedures to be followed, and interpreted the customary law. He also presided over the sessions of the Conseil Supérieur and forwarded appeals sent to the King.

The Conseil Supérieur acted as a court of appeal and the decisions of any court of justice, secular or ecclesiastical, could be challenged there. Very few of its members were jurists, but in the eighteenth century they were mainly merchants who were trained in business and who handed down decisions dictated by common sense. The Council normally sat in the Palais de l'Intendance, on Mondays. Justice was dispensed free of charge and *ni épices ni vacations* were accepted. On the other hand, if the plaintiff did not have important grounds, he could be fined for any *fol appel* ("impertinent appeal").

Courts of first instance

At this level, all cases—except those which were subject to seigneurial justice—had first to be referred to a court. The ecclesiastical court, the Admiralty Court, and the courts of royal jurisdiction were courts of first instance.

a) *Ecclesiastical courts*

An ecclesiastical court had existed since 1660, under the name *Officialité*, but it was not recognized by the State until 1684. It had authority over the entire diocese of New France in both civil and criminal cases between ecclesiastics, and in cases between ecclesiastics and laymen. Wherever a case occurred, the parties did not have to appear before a secular court or before the Conseil Supérieur, but before the Officialité, which sat in Quebec. Afterwards, if necessary, the case was taken to the Conseil Supérieur.

This ecclesiastical court was under the authority of the bishop and included the *Official* (judge), who was usually a canon, the *promoteur* (proctor), and the court clerk. Although it did not have the powers of a higher court, it maintained a prison which, at this time, was in the Hôpital Général in Quebec.

b) *The Admiralty Court*

This court was established in 1717 and was called the *Amirauté* (Admiralty Court) because the Amiral de France was responsible for it and presented its members to the King. It decided maritime cases and any disputes arising during navigation, and it provided the harbour police. Passengers and merchandise were not permitted to disembark before the officers had made their inspection. No ship was allowed to leave port without the permission of the Admiralty Court. This permission was granted only if the ship carried a minimum of 60 rations and two thirds of a barrel of water for each passenger, for it was reckoned that at least two months were needed for the crossing.

The Admiralty Court was presided over by a lieutenant-general, who was not necessarily a specialist in maritime law. As in every court of law, the judge was assisted by a proctor and a clerk. The Court also had a receiver who granted permits and a harbour-master who made sure that port regulations were observed. For example, he saw that ships discharged their ballast of stones in open water and not on shore.

c) *Courts of royal jurisdiction*

The courts of first instance under royal jurisdiction corresponded, as a rule, to the Governments. In fact, Canada—the area that was most completely organized—possessed four courts at the end of the French regime. In the Government of Quebec, there was the court of Quebec, called the *Prévôté*, and a court at Saint-Thomas-de-Montmagny, called the *Juridiction royale de la Rivière-du-Sud*. The third and fourth ones, at Trois-Rivières and Montreal, were known as Royal Courts.

Each of these courts was presided over by a judge appointed by the King—the *lieutenant-général civil et criminel*—assisted by a *lieutenant particulier*. A proctor investigated the case, organized the judicial inquiry, and brought actions on behalf of the State, or on behalf of absent persons. A clerk of the court, with an assistant, kept the records, and a *huissier et sergent royal* served writs on the parties and made arrests.

Part of a document drawn up by Notaire Chambalon

Archives de la province de Québec

Seigneurial or lower courts

Finally, at the bottom of this judicial structure, were the seigneurial, or lower courts, so-called because they were below any royal court of the first instance and were only entitled to two thirds of the retainers and fees set in royal courts. The right to hold a court was not granted to every seigneur. In the beginning, the seigneurs who had this right were also granted the powers of dispensing "higher justice," but after 1693, seigneurial courts were only middle or lower courts. As middle courts, they dealt with all civil cases and offences, if the fine involved did not exceed 60 *sols*. They also had jurisdiction over guardianship and took inventories of property. As lower courts, they also dealt with civil cases, but only if the amount at stake did not exceed 60 *sols*, and only if the offences were subject to a fine of less than 10 *sols*.

These middle and lower courts had the following names: *bailliage* in Côte-de-Beaupré, Sillery, and Trois-Rivières; *sénéchaussée* in the seigneury of Lauson: and *prévôté* in the Jesuit seigneury of Notre-Dame-des-Anges.

The court consisted of a judge (also called a *bailli*, a *sénéchal*, or a *prévôt*, as the case may be), a *procureur fiscal*—who represented the seigneur in the prosecution and

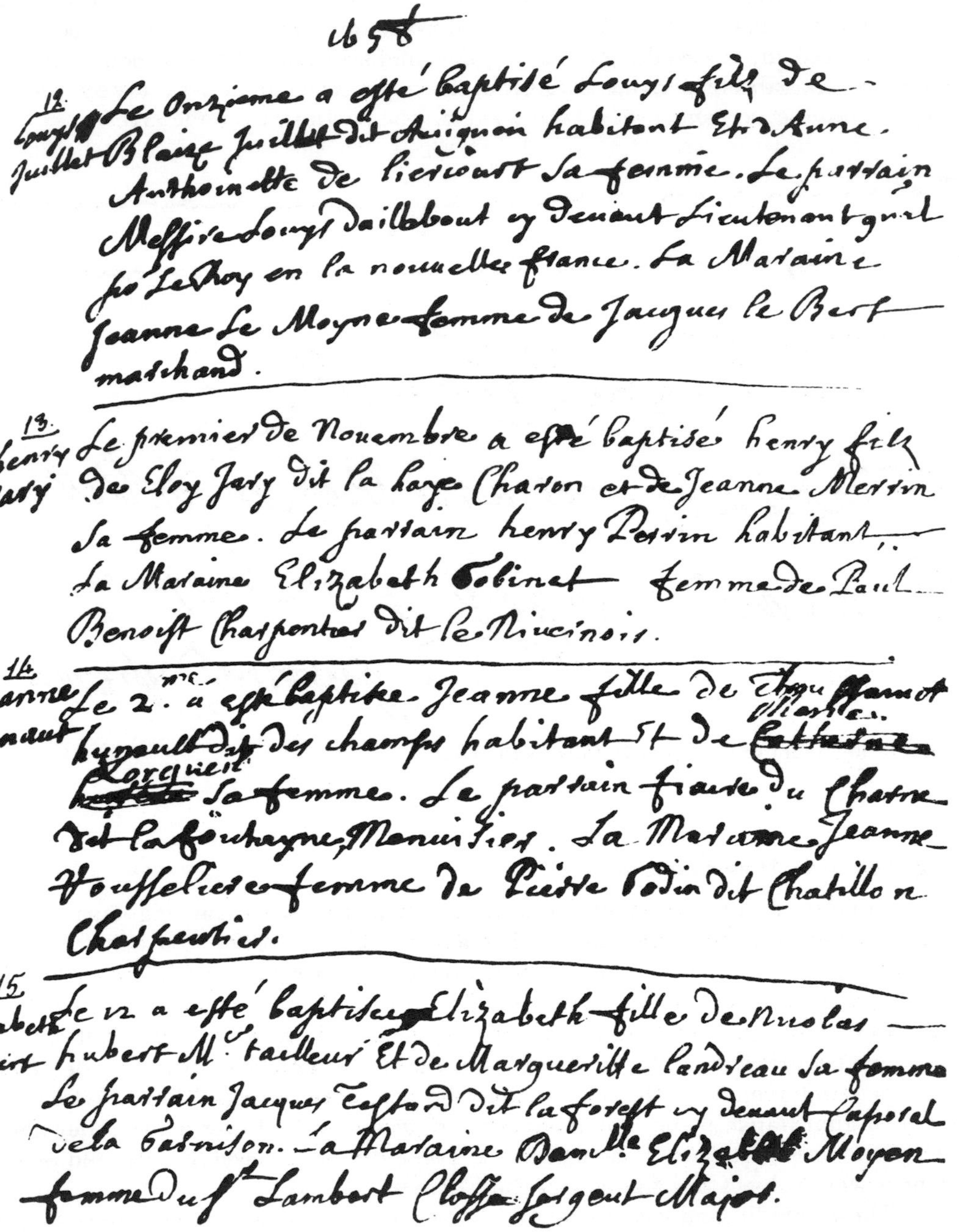

1658

12.
Louys
Juillet

Le Onzieme a esté baptisé Louys fils de
Blaise Juillet dit Avignon habitant Et d'Anne
Anthoinette de Liercourt sa femme. Le parrain
Messire Louys d'Aillebout cy devant Lieutenant genl
pro Le Roy en la nouuelle france. La Maraine
Jeanne Le Moyne femme de Jacques le Bert
marchand.

13.
henry
Jary

Le premier de Nouembre a esté baptisé henry fils
de Eloy Jary dit la haye Charon et de Jeanne Merlin
sa femme. Le parrain henry Perrin habitant.
la Maraine Elizabeth Sobinet femme de Paul
Benoist Charpentier dit le Niuernois.

14.
Jeanne
huraut

Le 2.me a esté baptike Jeanne fille de Thou Mamot
hurault dit des champs habitant Et de Catherine Charles
Corgueil sa femme. Le parrain fiacre du Charne
dit Lafourchayne, Menuisier. La Maraine Jeanne
Houssette femme de Pierre Dodin dit Chatillon
Charpentier.

15.
Elizabeth
hubert

Le 12 a esté baptisée Elizabeth fille de Nicolas
hubert Mr tailleur Et de Marguerite Landreau sa femme
Le parrain Jacques Testard dit la forest cy devant Caporal
de la Garnison. La Maraine Dam.lle Elizabeth Moyen
femme du Sr Lambert Closse Sergeut Major.

Register entries
Montreal, 1658

protected the interests of *censitaires* who were absent or under age—and finally, a clerk and a *huissier*. The seigneur paid and appointed these officials, but their appointments were confirmed by the *lieutenant-general civil et criminel* of the Government in which the seigneury was located. Judgments made in the seigneurial court could always be appealed to this lieutenant-general.

The following table may help in understanding the procedure followed in making an appeal.

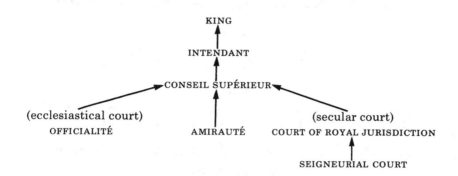

Table of Legal Recourse

Legal assistants

In addition to the regular officials who administered justice, there were legal practitioners, notaries, curés (in the absence of anyone else), and land surveyors, who acted as auxiliaries or legal assistants.

a) *Legal practitioners*

Lawyers as such had been officially prohibited in New France since 1678. By this means, the King hoped to avoid "chicanery," that is, interminable trials. It was not until 1764 that lawyers were able to practise in Canada. Since plaintiffs and defendants could not always plead or appear in person, they resorted to "practitioners." These were people quite familiar (at least, theoretically) with the legal routine, who drew up documents and acted as attorneys.

b) *Notaries*

It was not until the beginning of the eighteenth century that notaries became organized. Two sets of regulations, in 1717 and 1733, established order in the profession and settled the rules that were to be followed. The intendant or the seigneur appointed notaries, for there were two kinds: the royal notary and the seigneurial notary.

The royal notary held authority from the intendant and had jurisdiction—according to his letters of appointment—throughout the entire Government, or in a smaller area. He drew up contracts (of sale, agreement, apprenticeship, or marriage) and deeds of gift, as well as inventories and wills. He also served as a practitioner.

NOUVEAU
COMMENTAIRE
SUR
LA COUTUME
DE
LA PREVOSTE'
ET
VICOMTE' DE PARIS.

Par M. CLAUDE DE FERRIERE, *Avocat au Parlement.*

NOUVELLE EDITION.

Revuë, corrigée & augmentée.

Par M. SAUVAN D'ARAMON, *Avocat au Parlement.*

TOME I.

A PARIS, AU PALAIS

Chez PIERRE-MICHEL BRUNET l'aîné,
Libraire, Grand'Salle, au S. Esprit.

M. DCC. XXVIII.
AVEC PRIVILEGE DU ROY.

Title page from a Coutume de Paris

The seigneurial notary appointed by the seigneur had jurisdiction only within the seigneury to which he was appointed. His scale of charges for drawing up documents was only half of the sum the royal notary charged.

Notaries were scarce, and since the profession was poorly paid, legal knowledge was not considered absolutely necessary. It was not unknown for shoemakers, cabinetmakers, and innkeepers to become notaries. In order to survive, notaries were obliged to take on a number of duties: one might be a notary, a surveyor, and a bailiff at the same time; another, a notary and a doctor; another, a notary, a surveyor, and an architect. A notary in one seigneury might even be the *procureur fiscal* in another.

c) *The curés, legal assistants by substitution*

Curés and missionaries were authorized to take the place of notaries where there were none. However, their duties were limited to marriage contracts and to recognizing wills. Permission for such action was in accordance with the customary law of Paris, and the *Rituel* even contains a formula for wills to help the curés in their duty as substitute notaries.

d) *Land surveyors*

The main duty of the surveyor was to draw alignments and to make boundary marks showing the limits of land grants. There were royal and seigneurial surveyors with the same distinctions in their jurisdiction as the royal and seigneurial notaries.

Before they were appointed, both candidates had to prove their ability before the Professor of Mathematics of the Jesuit College. When they began their duties, they adjusted their instruments according to those of the same professor. Since the seigneuries of the Saint Lawrence followed a northwest to southeast orientation, four posts were set up in the town of Quebec to serve as landmarks: two on the northwest to southeast rhumbline, and two on the northeast to southwest rhumbline.

The Coutume de Paris

The administration of justice and the laws on which it was based were linked to the Coutume de Paris, that is, the body of customary law in force in the *Prévôté et Vicomté de Paris*. This was written in 1510 and reformed in 1580.

As early as 1627 the Compagnie des Cent-Associés chose the Coutume de Paris, from all the different law systems in France, as the one law it intended to follow. However, other law systems were introduced into the country (those of Orléans and Vexin-le-Français). In 1664, in article 33 of the Act that set up the Compagnie des Indes Occidentales, Louis XIV established the Coutume de Paris to the exclusion of all others. For this reason, it became and remained the basis of Law in New France.

However, after the Conquest, it was customary to speak of the "laws of Canada" instead of the Coutume de Paris, not only to avoid hurting England's feelings, but because the Coutume de Paris had to some extent become Canadianized. The various modifications that it went through, in particular in 1667, 1678, and 1685, soon made it quite a different body of law from the original customary law.

Neither lawyers nor chancellery existed in New France. Additional delays in law were authorized after taking into consideration the distance and the climate. Because of the poverty of the country, fees were left to the discretion of the judges. In certain cases for reasons of geography, witnesses were not insisted upon, although elsewhere they were required. There were no benefices and appeals were free of charge. These measures and many others speeded up the distinction between the true Coutume de Paris and that which was followed here.

The Coutume de Paris directed every action in a Canadian's life from birth to death. So, it is possible to appreciate the disaster created in 1764 by the decision to replace the "laws of Canada" by the laws of England.

Criminal law

Only in the domain of civil law was this substitution disastrous, for Canadians welcomed the introduction of English criminal law, which was much more humane than French criminal law.

a) *Trial*

In England, the suspect is presumed innocent until he is proven guilty. He enjoys the right of habeas corpus and is not forced to submit to questioning by torture. The French suspect, on the other hand, was presumed guilty. He had to prove his innocence,

The accused person was arrested by the *Maréchaussée,* presided over by a *prévôt,* called a *juge d'épée.* He was detained in the "Royal Prisons," which were guarded by a jailer, or in the case of a woman, in the Hôpital-Général controlled by a nun (the Mistress of Discipline, in the strongest sense of the word). The witnesses for both the prosecution and the defence gave their testimony without the accused person being present. Denied the assistance of a lawyer and still not knowing the nature of the evidence against him, the accused person was subjected to a harsh interrogation, sometimes accompanied by torture (this was called the *question préparatoire*). He was confronted with the witnesses to make him say whether or not he denied their allegations. Finally, the judge pronounced the sentence, which was read to the accused in his cell by a clerk of the court. Sentence was arbitrary, for it was left up to the judge to choose the punishment he thought appropriate to the crime.

The harshness of this procedure was nevertheless reduced in several ways: by the skill of the accused during the questioning; by the system itself, which left a good deal to the "sense of duty and religion of the judges," and to their natural kindness in estimating guilt (all of this being still a manifestation of paternalism); and lastly, by the Conseil Supérieur, because no punishment could be carried out before the sentence had been reviewed. After conviction, an appeal was obligatory, and it seems that the Conseil Supérieur proved less harsh than the lower courts.

b) *Punishment*

Before the punishment was carried out, the authorities subjected the condemned person to a painful interrogation, called the *question préalable (question ordinaire,* if it

Compass rose
(from a map by Champlain)
The fleur-de-lis shows the north: the engraver by mistake wrote *F* instead of *E* (east)

Public Archives of Canada

were a matter of simple torture—usually with the boots; *question extraordinaire*, if it involved the breaking of limbs). Then, they proceeded to the punishment.

If the guilty man was not condemned to death, he was whipped and branded with a red-hot iron on the hand, the shoulder, or the cheek (an indelible record in case of a relapse into crime), and then he was banished or sent to the galleys. Men were condemned to death very freely. Any theft committed, or even attempted, during the night; any theft of the slightest importance committed during the day; arson, rape, or attempted rape of a minor were all sufficient for the gallows. Once the condemned man was hanged, his body was burned or exposed at the crossroads, later to be "thrown into the ditch." The same harsh treatment was normal for suicides. The execution of the sentence was an event to which the settlers were invited. It was accompanied by a rite of horror, so that the punishment might serve as a warning.

The official in charge of torturing and punishing the condemned man was the executioner, called *exécuteur de la haute justice,* or *maître des hautes oeuvres.* He was appointed by the Conseil Supérieur and was housed at their expense. He received an annual remuneration of 300 *livres*. The hiring of this official was not an easy task, since he was detested by everyone. Except for Rattier, who filled the office for twenty-three years, their careers were often short. An Irish executioner aged nineteen was hanged for theft

Scale in leagues
Reproduction taken from a map by Bellin, 1755

Public Archives of Canada

only four months after his appointment. The executioner was recruited in the prisons from among those condemned to death. But, sometimes, the State purchased a Negro, like the one who was executioner at Quebec from 1733 to 1743.

The system of measurements

The system of measurements was closely connected with the administration of justice because it depended, as a rule, on the customary law that was in use.

The system of this period was a confusing mixture (something of the system still remains in the measurements of Quebec and even in English measurements). The confusion arose because measurements were based on variable standards (2 grains *d'orge* [of barley] made 1 *ligne* [line]) and calculations were made according to the *pied-de-roi*, the highest tide, and the height of a white horse's belly. The system was also confusing because the measurements were often given vague definitions, as in the case of the *tierçon* which, we are told, is the third part of a larger measurement. It is useless to look for a definition of the *ancre* and the *misérable*. Moreover, French measurements varied from one province to another (the *tun* of Bordeaux was larger than that of Orléans), and within the same province, there was an *ell* for silk that differed from the *ell* for wool; there was a *velte* of 3 *pots*, and another of 4 *pots*.

In New France, an attempt was made to correct this confusion by using only the measurements of Paris. The intendant made frequent checks, but in 1733, there were still millers who were using stones instead of standardized iron weights.

The following is a list of the most frequently used regular measures.

a) *Measurements of length*

2 *grains d'orge*	equal	1 *ligne*
12 *lignes*	equal	1 *pouce* (inch)
12 *pouces*	equal	1 *pied-de-roi* (foot)
5 *pieds* (feet)	equal	1 *brasse* (span)
6 *pieds*	equal	1 *toise* (fathom)
3 *toises*	equal	1 *perche* (perch)
10 *perches*	equal	1 *arpent* (in length)
84 *arpents*	equal	1 *lieue* (league, in length)

The *pied* (foot) equalled 12.789 inches, English measure. The *aune* (ell) measured 3 *pieds* 8 *pouces*. The *toise* of 6 *pieds* was the mason's *toise*. It must be distinguished from the carpenter's *toise*, which equalled 5.5 *pieds*. The *perche* of Paris was of 18 *pieds*, but there was also the *perche royale et forestière* of 22 *pieds*, and the *perche moyenne* of 20 *pieds*. The *arpent*, as a measurement of length, equalled 180 *pieds*, in the French measure; in the English measure, 191.8 or 192 feet.

In New France, no calculations were made in *verges* (yards) or *milles* (miles), which are English measures.

There were 3 kinds of *lieues*:

the *lieue légale* (official league):	2.42 English miles
the *lieue commune* (common league):	2.76 English miles
the *lieue marine* (nautical league):	3.45 English miles

b) *Measurements of surface-area*

144 *pouces carrés* (square inches)	equal	1 *pied carré* (square foot)
36 *pieds carrés*	equal	1 *toise carrée* (square *toise*)
9 *toises carrés*	equal	1 *perche carrée* (square *perch*)
100 *perches carrées*	equal	1 *arpent* (surface area)
7,056 *arpents carrés*	equal	1 *lieue carrée* (square league)

The acre (English measure) was larger than the *arpent*. An acre covered 120 *perches carrées*.

c) *Measurements of weight*

16 *onces* (ounces)	equal	1 *livre* (pound)
100 *livres*	equal	1 *quintal* (hundredweight)
2,000 *livres*	equal	1 (nautical) ton

A *ballot* (bale) of beaver fur weighed 120 *livres*.

d) *Measurements of volume*

The confusion is greater here than elsewhere. The following, however, are the main terms.

i. *Liquids:*

2 *roquilles*	equal	1 *demiard*
2 *demiards*	equal	1 *chopine* (pint)
2 *chopines*	equal	1 *pinte* (quart)
2 *pintes*	equal	1 *pot* (half gallon)
4 *pots*	equal	1 *velte* (2 gallons)

Larger than the *velte* (which would be equivalent to a half-gallon today) were

the *ancre*	probably equal to 32 *pots*
the *baril* (keg)	probably equal to 35 to 40 *pots*
the *tonne*	probably equal to 46 *pots*
the *quart*	probably equal to 80 *pots*
the *poinçon* (puncheon)	probably equal to 93 *pots*
the *barrique* (hogshead)	probably equal to 110, 120, or even 180 *pots*
the *muid* (hogshead)	probably equal to 140 *pots*
the *pipe*	probably equal to 210 *pots*
the *tonneau d'Orléans* (Orleans tun)	probably equal to 280 *pots*
the *tonneau de Bordeaux* (Bordeaux tun)	probably equal to 420 *pots*

There is no definition of the *misérable* (the very small quantity of brandy guaranteed to hired men at "break" time); yet, it is mentioned in many contracts. It would seem that the *misérable* was equivalent to one quarter of a *roquille*—a very small amount, only one or two nips!

ii. *Solids:*

2 *litrons*	equal	1 *quart*
4 *quarts*	equal	1 *boisseau* (bushel)
3 *boisseaux*	equal	1 *minot*
4 *minots*	equal	1 *setier*
12 *setiers*	equal	1 *muid*
1½ *muid*	equal	1 *pipe*

Other measures of capacity were as follows:

the *ancre de lard* (bacon), which contained at least 70 *livres*

the *barrique de sel* (salt), 6 *minots*

the *poinçon de pois* (peas), 9 *minots*

the *baril de farine* (flour), or *de boeuf salé* (salt beef), at least 180 *livres*

the *barrique de sucre* (sugar), a maximum of 1,000 *livres*.

Certain articles were sold *à la poignée* (by the handful): the amount that could be held in the hand (as in the case of cod). At other times, articles sold *au cent* (by the hundred). Cod was sold by the hundred, but in fact, this was a quantity of 132 codfish, from which came the word *quarteron,* to designate a quantity of 33 codfish.

iii. *La corde (cord):* A cord of wood measured 8 *pieds* in length by 4 *pieds* in height.

e) *Measurements of time*

i. *The calendar:* Since 1582, France had followed the calendar of Gregory XIII, but other countries adopted it a long time after her (the Netherlands in 1700; England in 1752), so that they were ten days behind and began their year on March 25.

Thus, an English document dated March 24, 1602, is, in the Gregorian calendar, April 3, 1603. The two "styles" are expressed in the following way.

Old Style (O.S.)	January 10, 1750	March 24, 1602
New Style (N.S.)	January 20, 1751	April 3, 1603

ii. *Abbreviations:* It has become the custom when editing documents of the seventeenth century to write gbi^{c}82 for 1682, because scholars though they had read gbi^c; in fact, these were the Roman numerals XVI^c, in a rather distorted form.

One should also note the method of abbreviating the last four months of the year.

7bre September
8bre October
9bre November
X^{bre} December

iii. *Other measurements of time:* In addition to clocks and hourglasses, a "candle" was sometimes used to measure the time at auctions (a candle had to burn before each of the three bids, to allow the bidder to consider the amount of his offer). It even appears that the "pipe" (here, the tobacco pipe is meant) was used as a measurement of time: such and such a village, it was said, is three pipes away, that is, the time needed to smoke three pipes.

Bibliographical Note

The general studies on the administration of justice are old, but they remain useful:

D. DU BOIS CAHALL, *The Sovereign Council of New France.* New York, Columbia University, 1915.

J. DELALANDE, *Le Conseil souverain de la Nouvelle-France.* Québec, Proulx, 1927.

G. LANCTÔT, *L'Administration de la Nouvelle-France.* Paris, Champion, 1929, pp. 83-124.

E. LAREAU, *Histoire du droit canadien.* Montréal, Périard, 1888-1889, 2 vol.

Recent studies are specialized studies of limited scope, but will give new life to historiography in this field.

On the profession of notary

A. VACHON, *Histoire du notariat canadien, 1621-1960.* Montréal, 1961.

On criminal law

A. MOREL, "La Justice criminelle en Nouvelle-France," in *Cité Libre,* (January 1963), pp. 26-30.

G. MALCHELOSSE, "Un procès criminel aux Trois-Rivières en 1759," in the *Cahiers des Dix,* XVIII, 1953, pp. 171-226.

R. BOYER, *Les Crimes et châtiments au Canada français, du XVIIe au XXe siècle.* Montréal, Cercle du Livre de France, 1966.

A. LACHANCE, "Les Prisons au Canada sous le régime français," in the *Revue d'histoire de l'Amérique français,* XIX, 4 (March 1966), pp. 561-565.

A. LACHANCE, *Le Bourreau au Canada sous le régime français.* Cahiers d'histoire no. 18 of the Société historique de Québec, Québec, 1966.

CHAPTER VIII

Public welfare

In the field of public welfare in New France, one must not look for the complex organization familiar to the society of the twentieth century. As in France and the other countries of the eighteenth century, organization was still only at an elementary stage, but other things being equal, the colony was no worse off than the mother country. The State adopted the greatest possible number of preventive measures to protect the health of the public. Society did its best to help illegitimate children and the poor, and in a haphazard way, an attempt was made to protect the towns against fire.

Health

In Canada, there were numerous epidemics that brought disaster. During a period of seventy-five years, we can cite ten of these, all of them unusually severe: in 1685, typhus; in 1687-88, smallpox or "purple fever," which was responsible for five hundred deaths; in 1700, influenza; in 1702-1703, another smallpox epidemic, which caused more than two thousand deaths in Quebec alone; malignant fevers in 1710 and 1718; smallpox in 1734; typhus from 1743 to 1746; typhus again in 1750; smallpox in 1755, which claimed five hundred victims; and new epidemics of typhus in 1756-1757 and in 1759. Two endemic illnesses (influenza and smallpox) every year carried off a number of adults, and with other childhood diseases, kept the death rate high among children.

a) *Preventive measures*

To reduce the conditions that led to these epidemics, preventive measures were laid down with respect to the ships that regularly carried with them "purple fevers" or "yellow fevers," typhus, and cholera. Officials from the *Amirauté* inspected the ships before passengers and merchandise were disembarked; if a ship were found to be carrying disease, it was put into quarantine and was disinfected with tar smoke.

In the country itself, the application of elementary health measures was supervised throughout the year (at least in the cities). In this field, the first important legislation was passed in 1673, and this was completed by stricter legislation in 1706. In 1673, for example, people building new houses were obliged to install "latrines or privies" in order to avoid the stench of this waste when it was deposited in the street. Where houses

A nun from the Hôtel-Dieu in Quebec

were already built without latrines, the owner had to clean the part of the street in front of his house each morning. By 1706, exceptions were no longer tolerated: every house in the town had to have its latrine.

In a general way, legislation in the eighteenth century prevented the streets from becoming dumps for night soil. Previously, all waste (human and animal dung, straw, and garbage) was thrown there. One could no longer throw anything from the windows, and night soil and refuse had to be carried to the river. (This rule was applied more strictly to butchers.) In the Lower Town, where pig-breeding was mainly carried on, it was forbidden to raise more than one pig per family and to let these animals "wander through the streets." Finally, an attempt was made to persuade people to pave the part of the street that lay in front of their houses. There was certainly a *juge de police* (equivalent to an inspector) to enforce these regulations; but though laws existed, they were not necessarily observed. At the end of the French regime, Quebec was considered an unhealthy and insanitary town because the inhabitants were neglectful. The authorities were not strict, and there was too much reliance on the optimistic policy that "every man must clean his own threshold."

Other measures concerning food were added to the fairly successful ones concerning public cleanliness. The important ordinance of 1706 required that bread should be good and "in good condition." Later, a baker was tried for making poor-quality bread liable to cause disease. The selling of meat from an animal that had died of disease or even by accident was forbidden. No meat was to be placed on sale before the *procureur du roi* had inspected it. Water was another cause of concern to the authorities, and so they checked the quality of wells and made sure that nothing liable to cause disease got into them.

b) *Medicine and surgery*

Physicians were extremely scarce, and this created problems in public health. They were still like the doctors described by Molière, without the exaggeration of caricature. New France had a total of four doctors: Jean Bonamour, Michel Sarrazin, Jean-François Gaultier and Antoine Briault, although there were plenty of surgeons. One must remember the distinction made both in France and New France between doctors of the Faculty of Medicine, who looked after the sick, and surgeons of the Society of Barber-Surgeons, who performed operations (barbers were finally excluded in 1743). Although the "First Barber and Surgeon of the King" controlled the association, surgeons were still considered to be only craftsmen. Their leader in the colony, who was called "Lieutenant to the King's Surgeon," had to make sure that the surgeons kept to the rules of their craft. They practised bleeding, lancing, amputation (all this, of course, without anesthetics) and substituted for apothecaries.

Both doctors and surgeons, as well as those numerous people who did without these "men of art," made use of ointments, infusions, purgatives, and enemas. The remedies of the Amerinds were popular: spruce gum, from which was made a syrup for colds; medicinal herbs to cure venereal disease; and beaver kidneys for nervous afflictions.

Admission to hospital was reserved for serious cases and those who were at death's door, for it was still believed that a hospital was simply a place in which to die. Hospitals

Montreal's Hôtel-Dieu in the eighteenth century

were provided by the religious communities: in Quebec, the Hôtel-Dieu was run by the Hospitalières de la Miséricorde de Jésus; in Trois-Rivières, there was the hospital of the Ursulines; and in Montreal, the Hôtel-Dieu was served by the Hospitalières de Saint-Joseph. Louisbourg and New Orleans also had their own hospitals.

In various places, one could find midwives (there were five of them in Quebec in 1742), who delivered babies, and if necessary, put the child out to nurse. They practised their profession, after taking the oath before the local curé, and received a salary from the State (six hundred *livres* in 1750).

Welfare work

The State worked hard to solve two important social problems: illegitimate children, who were called *enfants du roi* (children of the king), and the poor.

a) *Illegitimate children*

In the seventeenth century, illegitimate children were the responsibility of the seigneurial magistrates; but since there were very few of these (only the Sulpicians in Montreal, and the Jesuits in Sillery and Trois-Rivières), it was chiefly the State that took over this responsibility. In the eighteenth century, as the only high justiciary, the State took over this task completely.

If the father were known, and there were legal proceedings, the State made him pay for the support and education of the child. Most of the time, the child was of an "unknown father," or even of "unknown father and mother." When this latter happened,

Archives de la province de Québec

Quebec's Hôpital-Général
Part of the building dates from the eighteenth century

the *procureur du roi* gave the child into a nurse's care in the Government area where it had been born. The nurse kept the child, for seven or ten *livres* per month, until it was eighteen months old. After that, it was placed with a settler until it was old enough to earn a living. The number of illegitimate children looked after by the State rose in 1736 to 390. In 1757, their upkeep cost 18,500 *livres*; whereas, earlier, it had reached the sum of 24,000 *livres*.

b) *The poor*

For a long time, in the seventeenth century, the only action taken to alleviate the conditions of poverty was to deal severely with those who begged when they were capable of working. It was only in 1688 that the Conseil Souverain finally took a positive step: that of helping the poor. In each town, the Council set up (the same measures were planned for the countryside) a *Bureau des Pauvres* (Office for the Poor), presided over by the curé. With the help of a secretary, the director made inquiries about the needs of those who appealed for charity, and if they could work, he tried to find employment for them. He put orphans into apprenticeship. A treasurer administered the funds that came from church boxes and the collections made by two women for this purpose. In Quebec, the *Bureau* immediately founded a *Maison de la Providence* for the needy. When a Hôpital-Général was founded in Quebec, in 1693, the *Bureau des Pauvres* disappeared. But, in

Druggists' mortars   A fire bucket

1698, when it was realized that the Hôpital-Général solved only a small part of the welfare problem the *Bureau* was set up again. It was still in existence at the end of the French regime.

In order to provide for the sick poor, the property belonging to the Hôtels-Dieu was divided into two parts and administered separately, as the property of the community and as the property of the poor. A piece of land, for example, given to the Quebec Hôtel-Dieu might be intended to benefit either the nuns or the poor. So, after 1734, the poor became the owners of the seigneury of Maure or Saint-Augustin, and the nuns managed it for them.

The colony possessed two asylums: the Hôpital-Général of Quebec, founded in 1693 by nuns from the Hôtel-Dieu, and the Hôpital-Général of Montreal, founded in 1692 by the Charron Brothers. The work in Montreal was resumed in 1747 by Madame d'Youville and her companions, who still lived in the secular state. Elderly people who were alone or crippled were admitted there, as well as invalids and the insane of both sexes, in special cells. Because of the lack of women's prisons, prostitutes were also kept there.

Protection against fire

Only in the towns was care taken to protect the community against fire, for there, the burning of one house constantly threatened to turn into a conflagration. The buildings crowded close together, the thatched roofs, the straw and other garbage that was thrown into the streets, and the enormous quantity of firewood piled up in the courtyards or against the houses, all made the city a vast woodpile ready to catch fire. In 1685, Governor Denonville wrote about Quebec: "The city is still alarmingly open to fire; the houses are unnecessarily crowded together and surrounded by a fearful amount of firewood." It was the same in Montreal, which was famous for its spectacular fires. In 1721, more than one hundred houses were burned; in 1734, forty-six houses. Further fires occurred in 1754 and 1765. Even the Hôtel-Dieu of Montreal was burned three times in forty years (in 1695, 1721, and 1734).

The first preventive measures were taken in 1664, and the first coherent legislation passed in 1673. This was completed or renewed later by laws in 1676 and by some very important legislation in 1727. The State obliged the inhabitants to have their chimneys cleaned periodically (this was done by young *Savoyards*) and to install ladders against the houses and on the roofs. People were permitted to keep only a small quantity of gunpowder in the house, and this had to be stored in a special way. No fires were allowed in the courtyards. Shipyard workers had to put a "lid on their pipes." Smoking in the bedrooms of inns was also forbidden. Intendant Bégon tried, in 1721, to have houses built only of stone, with a tile roof replacing a thatched one. In 1727, Intendant Dupuy even proposed a special method of constructing gables so that they could be easily knocked down into the street in case of fire. But, after reading the numerous ordinances intended to remind people of their duties, one remains convinced that most of these regulations were not respected.

Methods of protection were still rudimentary. As late as 1781, the Lower Town of Quebec did not have a "royal and common well" (that is, a public well) to provide water needed for firefighting. In 1706, in Quebec, the State put into use one hundred leather buckets and ordered that, at the first sound of the alarm bell, the inhabitants must go to the scene of the fire with a bucket of water. Organization was a little better by the end of the French regime. In Montreal, the Intendant set up two squads of firemen in 1734. These were composed of workmen directed by two master workmen, and the State distributed throughout the town 280 buckets, 100 axes, ladders, battering rams, and various articles for firefighting. The same arrangement was planned for Quebec.

Bibliographical Note

Up to the present time, the subjects of public safety and welfare work in New France have been very little studied. In the fields of health and poverty, some general works give the main principles:

Georges and M.-J. AHERN, *Notes pour servir à l'histoire de la médecine dans le Bas-Canada.* Québec, 1923.

H.-R. CASGRAIN, *Histoire de l'Hôtel-Dieu de Québec.* Québec, Brousseau, 1878.
L'Hôtel-Dieu, premier hôpital de Montréal, 1642-1763. Montréal, 1942.

A. FERLAND-ANGERS, *Mère d'Youville, première fondatrice canadienne.* Montréal, Beauchemin, 1945.

A. G. REID, "The First Poor-Relief System of Canada," in *Canadian Historical Review,* XXVII, 4 (December 1946), pp. 424-431.

The following articles give interesting information on large fires:

"Les Catastrophes dans la Nouvelle-France," in the *Bulletin des Recherches historiques,* 53 (1947), pp. 5-19, 35-48.

"Les Conflagrations à Québec sous le régime français," in the *Bulletin des Recherches historiques,* 31 (1925), pp. 65-76, 97-103.

E.-Z. MASSICOTTE, "Les Incendies à Montréal sous le régime français," in the *Bulletin des Recherches historiques,* 25 (1919), pp. 215-218.

Mgr de Saint-Vallier

CHAPTER IX

Religious life

Like many of the American colonies, New France experienced a strict system of religious control. Admittedly, from 1611 to 1658, the country was under the authority only of the missionaries, but they very soon possessed great influence. In 1620, Champlain received instructions to undertake no new enterprise without first consulting the Récollet Le Baillif. In 1626, the Jesuit Lallemant became Champlain's spiritual director. Later, devout governors such as Montmagny, Mézy, Denonville, and influential or exacting bishops, like Laval and Saint-Vallier, made sure the Church held a predominant place. Although the eighteenth century saw the Church subject to the authority of the State, the ecclesiastical hierarchy retained supreme authority over the clergy and the people. Churchmen trained in the school of the Catholic Counter Reformation maintained strict control over religious life.

The Bishop

The first bishop was appointed in 1674. He resided in Quebec, and as head of the Church in New France, he had ecclesiastical authority over the entire French empire in North America.

a) *His powers*

The Bishop, usually called *Monsieur de Québec*, received his documents from the Pope, but was appointed by the king. Like the governor and the intendant, his position depended on the king, who could invite him to resign or could detain him in France, as Louis XIV had to do with Mgr de Saint-Vallier. As soon as he took possession of his see, the Bishop swore an oath of allegiance to the king, and in practice, he supported the interests of the Crown. Mgr de Saint-Vallier, for example, considered that a bishop could keep better watch over the King's interests than the apostolic vicars, "who seem more concerned with those of Rome." The Bishop ordered public prayer for the interests of the Crown and the person of the king, whenever these were threatened, or sometimes, a *Te Deum* when the king achieved a victory.

The eighteenth-century bishop was no longer the political force he had been in the preceding century. Certainly, he still had precedence over the intendant after the governor, but he confined himself to his religious duties and no longer took his seat on the Conseil Supérieur.

The Bishop retained the right to make ecclesiastical appointments. He appointed the *grands-vicaires* to represent him in the various parts of New France. He granted the "dignities" within the Chapter (except for the offices of *doyenné* [Dean] and *chantrerie* [Precentor]). He also appointed the priests who were to be curés or missionaries in the parishes, without the State's having any right to question this. However, in cases where religion directly affected everyday life, the State took precedence. It was the State that authorized, or forbade, the formation of communities of men or women and limited their number. It also approved, or prohibited, the foundation of parishes and fixed the amount of the tithe.

b) *The episcopal see*

The Bishop had his episcopal see in Quebec, where the church of Notre-Dame, with its double title of *Conception de la Sainte-Vierge* and of *Saint-Louis*, served as his cathedral. This claim to cathedral status was ceaselessly contested by the canons, who made the building their canonical church, and by the curés and churchwardens, who claimed it as a parish church. These disputes became very distressing for the first bishop of the English regime.

During the eighteenth century, the Bishop lived on the far east side of Cap-aux-Diamants, in an episcopal palace. The original plan would have made this residence very large, but because of the lack of money, only half of it was built. Even in this half, rooms had to be rented to the French administration.

The Bishop's annual income amounted to some ten thousand *livres*, whether the year was a good or bad one.

c) *The bishops of New France*

New France had six bishops in less than a century (between 1674 and 1760):

François de Montmorency Laval (1674 to 1688) had been apostolic vicar from 1658 to 1674. In the absence of his successor, he continued to carry out the duties of a bishop. Consecrated at 35 years of age.

Jean-de-la-Croix Chevrières de Saint-Vallier (1688 to 1727). Chosen by Mgr de Laval himself, he served first as *vicaire général* from 1685 to 1688. Consecrated at 35 years of age.

Louis-François Duplessis de Mornay (1728 to 1733). A Capuchin, he had been coadjutor to the previous bishop, from 1713 to 1727, but never came to New France either as coadjutor or as bishop. Consecrated at 50 years of age.

Pierre-Herman Dosquet (1733 to 1739). Coadjutor of the previous bishop, from 1729 to 1733. Consecrated at 34 years of age.

François-Louis Pourroy de Lauberivière (1739 to 1740) died on his arrival in 1740. Consecrated at 28 years of age.

Henri-Marie Dubreil de Pontbriand (1741 to 1760, the year of his death). Consecrated at 33 years of age.

Public Archives of Canada

View of part of the bishop's palace in Quebec
(from an engraving by Richard Short)

Not one of these bishops was Canadian, or Acadian, by birth; yet the last governor general of New France was born in Canada. These six bishops were all born in France, with the exception of Mgr Dosquet, who was of Flemish origin. The Conseil Supérieur did not even recognize him as a "French native." They were all nobles, and with the exception of the Capuchin Mornay, belonged to the secular clergy.

The youngest bishop was Mgr de Lauberivière who was only twenty-eight years old at his consecration; the oldest was Mgr de Mornay consecrated at the age of fifty.

The first two bishops ruled for the longest periods: Mgr de Laval, for thirty years, as apostolic vicar and titular bishop; Mgr de Saint-Vallier, for thirty-nine years.

With the exception of Mgr de Pontbriand, the bishops were conspicuous for their absenteeism. Of the thirty years spent in charge of the Church of New France, Mgr de Laval spent twelve in France. Mgr Saint-Vallier spent seventeen years in Europe of an episcopate of thirty-nine years, (from 1700 to 1713, he was detained by the French King and the English). Bishop Mornay did not come once during an episcopate of six years. Mgr Dosquet, titular bishop for six years, came for only one year. This voluntary or accidental absenteeism (sometimes necessary) did not occur without creating many problems in the diocese. These, however, did not have the tragic character of the episcopal vacancy that

Mgr de Lauberivière, Bishop at 28

happened between 1760 and 1766, at a time when all relations were officially broken off with France and with Rome.

d) *Vicaires généraux* and *grands-vicaires*

When the bishop was absent, a *vicaire général* took his place. This role was filled by Mgr de Saint-Vallier from 1685 to 1688, until the resignation of Mgr de Laval was duly accepted; it was also filled by Mgr de Laval, at this time called *Monseigneur l'Ancien*, while Mgr de Saint-Vallier was detained in Europe.

Mgr Dosquet began the custom of having a permanent *vicaire général* to represent the Bishop of Quebec in Paris. This *vicaire* served as an intermediary between the French king and Rome. He supervised the recruitment of priests for New France and looked after all the problems that could be solved in Europe. During the French regime, the *vicaire général* was Pierre de La Rue, Abbot of Isle-Dieu, whose title was *Aumonier général des colonies de la Nouvelle-France* (Chaplain-general of the colonies of New France). He kept the position until 1777.

In New France *grands-vicaires* helped the bishop administer a diocese which stretched across a continent. The bishop had a *grand-vicaire* in Acadia, one in each of the three Governments of Canada, and another in Michilimackinac. The one in Michilimackinac was the Superior of the Jesuit house, and he had authority over the whole of the *pays d'en haut*. The one in Louisiana was also a Jesuit, the Superior of New Orleans.

The clergy

The most distinguished group of clergy in New France was the *Chapitre* (Chapter) because it was closest to the bishop.

a) *The Chapter*

The Chapter first appeared in 1684 and was composed of contemplatives (so-called because their only role was that of prayer) who acted as the bishop's court and council. The members lived as a community, assembled in the choir three times a day to recite the canonical services, and sang High Mass every day.

The Chapter had thirteen members: five dignitaries (the dean, precentor, archdeacon, *théologal*, and *grand-pénitencier*) and eight ordinary canons. During the French regime, there was never more than one honorary canon, the curé of Quebec, and it was hoped that this would reduce the difficulties between the parish and the Chapter. A director of ceremonies, a sacristan, a choirmaster, and six choirboys, who were pupils of the Petit Séminaire of Quebec, served this institution.

The *grands-vicaires*, the members of the ecclesiastical court, and the chaplains and confessors of the religious communities were usually chosen from the Chapter. The canons, however, were not allowed to teach or to become curés. Their essential function was to pray together. In exceptional cases, when they lived in a presbytery, they were known as missionaries. Although it was first attached to the Seminary of Quebec by Mgr de Laval (an action that meant a new burden and a rival for the seminary) the Chapter, under Mgr de Saint-Vallier, became a distinct and autonomous body. As part of its income, it received the revenues from two abbeys in France (Maubec in Berry and Lestrées in

Normandy), which brought in some 6,500 *livres* per annum. A gift of 8,000 *livres* was the reward for allowing the King to appoint the dean and precentor. It also possessed one half of the Petite-Nation, a seigneury that remained unproductive because the State did not allow colonists to settle on the Ottawa River—the fur-trade route.

The history of the Chapter consists almost throughout of fruitless and childish disputes. The canons were taken to task for paying more attention to their interests than to their duties, because they were often absent from the services and lived outside the community. At the end of the French regime, the dispersal of its members hurt the Chapter. Three of the five dignitaries remained in France for years; three canons were in parishes; two others embarked in 1759, never to return.

It was only after the death of the last bishop of New France that the Chapter played an important role. It set up a temporary administration and on two occasions carried out an episcopal election.

No attempt was made to preserve this institution, and its disappearance was not as deeply felt as others in this period. It ceased to meet in 1773, and the last canon died in 1795. It was not considered worthwhile to re-establish the Chapter in Quebec until 1915.

b) *Secular clergy*

The clergy of the Church of New France included both secular and regular priests. Very few secular priests had lived in New France before the arrival of Mgr de Laval (the best-known are Flesché and Saint-Sauveur). Mgr de Laval in 1658 began to form his own secular clergy, and to ensure support for it, he founded the *Séminaire de Québec* (Seminary of Quebec) in 1663, and in 1668, the *Petit Séminaire* (Little Seminary), which was to provide recruitment and training. Here, the candidates for the priesthood were accepted and put through rigorous training. They spent the whole scholastic year at the Seminary, and after August 15 (marking the beginning of the summer vacation) they went to the farm of Saint-Joachim where they helped with the harvest and devoted some time to study each day. At the end of this vacation, they returned to the Seminary. Since this was only a training establishment, the students took courses at the Jesuit College.

It has been estimated that, of 843 pupils who went through the Little Seminary during the French regime (that is, over a period of ninety years), 118 attained the priesthood. In any case, the secular clergy rapidly became Canadian.

In 1760, out of 73 secular priests, four fifths were Canadian. This secular clergy, trained by the priests of the Quebec Seminary, went to serve the parishes and the missions but occupied only one urban *cure*—that of Quebec—after 1664.

The secular clergy in the countryside have been blamed too easily for a rather poor intellectual life. It must be remembered that they were *prêtres-habitants* with a difficult ministry. They yielded to local conditions because they were isolated among a largely illiterate population and were forced, most of the time, to resort to agricultural work.

c) *Regular clergy*

The title of "regular clergy" here includes not only the priests who lived within a religious order, but also every priest who belonged to the life of a community by observing

Archives de la province de Québec

Duberger's model of the Quebec Seminary
Completed in 1809, Duberger's model shows the Seminary much as it appeared during the French regime

a rule. The priests who were at this time "joined" to a seminary were members of a community, as were the canons discussed above.

i. *The Quebec Seminary:* It was officially called the *Séminaire des Missions étrangères* because its priests, all from France, came from the Seminary of Foreign Missions in Paris. The Quebec Seminary was the smallest of the communities of priests (at the end of the French regime, there were only five members), but it was very important because it recruited and trained the future members of the secular clergy.

The Seminary also devoted itself to missionary work. In 1698, it founded the mission of Sainte-Famille at Cahokia in Illinois, which still existed at the time of the Conquest. From time to time, it sent some of its members to Acadia.

It had been generously endowed and held, among other property, the seigneury of Sault-au-Matelot (in the town of Quebec), the seigneury of Beaupré, and Île Jésus.

ii. *The Montreal Seminary:* The Sulpicians of Montreal, secular priests living in a community, had also been part of a seminary in Paris—that of Saint-Sulpice.

They arrived in 1657 and immediately became curés of Montreal, which they acquired as a seigneury in 1664. In addition to the parish ministry that they carried on in Montreal (there was, strictly speaking, only the one parish of Notre-Dame, for the other

Archives de la province de Québec

The Montreal Seminary in the eighteenth century

areas received only parish services), they devoted themselves to teaching in the elementary schools. A few (less than ten) became missionaries in Acadia, while others looked after the Indians who lived in villages in the Montreal area. We owe the important exploration of the upper Saint Lawrence in 1669-1670 to the two Sulpicians, Dollier de Casson and Galinée.

The Sulpicians numbered thirty by 1760, all born in France. They seem to have been opposed to recruiting Canadians, and this attitude was to create serious problems for them during the English regime.

iii. *The Spiritains:* The Spiritains were priests from the Seminary of Saint-Esprit in Paris, and they did not found any branch in New France. They only made individual contributions to missionary work in Acadia. Of the few representatives of this order, the Abbé Le Loutre remains the most famous for his political role.

iv. *The Jesuits:* The Jesuits were the first members of a religious order to come to New France, and they worked as missionaries in Acadia from 1611 to 1613, going to the Saint Lawrence in 1625. Returning to France in 1629, they came back permanently in 1632. At first, they were the only missionaries performing the function of curés, in Ville-Marie until 1657, in Quebec until 1664, and in Trois-Rivières until 1670. When they had been replaced in these three towns, they dedicated themselves to missions, both stationary and itinerant, accepting the most unrewarding and the most dangerous ones (the Huron, Iroquois, and Montagnais missions). At the end of the French regime, they were also working in Acadia and Louisiana. They can be found involved in great discoveries: Father Albanel at Hudson Bay; Father Marquette on the Mississippi; and Fathers Aulneau, Messaiger, and Coquart accompanying La Vérendrye to the West. In the Quebec College, they maintained a high standard of education. They also played an important part in religious administration. A Jesuit, the Superior of Michilimackinac, was *grand-vicaire* to the bishop of Quebec for the *pays d'en haut*; there was also a Jesuit, the Superior of New Orleans, who fulfilled the same function for the whole of Louisiana.

The Jesuits had been endowed with considerable wealth. If all their lands were brought together in one place, the resulting area would form a seigneury with 6 miles of frontage and 171 miles deep. In 1728, these lands brought them an income of 20,000 *livres*; in 1726, perhaps 40,000 *livres*. For the support of their missions and for their Chair of Hydrography, they received an additional 13,300 *livres* a year from the King.

The Jesuits had a negligible Canadian membership (before 1760, they are known to have had three Canadians, of whom only one came to work in New France), and they were harshly treated in Europe by both Catholic and Protestant countries. The English forbade them to accept any new members, and before ceding Louisiana to Spain, the French were careful to expel most of the Jesuits from the area. The last Jesuit of the French regime in Canada died in 1800.

v. *The Récollets:* The Récollets, dressed in grey homespun, were the first missionaries on the Saint Lawrence. They arrived in 1615, re-embarked in 1629, and returning in 1670. They continued their role of missionaries without either the scope or the boldness of the Jesuits. They also became titular chaplains to the governor and the army. It was in this capacity that they served Louisbourg, Detroit, and other important forts. Already acting as parish priests in Trois-Rivières, they tended to become curés and priests in charge of parishes, living like the secular clergy in presbyteries. This led to a serious relaxation in the life of the community.

They were very popular and rapidly became Canadian (in 1760, 17 of their 24 priests were Canadian). However, they, too, were to disappear like the Jesuits, and the last Récollet priest of the French regime died in 1813.

vi. *The Capuchins:* Strictly speaking, the Récollets did not form an order, but only a branch of the Order of Friars Minor, founded by Saint Francis of Assisi. Another branch of this Franciscan order, the Capuchins, had representatives in New France.

They arrived in Acadia in 1632 and worked there until 1655, when the English conquest forced them to return to France. They reappeared in Louisiana in 1721 and confined their attention to the missions on the Lower Mississippi. *Vicaire général* L'Isle-Dieu took them to task, as with the Récollets, because they were not united and showed signs of insubordination.

Religious auxiliaries

To help the clergy and to minister to social needs, New France had a few Brothers and a much larger number of nuns, both cloistered and secular.

The Récollet monastery in Montreal

a) *The Brothers*

The *Frères Hospitaliers de la Croix et de Saint-Joseph* (Hospital Brothers of the Cross and Saint Joseph) were founded in 1692 by François Charron de La Barre. They devoted themselves to the running of an asylum and the Hôpital-Général of Montreal. They also taught school, and for a time, operated a real trade school. In the end, they were forced to dissolve because they were few in number and because the community to which they belonged was badly administered and was ruined by quarrels and defections. In 1737, the *Frères des Écoles chrétiennes* arrived to check the value of their work, but they preferred to withdraw, not to return until exactly one century later.

Louisbourg also had its Frères Hospitaliers after 1716. They were called the Frères de Saint Jean-de-Dieu and looked after the old and the sick. They returned to France when the fortified town capitulated.

b) *Nuns*

The communities of nuns were much more successful and were much more important than the communities of brothers.

i. *Cloistered communities:* In 1639, two groups of nuns arrived in Quebec from cloistered communities: the Ursulines, who came from Tours and Paris and were led by the mystic Marie de l'Incarnation; and the Hospitalières de la Miséricorde de Jésus, recruited from a convent in Dieppe. The Ursulines took charge of a *séminaire de filles* for French and

Huron girls, but the nuns soon had to give up the attempt to turn the little "savages" into French girls. The Hospitalières looked after the Hôtel-Dieu of Quebec, which took in the sick.

In 1659, a third group of nuns arrived from a cloistered community. The Hospitalières de Saint-Joseph were part of the convent of La Flèche (in Anjou) and came to carry on the work of Jeanne Mance in the Hôtel-Dieu of Montreal.

Then, the two cloistered communities of Quebec each founded a new community. At the request of Mgr de Saint-Vallier, some nuns from the Hôtel-Dieu went into the outskirts of the town, in 1693, and founded a Hôpital-Général for the infirm, the old, and the insane. Again, at the request of the same bishop, the Ursulines went to Trois-Rivières, in 1697, to establish another convent where they would devote themselves to education and hospital work.

Finally, a sixth cloistered convent was founded in 1727, when some French Ursulines arrived in New Orleans. There were only eleven of them in 1747, working in schools and hospitals.

ii. *Secular communities:* In a country as vast as New France, where settlements were small, cloistered communities could play a much less effective part than active communities. Marguerite Bourgeoys understood this when, in 1658, she founded the *Filles séculières de la Congrégation de Notre-Dame*, called *Soeurs de la Congrégation* (Sisters of the Congregation), in Montreal. She opposed Mgr de Saint-Vallier who was disturbed at seeing nuns living in the world and wanted to assign them to the cloister. The Sisters of the Congregation remained secular, going in pairs into the countryside, to dedicate themselves to the education of children of both sexes. They had several schools in the Government of Montreal, one in the Government of Trois-Rivières, four in Quebec, and one in Louisbourg.

Another community of secular nuns was founded in Montreal in 1737: that of Madame d'Youville, called the *Communauté des Soeurs Grises* (Community of the Grey Sisters), because of the grey dress they adopted, no doubt in imitation of the Récollets. The Grey Sisters took over the duties of the Frères Hospitaliers at the Hôpital-Général of Montreal. This was the first community founded by a Canadian woman.

iii. *General table:* New France thus possessed eight communities of nuns, the population of these communities, in 1760 (without counting the lay sisters) being distributed as follows:

Congrégation de Notre-Dame	70
Ursulines of Quebec	30
Hôtel-Dieu of Quebec	26
Hôtel-Dieu of Montreal	26
Hôpital-Général of Quebec	22
Ursulines of Trois-Rivières	15
Hôpital-Général of Montreal	15
Ursulines of New Orleans	11 (?)
Total	215

Marguerite Bourgeoys
A portrait done by the painter Pierre Le Ber, immediately after the founder's death in 1700.

Of these 215 nuns, 130 (or 60.5 percent) were in cloistered communities. There would have been more cloistered nuns if the State had not fixed a maximum number of members for each community, which number could not be exceeded. This action was done to prevent the upsetting of an exact balance.

What strikes one, particularly in this general table, is the concentration of nuns in the best-organized part of New France, Canada. While Louisiana had only eleven and Louisbourg three or four, all the others (some two hundred) were in the three Governments of the Saint Lawrence.

Note should also be taken of the rapid expansion made by the Congrégation de Notre-Dame, which can be explained in two ways. There was the fact that cloistered convents could not exceed a certain number of members, and the fact that their rule was less severe. In any case, it was this community that recruited more members from the lower classes.

On the other hand, it was the Convent of the Hôpital-Général of Quebec that proved more attractive to young ladies of good family, in spite of the unpleasant tasks that had to be performed there. In 1760, 59.1 percent of its nuns came from the upper classes (the Hôtel-Dieu of Montreal was second with only 30.6 percent), which made the Hôpital-Général of Quebec the aristocratic convent in New France.

Canadian membership no longer seemed a cause for worry because, in 1760, with the exception of the Ursulines of New Orleans, no nun was a native of France.

The parish

The parish in New France, was not legally established until fairly late. During the first half of the seventeenth century, the mission church was the centre of attraction for the settlers. The first parish, Notre-Dame-de-Quebec, was not set up until 1664, and it remained the only parish until 1678, when Mgr de Laval set up fourteen parishes, including Ville-Marie. Between 1692 and 1724, Mgr de Saint-Vallier set up twenty five. By the end of the French regime, there would be more than one hundred in Canada alone.

The parish, not the seigneury, served as the basis not only for the religious administration, but also for the civil and military administration. It was the parish church, not the seigneurial manor, which was the centre of social life in the countryside.

a) *The founding of the parish*

In France as a rule, the State did not interfere with the founding of parishes, but in New France it intervened constantly to allow or forbid the founding of a parish and to decide on its boundaries.

Before founding a parish, the first requisite was a sufficiently large population. Then, the church had to be endowed with the necessary lands. Finally, the settlers had to be consulted about the advantages and inconveniences of the proposed boundaries. (This was the so-called *de commodo et incommodo* inquiry.) In 1721, a program was initiated to lay out the future parish boundaries. Governor Vaudreuil made the *procureur général* institute an inquiry throughout Canada into existing and future parishes. As a result of this inquiry, the State ratified the boundaries that had already been settled and fixed those of future parishes in advance.

Interior of the church of Saint-Pierre, on Île d'Orléans

Archives de la province de Québec

b) *The cure*

Wherever a parish was set up in the proper way, there was a corresponding *cure*. The holder of this *cure* was called the *curé*, and he was the religious leader of the parish, while the captain of militia was its civil and military leader.

i. *The conferring of the cure:* There were three methods of conferring a *cure*, the first of which came about when the bishop made a *libre collation* (a free grant). By this method, the bishop appointed the holder without having to account to either the king or the governor. He could remove his candidate from office as he wished and appoint him elsewhere. In order to reduce the power of the bishop, the State tried, without success, to force upon him the idea that curés could not be removed.

In fact, curés could not be removed if they were appointed by the second method, which was *l'union des cures à une institution* (attaching *cures* to an institution). By virtue of this system, the *cure* of Notre-Dame-de-Québec was attached to the Quebec Seminary, which presented the candidate for this position to the bishop (this attachment was only brought to an end in 1768). In the same way, in Montreal, the Superior of the Sulpicians was titular curé of the "parish" of Montreal Island.

From 1679 to 1699 there was a third method: *la cure de patronage*. Any person who built a stone church at his own expense had the right to present the future curé to the bishop. Just three cases of this kind are known: in Saint-Joachim and on Ile Jésus, the Quebec Seminary had this right, while in Terrebonne, it was the curé and Seigneur Lepage.

ii. *Duties of the curé:* The possession of the *cure* was made official by letters of appointment and a special ceremony that was recorded. Then the holder carried out his duties: he provided spiritual ministrations, officiated at the services, and presided over the administration of the church revenues. He even had certain civil functions: to keep the registers of births and deaths; in the absence of competent people, to preside over cases of trusteeship and the making of inventories; and to receive and draw up marriage contracts and wills. After 1717, he was released from the obligation of making the ordinances of the State public at the sermon during Mass. But, at the time of the sermon and in the canon of the Mass, he still had to pray for the king by name, and at the time of the sermon, had to do the same for the seigneur and his family.

iii. *Housing and supporting the curé:* A priest only settled in a parish if it could support him. Yet, every year, the State granted eight thousand *livres* to the bishop for *cures* that could not be kept up without this subsidy.

The parish had to provide the curé with accommodation at least thirty feet square, called the presbytery. He was also provided with a male servant (female servants being forbidden). Fees were one of the sources of income possessed by the curé. These included the fees for Low Mass (from twenty to twenty-four *sols*), for High Mass, for the transcription of extracts from the register of births and deaths, and for marriage banns.

His most important source of income, however, was the tithe. The tithe was fixed in 1663 at one thirteenth, then at one twentieth, and finally, in 1667, at one twenty-sixth. It was collected only on threshed and winnowed grain (that is, wheat, rye, barley, and oats), but by a special agreement, it could be collected on other products if there was

Archives de la province de Québec

Tabernacle from the church of Lachenaie
Executed by Gilles Bolvin, from 1737-1741, based on a design by the Récollet Augustin Quintal.

no grain. The parishioner himself had to deliver the tithe to the presbytery, at a convenient time, without waiting for it to be claimed, as in France.

The State intervened, on the one hand, to decide the amount of the tithe and what form it should take, and no curé could change any part of this if the State showed its opposition. On the other hand, the State also intervened, when necessary, to force the parishioner to carry out his duty. Thus, the State protected both the Church, which had a right to claim support for its priests, and the parishioner, to prevent extortion.

On the whole, the tithe bound together the fortunes of the curé and the settler. Both suffered the effects of prosperity and want. Admittedly, the tithe was an extra obligation added to the seigneurial dues, but these latter were not high. In any case, in this area of taxation, the *habitant* was still in a better position than the French peasant, who was subject to the *taille* and several kinds of tithe.

c) *The Vestry*

Whenever a parish or simple mission was established, there was always a vestry, that is, a body entrusted with administering the property of the church. The vestry of Notre-Dame-de-Quebec, for example, was set up much earlier than was the parish.

i. *Organization:* Members of the vestry included the curé (*ex officio*), the former churchwardens, and the *marguilliers du banc* (churchwardens of the pew). These last numbered three, except in Quebec where there were four of them.

The churchwardens were elected by the parishioners, except in Quebec and Montreal where the election was held by the former and current churchwardens. The person elected did not have the right to refuse, unless he was a nobleman, a soldier, or an officer of militia serving a term of duty. However, women were not allowed to become churchwardens. The office carried no salary; so the churchwardens had to be satisfied with the special honours accorded them in the church, and with the pew that was reserved for them in a prominent position. In cases where a seigneurial pew and a pew for the captain of militia already existed, the "churchwardens' pew" was placed opposite the pulpit.

The board of administration consisted of the curé, who was its president, and the "pew churchwardens." The oldest of the churchwardens, called the "Head Churchwarden," had the duty of administering the revenues of the church during the current year. As a rule, he collected and looked after the funds and paid current expenses. When his period of office ended, he presented his accounts to the members of the vestry, or to the parishioners, and "left the pew." The bishop, when he visited the parish, inspected and approved the accounts.

ii. *Budget:* The income of the vestry could come from various sources: the rent on farmland, the Collection for the Infant Jesus (made by the curé at the time of his parochial visit), the *tasse* (a Sunday collection, so-called because a "cup" was used), oblations, the pew rents, fees for High Mass (one third of which went to the vestry), and burials. The tithe did not form part of this revenue, for it was the personal property of the curé.

The usual expenses included the cost of services (wine, candles, the beadle's salary, and firewood) and the maintenance, or repair, of the interior of the church. If it became necessary to carry out repairs to the outside of the church or to the presbytery, or if some

Archives de la province de Québec

Seigneurial pew from the church of Saint-Pierre, on Île d'Orléans

construction work was required, these expenses were considered to be "extraordinary" because they greatly exceeded the budget of the vestry. In such cases, the parishioners met to assign the work and contributions necessary, so that each one had to provide a certain number of workdays, planks, or nails.

The cost of maintaining a school and paying the salary of a schoolmaster—in places where the vestry provided a school—was also part of the unusual expenses.

iii. *Introduction to democracy*: The vestry was the only administrative body over which Canadians had any control, provided that they were or had been churchwardens. It often happened that the head churchwarden played no part in administration, either because he was illiterate or because the curé found it more convenient to manage the money himself. The budget of this body was very small in the majority of parishes: a short page for income and a short page for expenses. However, apart from the elections of officials (syndics), which were only carried out in the towns and in the presence of the intendant, the vestry provided the only opportunity for Canadians to hold regular elections. This introduction to democracy was restricted in Quebec and Montreal since, in these two towns, it was customary for former churchwardens and those currently occupying the office to be the only electors.

Religious observance

a) *Early Training*

The first ceremony that brought the newly-born child into the Catholic Church was Baptism. This rite was free of charge, but obligatory. The *Rituel* required the parents to have the child baptized within three or four days after its birth. In certain circumstances, private baptism was permitted, provided that the child was taken to church as soon as possible afterwards. The State sometimes had to intervene when parents made use of very special excuses to baptize their children privately or to put off the ceremony of Baptism for a long time. When the child received the sacrament, he (or she) was accompanied by both a godfather and a godmother. The priest who performed the baptism bore witness by the record he placed in the register of births and deaths.

Baptism was followed by the sacrament of Confirmation, conferred by the bishop when the child had reached, as the *Rituel* expressed it, "the appropriate age." This sacrament was also obligatory and was duly recorded by the priest.

The young Catholic was prepared for Confirmation and for the whole of his religious life by the study of the catechism. He studied the catechism composed by Mgr de Saint-Vallier, which was divided into two parts: the "Larger Catechism" or "fuller explanation of the doctrine of Jesus Christ," and the "Shorter Catechism," which was a summary of the other, "intended for the youngest children, or uneducated people." The child was required to know his prayers from memory, many of these prayers being in Latin.

b) *The Eucharist*

When the believer had been adequately introduced to the Faith and had reached the age of reason (according to the norms of that time, about twelve years of age), he began to receive the Eucharist.

Public Archives of Canada

Confessional from the Récollet Church in Quebec
(from an engraving by Richard Short)

From then on, he had to make at least one communion per year, which had to be at Easter time and was recorded by the curé. If the believer fulfilled this duty in another parish, he had to present written proof of this fact to his own curé. The Church required the fulfilment of certain conditions before allowing a person to approach the altar. These were fasting since the previous midnight; the removal of weapons by the men; and the covering of breasts and shoulders by the women. Women were also asked to veil their heads and to let down their dresses. (They wore long dresses anyway, but they used to turn up the skirts and tuck them into the waistband in order to allow freedom for walking).

The *Rituel* encouraged frequent communion, but there were so many reservations and so much advice on the long preparations necessary beforehand that the faithful were convinced, on the whole, to take communion infrequently.

c) *Penitence*

Confession was obligatory at least once a year, and this minimal duty had to be completed at Easter time with the curé of one's parish. If an Easter confession was made in another parish a "certificate of confession" had to be obtained to be given to one's own curé. The *Rituel* was strict about women's confessions. They could not confess in the sacristy, or in the church after sunset, unless there were witnesses and lighted candles. The confessor could impose public penance upon his penitents, but only with authorization from the bishop. For example, the guilty person might be obliged to kneel at the door of the church when the faithful were coming in.

The entire year was marked by days when one did penance, either through abstinence (abstaining from eating meat) or by fasting. Fasting was harsh: meat, eggs, and milk products were forbidden,* and only one meal was allowed, to be taken at midday, with a light snack in the evening. Many days were fast days: the forty days of Lent, except for Sundays (which were meatless), the vigils of ten religious holidays, the Ember Days, which alone included twelve fast days, for a total of some fifty-seven fast days during the year, or nearly two months. The days of abstinence must be added to those days on which meat was forbidden: the three Rogation Days, the feast of St. Mark, and every Friday and Saturday. Altogether, through both fasting or abstinence, one did without meat for almost five months of the year.

d) *The Lord's Day*

There were also many days when Sunday rest was compulsory. To the fifty-two Sundays of the year were added some thirty-seven Holy Days of Obligation before 1744.

During the year		The Patron Saint of the parish
January	1	Circumcision
	6	Epiphany
February	2	Purification
	24	St. Mathias, Apostle

---

*The catechism forbade eggs and milk products during Lent, but it appears that from the time the colony began the consumption of eggs, butter, and cheese was tolerated.

March	19	St. Joseph, First Patron Saint of the Country
	25	Incarnation and Annunciation

In the spring		Easter
		Easter Monday
		Easter Tuesday
		Ascension
		Whit Sunday
		Whit Monday
		Whit Tuesday
		Feast of the Holy Sacrament
		Thursday of the Octave of Feast (until noon)

May	1	St. Philip and St. James, Apostles
June	24	St. John the Baptist
	29	St. Peter and St. Paul
July	25	St. James, Apostle
	26	St. Anne
August	10	St. Lawrence
	15	Assumption
	24	St. Bartholomew, Apostle
	25	St. Louis, Second Patron Saint of the Cathedral
September	8	Birth of the Holy Virgin
	21	St. Matthew, Apostle
	29	St. Michael
October	28	St. Simon and St. Jude, Apostles
November	1	All Saints
	30	St. Andrew, Apostle
December	3	St. Francis Xavier, Second Patron Saint of the Country
	8	Conception of the Holy Virgin
	21	St. Thomas, Apostle
	25	Christmas
	26	St. Stephen
	27	St. John, Apostle

It should be noticed, in particular, that people did not work on the several feasts of the Holy Virgin, as well as on the feasts of all the Apostles. When certain of these feast days fell on a Sunday, they were put forward to the Monday, which thus ceased to be a working day. If July 24 or 27 was a Sunday, there were three successive days on which work was forbidden at a time when farm work was at its busiest. It was the same when August 23 or 26 fell on a Sunday. Spring, with its twenty Sundays and holidays, and the month of December, after the twenty-first, carried the heaviest burden. Altogether, one can count eighty-nine Holy Days, or one quarter of the year. In 1744, the bishop put seventeen of these Holy Days of Obligation on Sundays, but Sundays and Holy Days of Obligation still occupied one fifth of the year.

The Lord's Day was strictly observed and the State dealt harshly with those who undertook manual labour. On those days, the faithful had to attend High Mass (where each head of the family in turn was expected to give the consecrated bread), the sermon, Vespers (Mgr de Saint-Vallier was strict on this point), and any additional religious ceremony that the curé considered suitable.

e) *Marriage*

Marriage was surrounded by detailed regulations with both religious and civil aspects. To enter into a contract of marriage, the groom had to be at least fourteen years old, and the bride, at least twelve. Both required parental consent, the boy, until the age of thirty, and the girl (even a widow), until the age of twenty-five. If the parents refused to give their consent (for no good reason), the young couple, through a notary, could have three *sommations respectueuses* (summonses) instituted. After a further refusal, they were free from the guardianship of their parents. Moreover, strangers (that is, those who had just arrived) had to have drawn up "evidence of freedom," certifying that they were not already married.

One also had to make sure that one did not fall within the provisions of the numerous canonical impediments. Fourteen of these were diriment, that is, they rendered marriage null and void. Diriment impediments were those such as consanguinity to the fourth degree inclusively; affinity, which prevented a man from marrying (also to the fourth degree inclusively) the relatives of his deceased wife; and propriety, which prohibited marriage with the mother, sister, or daughter of his deceased fiancée. There were also impediments that made marriage unlawful: for example, marrying during prohibited periods (between the first Sunday of Advent and Epiphany or between Ash Wednesday and Low Sunday). Admittedly, it was possible to obtain dispensations, but only by paying a fairly large sum, which varied according to the impediment to be overcome.

There were other procedures: the prenuptial examination, in which the curé questioned the future couple on marriage and made sure that they knew their prayers. In the eighteenth century, one curé even tried to refuse the sacrament to a poor man who did not know his prayers in Latin. Finally, there were the banns, which were published on three successive Sundays. By paying a sum of money, one could dispense with two of them, or even with any publishing at all.

Attempts were sometimes made to avoid these regulations by resorting to a *mariage à la gaumine*. The bride and groom went to Mass in the company of their witnesses, and at the moment when the priest turned to bless those present, they stood up and declared themselves man and wife. Both Church and State, of course, denounced and proceeded against those who made use of this imitation of the sacrament.

After the marriage ceremony, the priest recorded it in the Register of Marriages. The ceremony could be completed by blessing the marriage bed, provided that, as the *Rituel* put it, this blessing was not left until the evening.

Finally (but here we are not dealing directly with the sacrament), if the difference in age between the spouses was too great, or if one of them had remarried too soon after the death of his or her former spouse, the couple could be subjected to a *charivari*: a disturbance they had to endure until they paid a fine considered sufficient by the kill-joys.

In 1683, in Quebec, such a charivari lasted for a week and Mgr de Laval threatened to excommunicate all those who, in future, took part in similar demonstrations, but the custom did not disappear.

f) *Death*

A sick person received the assistance of religion until the hour of death, but it was still customary, at this time, to wait until the person was at death's door before receiving Extreme Unction. The dead person was displayed *sur les planches* and not in his bed, as was done in France. The "visit to the body" provided the opportunity during the evening for a "wake," which was sometimes reminiscent of the midnight supper at Christmas. Since embalming was used only by the rich, it was necessary in summer, for the ordinary people to hurry with the burial, and it was very often on the same day.

People were rarely buried under the church. This privilege was reserved for priests, who had a place under the choir, and for seigneurs, under their seigneurial pew. Others, on payment of a large sum (fifty *livres* in the country), could be buried under the church. This custom had to be limited little by little, because the graves were not dug very deep, and pestilential odours spread through the church. In the towns, certain wealthy people had themselves buried out of piety in the paupers' cemetery. There was even a priest from the Quebec Seminary who, at his own request, was buried with his face to the ground to "make amends to the Holy Sacrament until the Resurrection of the Dead."

Special characteristics

a) *A strict observance*

The Canadians of the eighteenth century lived in an atmosphere of religion. The days dedicated to prayer (Sundays and Holy Days of Obligation) took up a quarter of the year, fast days totalled almost two months, and meatless days, including fast days, totalled almost five months. Many everyday activities required a liturgical blessing. Votive offerings and processions were often used. Prayers in the home were a daily and a lengthy event. The curé made certain that each person completed all his religious duties, and he frequently intervened in personal affairs. Religious brotherhoods, like the *Confrérie de la Sainte-Famille*, founded in 1664, helped to keep the believer within the widespread framework. All this did not necessarily make people devout, but it may be said that Canadians had a predilection for strict observance of religion.

So strict was this observance that superstition eventually became intermingled with religion. Not only did the religious rites themselves take on the values of religion, but sometimes the mysterious forces of nature became manifestations of the Divine. This was proved at the time of the famous earthquake of 1663, and another time when showers of cinders, originating in faraway forest fires, came down upon the people like the hand of an avenging God. It was established again in many displays of witchcraft: poor Gadois dit Mauger, for example, was "rendered impotent" by an unhappy rival. The curé could do nothing to help and the marriage was nullified. Gadois later married another girl and produced as many children as he wanted.

b) *Rigorism or Jansenism?*

The religious atmosphere was an austere one. The observance of Sunday rest was peremptory. During Lent, butchers' shops were closed. The curé kept a record of the confessions and annual communions, and he did not usually allow his parishioners to make their confessions to another priest. After confession, if there had been a public scandal, public penance was imposed. The marriage sacrament was surrounded by a great number of impediments. Loans at interest were forbidden in the Pastoral Letters, as were certain hairstyles (described as immodest), plays in general, and dancing between boys and girls. The *Rituel* contains a terrible form of excommunication that certain bishops, like Mgr de Saint-Vallier, used more often than was absolutely necessary. The catechism reminded men that, in the evening, they should go to bed "with the preparations of a person about to be laid in his tomb." In all this, the love of God had very little place: the God that one received at communion was not so much the God of Love as the God of Justice.

Must we conclude that this was Jansenism? Canadians of the French regime lived in a spiritual atmosphere that came directly from Mgr de Laval and Mgr de Saint-Vallier, both determined enemies of Jansenism. The bishops remained faithful to the King in this matter, as in all the others, and proved themselves alert on each of the rare occasions on which they thought they were dealing with a Jansenist infiltration. In any case, could Jansenism (a theological doctrine) have reached the lower classes who, in religious matters, knew scarcely more than their catechism? Nevertheless, even if Jansenist theses found only opponents in New France, the doctrine may well have influenced the religious mentality there, just as it did in France. It certainly seems that the great Arnauld was in touch with certain spiritual groups in New France, and there is reason to believe that Mgr de Saint-Vallier took part of his *Rituel* from another *Rituel*, with a strong Jansenist flavour, published in 1677 in the town of Alès, where the followers of Jansenius were predominant.

Rigorism was not peculiar to New France alone; the Catholic Counter Reformation in Europe at this time was strict in everything—as strict as certain groups of the Reformation. Nothing, for example, resembles the religious stringency of New France more than that of the Puritans of New England during the same period.

c) *The Church was within the State*

If Mgr de Laval in the seventeenth century had led people to believe that the Church in New France could rival the State and could keep governors in check, or change them, this was no longer true in the eighteenth century. The Church certainly occupied a prominent position, but it was subordinate to the State.

The eighteenth-century bishop no longer intervened in affairs of State. Except on State occasions, he did not even sit on the Conseil Supérieur. The ecclesiastic who replaced him there was examined on his life and morals like any other civil servant, and he had to present a certificate of Catholicism from his curé. Two members of the Chapter were appointed by the King, instead of by the bishop. The setting up of a parish was now possible only if the State first gave its approval, which it sometimes refused to do. It was not the bishop but the State that fixed the tithe, and what is more, it was the governor who was asked by the King to report every year on the state of religious affairs. The King exercised his authority over the religious communities. He fixed the number of members; he did not allow the Frères Hospitaliers to wear a uniform or to take vows; and in spite of the bishop, he did not allow the Sisters of the Congrégation to do so either. He no longer permitted the religious communities to acquire property in mortmain. It should also be added that it was the State that decided upon the honours to be accorded in church to lay and ecclesiastical dignitaries.

This submission to the State, in areas that had nothing to do with dogma or freedom of expression, was a help rather than an obstacle to the Church. The State enforced the observance of order in the churches, Sunday rest, the regulations on fasting and abstinence, the presentation of the consecrated bread, the service of churchwardens, and the collection of the tithe. It prevented the religious communities from undertaking too much, or from developing too quickly. Through annual subsidies (in addition to seigneuries and lands), the State contributed to the expenses of worship and supported the bishop, the Chapter, the poor parishes, and the missions. Every year, the Church received a large sum from the King's Domain. Thus, in 1744, it received 58,200 *livres*, or one half of the budget of the King's Domain and 11.5 percent of all the colony's expenses.

The Church does not appear to have complained when its material life was put into trusteeship in this way. The reason was that the King in his life as king (his private life is of little importance here) was responsible before God and the Church for the advancement of religion, and from this point of view, Louis XV was as careful to carry out his royal duties as Louis XIV had been. As the historian Frégault writes: "The State, sure of its power, did not seem too inclined to abuse it, while the clergy did not reveal any tendency to be easily offended by the State. The statesmen were Catholic; the Churchmen were the servants of the king." The Church gained strength from this, but its fate was seriously jeopardized after 1760 when the English King claimed that he had acquired the privileges of the French King over the Church.

Bibliographical Note

Much has been written on religious life and the Church in New France, but too often authors have acted as pious hagiographers (as in the case of Mgr de Laval) or have been unable to be objective enough in their approach.

For the history of events, the following work is still useful.

A. Gosselin, *L'Église du Canada depuis Mgr de Laval jusqu'à la conquête*. Québec, Laflamme et Proulx, 1914-1917, 3 vol.

On the position of the Church vis-a-vis the State, two studies should be mentioned.

G. Lanctôt, "Situation politique de l'Église canadienne sous le régime français", in the report of the *Société canadienne d'histoire de l'Église catholique*, 1940-41, pp. 35-36.

G. Frégault, "Les Finances de l'Église sous le régime français", in *Écrits du Canada français*. Montréal, 1959, V, pp. 147-171.

C. E. O'Neill, *Church and State in French Colonial Louisiana: Policy and Politics to 1732*. New Haven and London, Yale University Press, 1966.

The study by Porter gives information on the content of religious education in the eighteenth century.

F. PORTER, O.F.M., *L'Institution catéchistique au Canada: Deux siècles de formation religieuse, 1633-1833.* Montréal, Éditions franciscaines, 1949.

On the *cures,* one may consult

REV. H. PROVOST, "Le Régime des cures au Canada français", in the report of the *Société canadienne d'histoire de l'Église catholique,* 1954-1955, pp. 85-103.

Finally, some studies on the observance of religious life or on marginal problems should be mentioned.

V. ROY. "Le Sacrement de Pénitence ou la confession sous le régime français", in the *Revue d'histoire de l'Amérique française,* XVI, 3 (Dec. 1962), pp. 409-437; 4 (March 1963), pp. 567-580.

REV. P. A. LECLERC, "Le Mariage sous le régime français", in the *Revue d'histoire de l'Amérique française,* XIII, 2 (Sept. 1959), pp. 230-246; 3 (Dec. 1959), pp. 374-401; 4 (March 1960), pp. 525-543; XIV, 1 (June 1960), pp. 34-60; 2 (Sept. 1960), pp. 226-245.

E.-A. MASSICOTTE, "Le Charivari au Canada", in the *Bulletin des Recherches historiques.* 32, 1926, pp. 712-725.

R.-L. SÉGUIN, *La Sorcellerie au Canada français, du XVIIIe au XIXe siècles.* Montréal, Ducharme, 1961.

CHAPTER X

Intellectual life

New France developed only a limited intellectual life, for it was a society largely composed of individuals from the needy lower classes—a society unable to provide itself with a printing works or to support a book trade.

Education

Illiteracy, at that time, was a phenomenon not limited to New France. No help in solving the problem is provided by the fact that we find signatures at the bottom of civil documents, by the fact that the curé neglected to make those people sign who were capable of doing so, or as has been observed, by the fact that the settlers found it less compromising to sign with a cross. There is lack of evidence to show whether those who signed their names could also write fluently, read with ease, and obtain books.

Here, as in France, the State left the task of education to private institutions, or to individuals. The State either made endowments for this purpose, or remunerated those concerned in one way or another. Nevertheless, it played a supervisory role. In 1727, Intendant Dupuy, who seems to have been the first intendant to intervene in education, required lay teachers to possess a permit from himself and the bishop, and to sit for an examination set by the ecclesiastic who was a member of the Conseil Supérieur. If these teachers were unmarried, they were not allowed to teach children of the opposite sex. This, it seems, was the only legislation on schools passed during the French regime.

a) *The petite école (elementary education)*

At the primary level, the child learned to read (in Latin first), to write, and to count. Some ideas about manners, and particularly the catechism, were also taught. When he had passed the examination in this and had taken his first communion (around the age of twelve), the child normally went no further with his studies. During the French regime, people who wrote on education regretted the fact that the schoolchild was not better prepared for his career; for example, no primary course included history or geography. Certain of these schools were given the name of *Latin Schools*. In fact, they were no more than preparatory schools for the Jesuit College.

It is not easy to find out what the school situation was like in the countryside. It seems to have been unreliable, for the fact that a school existed at a given time is no proof that it was still there ten years later. In any case, in the Acadian missions, the priests must have devoted some of their time to teaching. In Côte de Beaupré, the Château-Richer school seems to have been important as were those of Saint-Famille (on Île d'Orléans), Neuville, and that of Curé Boucher at Pointe-Lévy. There were also schools in the countryside around Trois-Rivières (for example, the one at Champlain). In several places around Montreal, the Sulpicians and the Sisters of the Congregation maintained schools. Church schools already existed in certain country areas.

Kalm wrote that every parish had its school, but this can only be true of the parishes that he visited. Whatever the truth is, there were lay teachers here and there. Sometimes, they were settled in one place; sometimes they were travelling teachers. It has not been proved that curés often became schoolmasters. Those who did so seem to have limited themselves to preparing candidates for the seminary.

It was the towns that profited most from teaching. Louisbourg had a school run by the Sisters of the Congregation. In the Lower Town of Quebec, the same sisters had a school, while there was another one run by the seminary and a boarding school in the Hôpital-Général. In the Upper Town, the Jesuit College included a primary school. Next door, the Ursulines had a day school and a boarding school. Trois-Rivières possessed a Church school, where there was a lay teacher and the Ursuline convent. It is possible that the Récollets also did a little teaching. In Montreal, the Charron Brothers (until their dissolution) and the Sulpicians ran primary schools for boys, while the Sisters of the Congregation took care of the girls. New Orleans had an Ursuline convent.

b) *The école d'arts et métiers (trade school)*

At the same level as the *petite école* were two *écoles d'arts et métiers* (trade schools) where young people learned reading, writing, and arithmetic besides being prepared for special trades. The first and oldest one was founded by Mgr de Laval at Saint-Joachim in the last quarter of the seventeenth century. It was afterwards supported by the Quebec Seminary and continued to exist into the eighteenth century until it disappeared, well before the Conquest. Many cabinetmakers, sculptors, painters, and gilders began their careers in this institution. In the Hôpital-Général of Montreal, the Charron Brothers also taught trades for a few years. At the end of the French regime, New France no longer seems to have had any trade schools.

c) *College*

The only college in New France was that of the Jesuits in Quebec. It was started in 1635 and was finally established in a house admired by the Swede Kalm for its architecture. All those who wished to follow the curriculum of college study attended this institution, unless they could go to France. The pupils of the Little Seminary of Quebec, who lived next door, followed its courses regularly. It has been calculated that the Jesuit College, on the average, took in some 150 pupils each year, of whom 50 or 60 were from the Seminary. In 1732, it boarded about thirty pupils. The occupation of the house by the English army and the dispersal of the Jesuits put an end to its courses in 1759. However,

Public Archives of Canada

The Jesuit College in Quebec
(from an engraving by Richard Short)

the elementary school was kept up until 1776. After 1765, the Quebec Seminary took over the work of the college.

The College followed the *Ratio Studiorum* of the Jesuits: three years of grammar, one year of humanities, one year of rhetoric, two years of philosophy (pupils of the seminary wore the cassock at this time), and for those destined for the priesthood, two years of theology. The Professor of Mathematics of the College had an important role, for it was his duty to check the competence of surveyors and the accuracy of their instruments.

In addition to the Ratio Studiorum, the Jesuits, with the aid of the State, maintained a Chair of Hydrography. The professor trained pilots by teaching chemistry, physics, geometry, and navigation. Among the professors who held this chair were Jean-Baptiste Franquelin, Louis Jolliet, and the Jesuit de Bonnecamp.

No regular system existed in New France to train for professions other than that of pilot. One became a notary after being apprenticed as a clerk, or quite often, by assuming the role of a notary. To prepare for a career in medicine, one had to go to France, or become a doctor's apprentice. Lawyers (who in any case were not allowed to practise here) came from France to become important civil servants. The Procureur général Verrier gave lectures on Law, not in order to train lawyers, but to prepare a few young men for the position of Assessor with the Conseil Supérieur.

Libraries

With the exception of a rudimentary apparatus used for printing pastoral letters and ordinances, New France had no printing press. The King was ready to grant a licence, but the country was in no condition to support a printer.

Just as the presence of a printer living on Île d'Orléans in 1666 does not establish the existence of a printing works in Canada, so the mention of one or two booksellers is not sufficient evidence to prove that there was a trade in books. Those who wanted books for teaching or those who wished to enrich their own libraries had to buy individually from French booksellers.

As in France, there were still no public libraries. The English colonies, however, had had these since 1730. All libraries were privately owned by religious institutions, by ecclesiastics, or by laymen. They were even found in far-off missions, like Illinois, for the Quebec Seminary had provided its priests with many books.

There is no record, accurate or otherwise, of the books in New France. The collections that it has been possible to list (about fifty) have altogether about 20,000 volumes. Among these collections, we may mention the thirty volumes belonging to an *homme du peuple* Jean Nicollet. Also Michel Sarrazin, a learned doctor, possessed 200 volumes; Intendant Dupuy, 300 volumes; Curé Philippe Boucher, 500 volumes; and the jurist Cugnet, 1,250 volumes. The largest private library, that of Procureur général Guillaume Verrier, contained more than 3,000 volumes.

In the libraries of institutions, as well as in those of private citizens, there were many literary works (mainly classical authors, but also others like Lesage, Abbé Prévost, the authors of the Encyclopedia, and Voltaire), books on history, geography, Law, sciences, and the fine arts. However, religious works make up the major portion of these libraries.

Literature

a) *Written literature*

Written literature could hardly develop in a country lacking a printing press or a bookstore. In any case, the necessity of *primo vivere*, in the upper classes as well as among the poorest people, did not allow leisure time for intellectual pursuits.

Nevertheless, there was a written literature, but no work was printed in the country, and literary production, whether by Canadians or by Frenchmen, satisfied a concern for usefulness. There were accounts of voyages (like those of Champlain, or the Jesuit Charlevoix), the accounts of missionaries, annals (those of Sister Marie Morin), religious writings (those of Mother Marie de l'Incarnation), works of publicity (the *Histoire* of Pierre Boucher, the first to be written by a Canadian), the tales of La Hontan, and the letters of Madame Bégon. With the exception of certain rare works, such as the *Muses* of Lescarbot and certain mock-heroic poems, there is a complete absence of imaginative literature.

However, the written literature of the French regime had some good qualities. Lescarbot; the Jesuits Biard, Le Jeune, and Brébeuf; Mother Marie de l'Incarnation; La Hontan; and Madame Bégon are authors whose writings are still a pleasure to read.

Archives de la province de Québec

A letter writer of the French regime, Elizabeth Bégon

In any case, this literature is especially valued for the documentary evidence that it gives us on men and events in New France.

b) *Oral literature*

Although the inhabitants of New France produced little written literature, story-telling was a favourite pastime, for books had not yet replaced the memory. The precise content of this oral literature of the French regime is still largely unknown since research in this field has begun only recently. However, what is known convinces us that the people were thoroughly familiar with the great traditional stories of European civilization. From Quebec, Acadia, and Louisiana—where people could not have learned them from books—tales and songs have been obtained that come from the collections of the seventeenth and eighteenth centuries in Europe. Some like the *Chanson des Écoliers de Pontoise* (Song of the Scholars of Pontoise) are connected with the dim traditions of the Middle Ages, or like the *Conte des Trois Voleurs* (Tale of the Three Robbers), with the Egypt of ancient times. The survival of these tales and songs makes it clear that the mass of the people enjoyed imaginative stories for the pleasure they gave, even though actual authors merely fulfilled the requirements of daily life.

The Arts

The arts served a useful purpose, as did literature. Music, painting, sculpture, architecture, and the making of jewellery were mainly employed in the service of the Church. There was hardly any originality in these. Either the artist or the style was imported, sometimes both. In general, the arts followed a simplified Louis XIV style. At no time did New France possess its own artistic movement.

Little is known about music. Poutrincourt was a musician, and divine service in Acadia was sung to music that he composed. Maisonneuve played the lute, and Madame de La Peltrie, the viola. Louis Jolliet played the organ; Archdeacon Serré de La Colombière wrote a Christmas carol. However, it appears that musicians were little more than simple amateurs.

With the exception of some portraits of dignitaries, painting was inspired by religion. Almost from the beginning, it was customary to cover the inside of churches with paintings. Of the many painters, only one artist is at all distinguished—the Récollet Claude François, or Frère Luc, who had been a painter in the service of Nicolas Poussin before taking religious vows. He lived in Canada for only a short time (1670-1671), but was able to produce some thirty paintings for various churches in the region of Quebec.

The art of sculpture was widespread in New France, both for decorative sculpture (tabernacles, altar pieces, and wall ornaments) and for statuary. But, except for household furniture, it was used only for religious subjects. Sculptors who worked in wood were very numerous, and it is often hard to distinguish them from master carpenters. The Le Vasseur family, as much as any other group, contributed to the art of statuary and to craftsmanship in general. Others include Gilles Bolvin, the Cirier family, and the Jourdain dit Labrosse family.

The Canadians of the French regime showed a little more originality in the working of gold and silver, which was also prompted mainly by religion. Jacques Pagé, Jean-

Archives de la province de Québec

The young Jesus painted by Frère Luc, about 1671

François Landron, Paul Lambert, and Ignace-François Delzenne brought the silver-smith's art to a high level of accomplishment. Among other pieces, there is a chalice Delzenne made for the Montreal Hôtel-Dieu, around 1755, which is considered the most perfect Canadian work of its type and period.

Although palace architecture displayed a lavish splendour in the bishop's palace, the Palais de l'Intendance, the Château Vaudreuil, and the Jesuit College, church architecture remained very simple, and the Jesuit style did not come into general use in New France. Architects were satisfied with the transept church that had a pointed roof and a semicircular apse, or with the church in the Récollet style of a single nave covered by a false vaulted roof in the shape of a semicircle and with a square apse.

Public speaking was employed in the pulpit and on the stage. The large amount of preaching during the French regime—consisting of sermons on Sundays and holidays, sermons and speeches on particular occasions, and funeral orations—was not enough to produce great speakers. Only one speaker—the Archdeacon Serré de La Colombière—can be considered at all famous. It should be added that Canada at this period produced a preacher of great distinction—the Jesuit François-Xavier Duplessis—but his success was achieved in France.

Drama began in New France in 1606, with a work by Lescarbot, *Le Théâtre de Neptune* (a *jeu scénique* accompanied by amusing verses). The next production was in Quebec in 1639, a tragi-comedy, the title of which still remains unknown. There were, on some rare occasions in the seventeenth century, interpretations of works by Corneille (*Le Cid* and *Nicomède*) and of Racine's *Mithridate*. However, either the strictness of Mgr de Saint-Vallier (who disapproved of the theatre as such), or perhaps the lack of money put an end to these modest beginnings. There was no other performance of impor-tant works anywhere and no creation of new plays. Canadians had to be satisfied with short, improvised plays or social skits.

The Sciences

Just as New France had no artistic movement but only artists, so also, in spite of a few men of science, it experienced no scientific movement. In the seventeenth century, New France did not possess men who made careers in the sciences but only observers who did not wish to present anything systematic. These men described, sometimes with great skill, merely what they saw. Champlain, Lescarbot, and the Récollet Sagard made important contributions to American ethnography, but it was the Jesuits Brébeuf, Le Jeune, and Lafiteau, who showed themselves to be masters in this field.

In the eighteenth century, the higher authorities in France encouraged research in the colonies, so that some talented men spent their time making collections. In partic-ular, they looked for rare specimens to enrich the *Jardin des Plantes* or the King's Menagerie, and their specimens made a valuable contribution to scientific research. The Frenchman Michel Sarrazin, a doctor of medicine and a corresponding member of the *Académie des Sciences*, exchanged observations with Réaumur. Until his death, in 1734, Sarrazin carried out investigations in anatomy and chemistry, and studied plants enthu-siastically. The most learned of the governors, La Galissonière, in whom the Swede Kalm saw "another Linnaeus," was an associate member of the *Académie des Sciences*. He

Michel Sarrazin

Public Archives of Canada

collected much material and composed interesting treatises. He corresponded regularly with the scholars of the period, while Doctor Jean-François Gaultier, a corresponding member of the same Academy, devoted himself to the study of nature—in particular to botany. To these men of science must be added the names of the Jesuit de Bonnecamp, Michel Chartier de Lotbinière, and Gaspard-Joseph Chaussegros de Léry. However, they seem to have gone little further than simple observation and the preparation of works of reference.

The intellectual richness of the English colonies

The trading colonies on the Atlantic—New England, New York, Pennsylvania, Virginia, and South Carolina—developed an intellectual life of their own that reached a very high standard. This development was due to the influence of a wealthy middle class and to the connections with the mother country that were maintained throughout the year. Also, the English colonies were endowed with numerous elementary schools, both private and public (the latter offered free instruction). They possessed three great colleges: Harvard, Yale, and William and Mary, which rivalled those of England. Regular courses in Law and Medicine were given there.

A score of public libraries were added to these centres of culture, including a travelling library at Boston and other private libraries. Unlike New France, most of these were owned by laymen. Moreover, a flourishing book trade was carried on in Boston, New York, Philadelphia, and Williamsburg. Early possession of the printing press definitely contributed to the development of culture. Especially important were the Gazettes that circulated in all the colonies, and the Magazines that fostered the expression of ideas and literary creation.

The intellectual life of this colonial period in United States history is revealed much more in the arts and sciences than in literature. Architecture (in the Georgian style) and town planning (as in Philadelphia) were making great strides. Two great names in painting were Benjamin West and John Singleton Copley. Kühn was a celebrated portrait painter. The work of goldsmiths from New York was sought after, thanks partly to the French Huguenots. New York and Charleston (South Carolina) were centres already famous for their concerts. Handel's *Messiah*, with a choir and musical accompaniment, was presented in New York.

In the American colonies, drama was already surprisingly successful. Although it was condemned by the Puritans and Quakers, it appeared at a very early date in New England and Pennsylvania. In New York and Charleston, people showed tremendous enthusiasm for drama. Here, there were permanent theatres in which professional troupes put on important works such as Shakespeare's plays.

The contribution made in the sciences was both brilliant and original. The attention that the Puritans, for example, refused to give to the "frivolity" of the arts was directed towards the sciences. In his writings, researches, and important collections, the Reverend Cotton Mather is a good representative of this type of thinking. In botany, Virginia produced a first-class scientist, John Clayton; South Carolina fostered a renowned naturalist, Alexander Garden, and great doctors. Benjamin Franklin played a part of international importance in this scientific movement that constantly enlivened

Cupboard dating from the end of the eighteenth century

Archives de la province de Québec

Cherub by Pierre-Noël Le Vasseur

the English colonies. During the second half of the eighteenth century, his writings and experiments (in particular those regarding electricity) surprised England and France.

Scientific study did not remain at the stage of pure speculation, but often influenced economic life. The research of John Rolfe gave Virginia a new economic foundation (tobacco), which was to determine its fate and that of the neighbouring colonies. Henry Woodward's work with rice brought prosperity to South Carolina.

The intellectual life of the English colonies was very active. But, taking their population into account, one would have expected an even greater activity, and it is surprising that with all the resources at their disposal, these colonies did not produce more literature of the imaginative kind. However, in comparing the intellectual activity of these colonies with that of New France, the latter appears deficient beside the printing work, the gazettes, the bookselling trade, the public and private libraries, the works of art and the men of science found in the English colonies.

Bibliographical Note

Not much research has been done into the intellectual life of New France, but since this intellectual life was restricted in its activity, this research goes much deeper into its subject than the studies in other fields. However, much still remains to be done. In particular, we lack a complete and systematic study of the literature of the French regime. The following works may be consulted:

Education

A. GOSSELIN, *L'Instruction au Canada sous le régime français, 1635-1670.* Québec, Laflamme et Proulx, 1911. This work has not yet been superseded.

Libraries

A. DROLET, *Les Bibliothèques canadiennes, 1604-1960.* Montréal, Cercle du Livre de France, 1965.

A. DROLET, "La Bibliothèque du Collège des Jesuites," in the *Revue d'histoire de l'Amérique française,* XIV, 4 March 1961, pp. 487-544.

Arts and Letters

Sculpture traditionelle du Québec. Musée du Québec, 1967.

Peinture traditionelle du Québec. Musée du Québec, 1967.

A. ROY, *Les Lettres, les sciences et les arts au Canada, sous le régime français.* Paris, Jouve et Cie, 1930.

A. VIATTE, *Histoire littéraire de l'Amérique française.* Paris and Québec, Presses Universitaires, 1954, pp. 1-43.

Les Archives de Folklore, published by Laval University through Les Editions Fides, Montreal: 8 issues have appeared to date.

G. MORISSET, *Coup d'oeil sur les arts en Nouvelle-France.* Québec, 1941.

G. MORISSET, *La Peinture traditionelle au Canada français.* Montréal, Cercle du Livre de France, 1960.

R. TRAQUAIR, *The Old Architecture of Quebec.* Toronto, Macmillan, 1947.

J. PALARDY, *Les Meubles anciens du Canada français.* Paris, 1963. Translated into English under the title *The Early Furniture of French Canada.* Toronto, 1963.

M. M. CAMERON, "Play-acting in Canada During the French Regime," in *Canadian Historical Review,* XI, 1 (March 1930), pp. 9-19.

A. GOSSELIN, "Un épisode de l'histoire du théâtre au Canada," in the *Mémoires de la Société royale du Canada,* IV, 1, pp. 53-72.

L. SPELL, "Music in New France in the Seventeenth Century," in *Canadian Historical Review,* VIII, 2 (June 1927), pp. 119-131.

Science

R. Lamontagne, "La Contribution scientifique de la Galissonière au Canada," in the *Revue d'histoire de l'Amérique française,* XIII, 4 (March 1960), pp. 509-524.

R. Lamontagne, "Les Échanges scientifiques entre Roland Michel Barrin de la Galissonière et les chercheurs contemporains," in the *Revue d'histoire de l'Amérique française,* XIV, 1 (June 1960), pp. 25-33.

A. Vallée, *Un biologiste canadien. Michel Sarrazin, 1659-1735.* Québec, Proulx, 1927.

Subjects of research to last for a century or two

Although for a good half-century New France's resources were more limited than those exploited by the English colonies, she possessed the basic framework for establishing a stable society. In many respects, this society contained elements common to all the other groups transplanted from Europe (the English, Dutch, Swedish, and Spanish), but it was also truly Canadian. Not only their language, but also their religion and government, their mentality, their habits and feelings of a common adventure, made the Canadians into a distinct social group that reacted as a unit when confronting other peoples, even those as similar as the Acadians.

Since men in Europe were concerned only with the European economy, there had been no attempt made to enable New France to exist independently of the mother country. However, the colony underwent a sudden change. (Although still subject to European influence, it had become American and Canadian.) It lost its natural mother country and had to become part of that English world against which it had struggled for three quarters of a century. It is true that the new mother country, England, resembled the old one in many ways. From the religious point of view, she was Christian and called herself Catholic. Church and State, throne and altar had the same close relationship. Socially, the new system she introduced was hierarchical. Politically, she was monarchic, and the King of England persisted in bearing the title of *King of France*. Economically, London was mainly interested in the great fur companies, as Paris had been. However, in conjunction with these similarities, there were differences that would strongly influence the future of Canadian society. England had separated from Rome, and her King had sworn at his consecration to destroy popery. Her culture differed from that of France, as did her language. Her monarchy, too, was based on free acceptance by the people. The English political system was not paternalistic, providing for and arranging everything in advance, but rather, it encouraged free initiative. English land tenure and the French seigneurial system provides a good illustration of the great differences between the two ideologies.

New France disintegrated after the Conquest, but a French society with its own social framework remained, continuing to carry on a traditional way of life. What future

Archives de la province de Québec

Chalice by Ignace-François Delzenne
Silver chalice made about 1755

might it expect as part of the English empire? Did Canadian society realize that it had entered a dramatic period in its history? Was this change from French to English control as tragic as had been claimed?

To reply to these questions, and to measure the influence of the Conquest upon the fate of Canadians, we would have to know much more about society under the French regime than merely its social structures. However, we still know very little about this society and important problems remain that historians have not yet sufficiently resolved. Subjects for study in this field abound.

For example, what were the relations between this society and the one in France, and between the various groups in this society itself? To what extent did distances and isolation influence the mentality of the people? What is known of the original settlers?

Even though we know the numbers of people each province of France provided, we are not familiar with the special circumstances that prompted them to emigrate. Nor do we yet know what was the value of the tradesmen who came, nor what happened to military recruits who became farmers, nor the background of the "king's daughters" and their relations with the strangers whom they were made to marry so quickly. The behaviour of those people deported from France, as well as the numbers and the social role of the Huguenots after the Revocation of the Edict of Nantes, are also unknowns. We still have not assessed the contribution of the non-French Europeans and the Amerinds to the growth of population under the French regime, and we may never know in what proportion the French Canadians of today are of English or native descent. Lastly, we know little of how social groups were formed and developed in this population or of what exchanges they had with one another. We do not know who constituted the nobility and the bourgeoisie; what is the meaning of the term "common people;" how men improved or lowered their social standing; or even the differences between the Canadian culture and that of the mother country, France.

The mechanics of government are familiar to us, but can we be certain that the administration functioned as intended? There is often a great difference between theory and practice, between the law and its execution. Again, we would wish to know a good deal more about the behaviour of the civil servants. Being so poorly paid, how did they augment their income? To what extent did public service, and consequently, the common good suffer from these practices? How were important posts accumulated by a few, and what harm resulted? Above all, we still do not possess a study of the behaviour of the common people under an absolute authority that either mitigated or increased the weight of paternalism. Such a study would make it easier to analyze the adaptation of the masses to free initiative and to the parliamentary system introduced under the English regime.

We think we know a great deal about the military organization; but what do we know of the lives of the officers and soldiers of the regular army, or of their relations with the civilian population and the latter's attitude towards them, and of the effect of their presence on economic life? What do we know of the army's role and the conditions of service? And what do we know of that minor parish leader, the captain of militia?

Indeed, it is only in our day that the seigneurial regime has been approached from the point of view of social history. Here, much study remains to be done. We still await the definitive seigneurial map that will reconstitute, on paper, the overall plan of the colony and enable us to appreciate the material advantages and disadvantages of this system in a given area. The role that laymen and religious institutions played in the development of the system; the rights and duties which seigneurs and *censitaires* really exercised; the importance these rights and duties had in social and economic life; the history of the abolition of the system in 1854 and its late disappearance; the extent to which two centuries of seigneurial life may have helped to form a characteristic French-Canadian personality — all these, as well as many more, are problems that historians must consider.

In spite of some wide-ranging studies, the greater part of the economic history of the French regime still has to be examined. We still await methodical work on the monetary system (paper money alone is a vast field of research), on financial administration, and on internal communications. Much has been said on the subject of trade — above all, the fur trade — but what few definite facts are known about those who practised it? We would first need a list of the merchants, since so many questions can be asked about their origins, the principal trade centres, their volume of business, their manner of life, their real wealth, their social rank, their mentality, their aristocratic ambitions, their influence on the fate of the colony, their rise and fall in importance, and their continuance through their sons or their extinction. Perhaps when answers have been provided for these questions, we will be better able to explain why these merchants lost control over business at the end of the eighteenth century. We still need to examine the mechanism of small-scale trade: the retail merchants, the speculators, the shops and markets, the goods in circulation, and the price fluctuations.

On industry, we still have only a short and primarily chronological listing that cannot give answers to the questions now being asked. Why, for example, was this country —although it was rich in wood—incapable, under the French regime, of supporting a shipbuilding industry as strong as that of New England? Concerning the Saint-Maurice Ironworks—the only heavy industry—there is need for a more thorough economic and social history than the one we have now. What do we know of the fisheries in the river and the Gulf, of the amount of business carried on in this area by the merchants of Quebec, or of the men who did the actual fishing? Why did small industries producing essential goods have such little success? What do we know of the nature and role of craft work done in the home? Lastly, what was the actual system of weights and measures? Without a knowledge of this system, no worthwhile economic study can be made.

Agriculture is another area in need of research. We are still not familiar with the changes in the lives of those immigrants who left either a trade or the army to become *habitants*. Also, we know neither the income provided by agriculture in the seventeenth and eighteenth centuries, nor the true condition of agriculture at the moment when the colony of the Saint Lawrence was forced by its new masters to become an agricultural colony. And we know very little about the average *habitant*: how he lived, what he ate, what his economic situation was, or what his outlook on life and his social habits were.

We have a fairly good idea of the overall functioning of the courts, but a detailed study is still necessary. Many avenues are yet to be explored. We know nothing of ecclesiastical justice because no one has yet had access to the records. Because of the lack of documentation, we still have little information on the various seigneurial courts. Neither the history of the legal practitioners nor that of the surveyors has yet been written. We also need an account of the adaptation of the *Coutume de Paris* to the needs of a new country, as well as the details on its transformation into the system called the "Laws of Canada."

An account of public health under the French regime has not been written, nor has that of social aid to the poor and to illegitimate children. On medicine and surgery, the only studies we have do not answer the questions posed by economic and social history.

To mention religious history is to bring up an immense number of historical problems. What was the exact position of the Church with respect to the State, and how did the bishops carry out their relations with the lay authorities? Light must be thrown on the biographies of the bishops: their backgrounds and their relations with the clergy. The life of the Chapter, which formed a community of contemplatives, has not been related; nor has the secular clergy's way of life, its sources of income (nor for example, the amount yielded by its contribution in the intellectual field and in everyday life). We have no study of the phenomenon of *Canadianization*. Little study has been carried out on the regular clergy. The priests of the Quebec Seminary have not yet found a historian, and those of the Montreal Seminary await the rewriting of their history in accordance with the needs of the present day. The role of the Priests of the Holy Spirit in Acadia has been recorded but only in a strongly biased version. The history of the Récollets has been written only for the region of Trois-Rivières, and we have nothing at all on any foundation of the Capuchins. Of all the communities, the Jesuits have best been served by historical studies, but even here only their beginnings in the seventeenth century have been thoroughly examined.

When we come to the auxiliaries of the clergy, there are great gaps. There is still much to be said on the Charron Brothers who ran hospitals and schools, as well as on the communities of women, both cloistered and secular. The pious or simply chronological histories that have been written of these do not take economic and social problems into account.

The institution of the parish has been well documented, but the curé himself has not, except for customary eulogies. The important role ascribed to him has yet to be proved, for his position and power in the parish, his relationships with the seigneur and the captain of the militia (those responsible for civil and military matters) and with the parishioners themselves have not yet been investigated. Also, any work on the sermons of the French regime will be of great use when original manuscripts are found. As for the vestry, we need to know the real role played by the churchwardens in administration but must wait for a far-reaching economic study in this field. Furthermore, an attempt will hopefully be made one day to evaluate the importance that the body of institutions dependent upon the Church had for the economic life of New France.

The areas to be studied are also very numerous when we wish to deal with religious observance. From what sources did religious life draw its support; what effect was exerted on the Church's outlook by the Catholic Counter-Reformation and the Jansenist and Pietist quarrels; what influence did the *Compagnie du Saint-Sacrement* have? In short, what was the nature of spirituality in New France?

The rules of religious observance are no better known. Of the seven sacraments, the observance of only two (Penance and Matrimony) has been described in detail. The observance of Sundays and Holy Days of Obligation, as well as the observance of abstinence and Lent, deserve well-documented research—not only to produce a description, but also to discover their socio-economic implications.

Finally, the intellectual life of New France is another field in which much study remains to be done. Little is known of education in rural areas and nothing of Church schools. A history of the Jesuit College has still not been written. There exists a general list of the libraries, but this is still incomplete and does not give a methodical analysis of their contents. On written literature, we still do not have a satisfactory overall study; as for oral literature, much material has been accumulated, but a general interpretation of it which will be helpful for knowledge of the French regime, remains to be published. In the arts, monographs are constantly appearing; in the sciences, the communications between our scientists and those of Europe have begun to be studied. But in both these areas, there is an equal lack of works of a general nature.

The above are some of the many questions the present continues to ask of the past. New generations of historians will, year by year, provide the answers. However, then, with the passage of time and in order to meet the needs of a new era, it will perhaps be necessary to start all over again.

INDEX

Abenakis, 25, 72, 93

Abénakise, 201

Abercromby, James, 95, 96

Abitibi, Lake, 82

Abitibi River, 82

Abitibis, 124

Abraham. *See* Plains of Abraham

Absolutism, 157*f*

Abstinence, 253

Acadia, 9, 21; natives, 25, 33; origin of name, 12; and de Monts, 36*f*; dissensions, 39, 49; English conquest, 1613, 39; in 1627, 46; trading network, 41; under Razilly, 46, 49*f*; map, 1630-1654, 48; English conquest, 1654, 49; settlement, 49*f*; seigneuries in, 50; religion in, 50; in 1663, 57*f*; English conquest, 1690, 72; English conquest, 1710, 72, 75; given up in 1713, 75; from 1668-1713, 71*f*; reconstruction of French Acadia, 79-80; general description, 116-117; in 1754, 85; English conquest, 1710, 72, 75; given up of Acadians, 93-94; missionaries, 115; eighteenth-century map, 117. *See also* Nova Scotia

Acadians. *See* Acadia

Adam of Bremen, 6

Administration. *See* Government

Africa, and Ancient World, 3; and Portugal, 6, 7

Agniers. *See* Mohawks

Agriculture, haphazard, 203*f*; absence of agricultural policy, 204; absence of outlets, 205-207; under Talon, 67; under Hocquart, 84; crops, 207; farm, 207-208; peasants, 204; barns, 205; house, 208;

social position, 209; subjects for research, 277

Aigremont. *See* Clairambault

Ailleboust de Coulonge et d'Argentenay, Louis, 151

Ailly, Cardinal d', 4, 6

Alabama, 19

Albanel, Charles, S.J., 69, 241

Albania, 4

Albany, Fort, 73

Albany River, 69, 82

Alcohol. *See* Brandy

Alès, 257

Alexander, Sir William, 42

Alexander VI, Pope, 7

Alfonse dit Fonteneau, Jean, 19

Algonkians, family of, 25-27; language, 33; and Celts, 4; canoe, 32

Algonkins, 29, 31, 33, 37, 41, 42, 51, 55; description, 26

Algonkins of the Island, 26, 33

Algonkins, River of, *See* Ottawa River

Algonquin, l', 201

Alleghenies. *See* Appalachians

Allumette Island, 26, 33

Almouchiquois, 33

Ambault. *See* Duchesneau

America, and Ancient World, 3; and Middle Ages, 3-6; origin of name, 10; discovery of, 3, 7; explorations in 16th century, 8*f*; vain European endeavours, 19*f*

Amerinds. *See* Natives

Amherst, Jeffrey, 96, 100, 101, 102

Amirauté, 148, 225; formation, 211; description, 212